RELIGIOUS FREEDOM

RELIGIOUS FREEDOM

A Conservative Primer

John D. Wilsey

WILLIAM B. EERDMANS PUBLISHING COMPANY
GRAND RAPIDS, MICHIGAN

Wm. B. Eerdmans Publishing Co.
2006 44th Street SE, Grand Rapids, MI 49508
www.eerdmans.com

Book design by Lydia Hall

Printed in the United States of America

31 30 29 28 27 26 25   1 2 3 4 5 6 7

ISBN 978-0-8028-8190-8

Library of Congress Cataloging-in-Publication Data

A catalog record for this book is available from the Library of Congress.

To my daughters, Caroline and Sally,
and to their generation

Persta atque obdura

Contents

America's Two Spirits

Hereafter the material strength of the West will not suffice without a unifying purpose of our own, not class hate and race hate but ethic and reason. The fate of mankind may depend on whether the moral, reasonable, rooted appeal of liberty can inspire as much unity as the romantic, emotional, apocalyptic appeal of its enemies.

—Peter Viereck, *Conservatism Revisited*

This is a book that considers how to think about and maintain a uniquely American tradition: the harmony between liberty and religion that each generation has received as an inheritance from the generations preceding it.

Today, such a tradition may be enjoyed in other lands and by other nations. The harmony between liberty and religion is not necessarily exclusive to America in our day, but such a societal harmony began here. Broadly considered, Americans have enjoyed this harmony since the national founding in 1789 when the Constitution went into effect. Are there exceptions to this rule? Have there been outrages against religious liberty in America, outrages inflicted by even religious people? Most certainly there have been, because every nation is made up of people, and people are morally flawed, sinful, prone to selfishness and abuse of liberty. Still, the observation that Alexis de Tocqueville made in 1835 represents the predominant tradition pertinent to the relationship between liberty and religion in America. He wrote in the first volume of *Democracy in America*, "[Anglo-American civilization] is the product . . . of two perfectly distinct elements that elsewhere are often at odds. But in America, these two have been successfully blended, in a way, and marvelously combined. I mean the *spirit of religion* and the *spirit of liberty*."[1] Liberty and religion have historically enjoyed a symbiotic relationship in America. The more expansive liberty has been, the more religion has flourished. And as religion has flourished, liberty has also deepened in American culture. This was one of the central observations that Tocqueville made when he and Gustave de Beaumont toured the United States between May 1831 and February 1832.

The tradition of harmony between liberty and religion goes back to the American founding. Protestant theology was one of the predominant intellectual traditions that animated the founding. This is not a controversial statement, nor is it the equivalent of saying that America was founded as a Christian nation. Protestantism was essential to the ideas of the American founding, and this has been demonstrated decisively by scholars in the fields of American history and political theory.[2] And yet, that harmony which has defined American culture for over two centuries has come under the greatest pressure seen in the nation's experience. Patriotism and religion have sharply declined as priorities among Americans since 1998. For example, whereas 70 percent of Americans considered patriotism to be very important to them in 1998, only 38 percent thought so in 2023, twenty-five years later. Sixty-two percent of citizens polled in 1998 considered religion to be very important, but in 2023, only 39 percent thought the same. To compound the problem, people have become inordinately preoccupied with racial diversity, valuing it over competency, and have become obsessed with trivialities and absurdities like the use of artificially contrived personal pronouns.[3] Moreover, there is a growing trend among Americans, from left and right, who favor authoritarian, antidemocratic leaders and means of governance over and against the traditional American order of democratic-republican constitutionalism.[4] The federal order, envisioned by the framers of the Constitution and enduring since the eighteenth century despite the realities of economic depression, civil war, world war, territorial growth, the rise of industrialism, demographic changes, exponential population growth, deepening religious diversity, social changes, urbanization, racial strife, and a myriad of other challenges and contexts, has sustained and advanced the American experiment in self-government. Now that experiment seems to be under threats emanating not from abroad but from home, to an extent not seen in three generations and perhaps not since the Civil War.

Amazingly, it is difficult to find enthusiasm among Americans for, or even agreement on, the term "American." What is an American? Does America represent equality under the law, unalienable rights, and the blessings of liberty? Or does America best represent racial oppression, violence, jingoism, genocide, and anything else nasty the imagination can conjure? Is anyone proud to be an American anymore? Or is such a concept now considered to be mere kitsch from the 1980s inspired by a cheesy song by Lee Greenwood? There are movements afoot emerging from both the left and the right that denigrate Americanness, or what Theodore Roosevelt called "true Americanism."[5] On the left, the writers who produced *The 1619 Project* sought to reimagine the American founding as dedicated principally to the preservation of slavery, and not to the professed ideals of equality, rights, liberty, and the pursuit of happiness. Even though *The 1619 Project* was repeatedly criticized for its portrayal of the American Revolution, and even though Nikole Hannah-Jones, the architect of the work, suggested that she planned to correct the historical inaccuracies pointed out by academic historians like Gordon S. Wood, Allen C. Guelzo, Victoria Bynum, and others in the production of the book, *The 1619 Project* continues to place slavery and racial oppression at the center of American identity.[6] Nobody of any consequence would deny the thesis that racial oppression must be thoroughly understood and studied in order to make sense of American history and identity. It is also indisputable that the history of Black people in America has too often been neglected in American history. The irony of these two conflicting realities is telling. Still, the effect of *The 1619 Project*, and books like it, is to call into question the moral legitimacy of love for country, and of the American project writ large.

Then there is the movement on the right advancing Catholic integralism or magisterial Christian nationalism. Both ideas are based on the premise that classical liberalism has had its day. Radical feminism; endless racial strife; endless war; crony capitalism; the abuses of Big Tech; the dehumanization that attends abortion; and the sexual revolution that gave us no-fault divorce, then same-sex marriage, and now drag queens and hormone suppression for teens have all been the products of classical liberalism, at least according to so-called postliberals. "A political philosophy that was launched to foster greater equity, defend a pluralist tapestry of different cultures and beliefs, protect human dignity, and, of course, expand liberty, in practice generates titanic inequality, enforces uniformity and homogeneity, fosters material and spiritual degradation, and undermines freedom," wrote Patrick J. Deneen in 2018.[7] Catholic integralists have argued that American government should thus be entirely reimagined from the ground up. The purpose, or end, of a society should not be to secure unalienable rights for its citizens, as our Declaration of Independence stated. The end of society is the common good, defined in extrinsic and intrinsic terms. The upshot of this understanding is that temporal authority should be subjected to spiritual authority, in that the spiritual authority directs the temporal authority to citizens' heavenly good, or "beatitude."[8] The best polity will be a mixed one, including monarchy, aristocracy, and democracy. Furthermore, such a polity should include "an element of hereditary power" based on prudence.[9]

Similarly, Protestant magisterial Christian nationalist Stephen Wolfe argued for a newly imagined government from top to bottom.

He wrote that America is dominated by pagan nationalists, and that the only way out of pagan nationalism is via Christian nationalism.[10] Wolfe built his case for a Christian nation in a book of nearly five hundred pages, in which he attempted to orient citizens (better described as subjects) to heaven and be ruled by a "Christian prince." The Christian prince governs by divine right—"the civil power of the prince comes immediately from God" and "the prince mediates God's divine civil rule." Furthermore, the Christian prince "holds the most excellent office, exceeding even that of the church minister, for it is most like God."[11] Wolfe's Christian prince is to possess executive, judicial, and legislative power in contrast to the mixed polity of the Catholic integral model proposed by Thomas Crean and Alan Fimister.

The common denominator between integralism and magisterial Christian nationalism is postliberalism. The idea here is that classical liberalism is dead—it is a victim of its own success, but it is dead. Christians must rise and champion a new order. Wolfe even has an entire chapter in which he justified violent revolution and came tantalizingly close to calling for it outright. "Let us train the will and cultivate the resolve," he wrote.[12]

But what is an American? Rather than attempting to make an abstract, *a priori* claim about what an American is, let us consider some real examples. Was Booker T. Washington an American? He was born in slavery. His mother was enslaved, and he never knew the identity of his white father. He rose to become the most prominent African American in the nation, having founded Tuskegee Institute in 1881 and being the first African American to be hosted as a dinner guest at the White House in 1902 by President Theodore Roosevelt. Washington's biographer, Robert J. Norrell, wrote, "Optimism was in his view the only practical posture, even if the present often made hopefulness about the future seem like folly."[13]

What about Rosa Parks? Was she an American? Parks was a freedom fighter, famously refusing to give up her seat to a white man on a bus in Montgomery and being arrested as a result. Her actions gave birth to the civil rights movement beginning with the Montgomery Bus Boycott that ended when the Supreme Court struck down segregation on public transport in 1956. "I had no idea when I refused to give up my seat on that Montgomery bus that my small action would help put an end to segregation laws in the South. I only knew I was tired of being pushed around," Parks wrote in her autobiography.[14]

What about Clare Boothe Luce? Was she an American? A prolific writer, political thinker, a member of Congress from Connecticut, and the first woman to serve as an American ambassador (to Italy), Luce received the Presidential Medal of Freedom in 1983 from President Ronald Reagan. Born out of wedlock in 1903, she became one of the most influential anti-Communist conservatives of the twentieth century. She was famous for her way with words and her high-spirited wit. After Sandra Day O'Connor took her seat on the Supreme Court as the first female justice, she invited Luce and Sylvia Jukes Morris (who became Luce's biographer) to join her for lunch and then to attend a hearing in the Court. According to Morris, Luce got impatient after twenty minutes of the hearing. Upon receiving a note from Chief Justice Warren Burger about the hearing that said, "Welcome, but what a sad case," Luce turned to Morris and said, "Now we'll have to stay another ten minutes."[15]

Washington, Parks, and Luce are irresistible, in part, because we instantly recognize their Americanness. We could consider countless examples of Americans who exude Americanness in their biographies. Washington, Parks, and Luce each had a few things in common that we might identify as American traits. They lived with purpose. They set out to leave their worlds better than they found them. They were optimistic, not cynical, sentimental, or utopian. They were realistic about their world and about the obstacles in front of them. But they lived for ideals that transcended their individual experiences, feelings, and realities. Their lives exuded optimism, not only by what they said, but more importantly, by what they did. They lived by both precept and example, and we will always have the testimony of their lives from which to benefit.

Not everything about Americans is good, true, or beautiful. And not every American has been faithful to American ideals. It is also true that people of other countries and traditions exhibit similar virtuous traits as Americans, and they are also worthy of emulation. Americans are not ontologically or morally superior to others. But Americans, as the lives of Washington, Parks, Luce, and countless others exhibit, have always been an intentional and aspirational people. Purpose and aspiration are at the core of our founding and have remained so ever since. Being an aspirational people, Americans generally have been able to assess their situation as they found it, formulate what they wanted to achieve, and come up with plans for how to make it happen. Consider Levi Preston, who fought at Concord in April 1775. When asked by Mellen Chamberlain in 1843 why he decided to join the fight against British regulars at Concord, the ninety-one-year-old Preston said that he felt no oppression, had never purchased any stamps, neither did he drink tea. He had never read John Locke or the English Commonwealthmen. With some exasperation, Chamberlain said, "Well, then, what was the matter?" Preston replied, "Young man, what we meant in fighting the British was this: we always had been free and we meant to be free always!"[16]

Ronald Reagan was a supreme storyteller, and he was fond of telling a particular story that captures this optimistic and intentional quality of Americans. A family had two young boys, one a gloomy pessimist, the other a cheerful optimist. One Christmas, the parents came up with a small test for the boys to see just how deeply their respective pessimism and optimism went. So, on Christmas Eve, the parents placed several gifts under the tree—glittering gifts for the pessimistic boy, but only one drab package for the optimist, a canvas bag of horse manure. Keep in mind, it was only a test; both boys were eventually receiving gifts of equal value. But when they saw the gifts that were there under the tree, they were unaware of their parents' experiment. The father asked the pessimist how Santa had treated him this year. "Okay, I guess," the surly boy replied. "I got a bicycle, but I will have to keep the tires pumped. Also, I will have to keep it locked up in case someone steals it. I got a basketball, but I don't have a basketball hoop. And I got a football, but I don't know how to throw it. I did get this nice camera, but you know how it is. I'll have to get someone to show me how to use it." All this time, the optimistic boy had found his bag of manure, opened it up, and began searching meticulously through the house. When the father asked him about his Christmas, and why he seemed to be so distracted, the boy triumphantly exclaimed, "It's the best ever! Santa brought me a pony, but I haven't found him yet!" Americans have been characterized as optimists like that boy seeing in a bag of offal the representation of the most wonderful gift he could imagine. Americans have historically rejected gloomy pessimism since the beginning of their existence on this continent.

Intentional optimism like that is historically characteristic of Americans. So is their collective sense of humor. Writers like Artemus Ward (Charles Farrar Browne, 1834–1867), Seba Smith (1792–1868), Bill Nye (1850–1896), Mark Twain (Samuel Clemens, 1835–1910), Finley Peter Dunne (1867–1936), and Will Rogers (1879–1935) were some popular humorists in the nineteenth and early twentieth centuries. American humor during that time was earthy, satirical, and expressed through various forms of media. "The humor of the stage and the humor of politics brought popularity to the American jesters of the nineteenth century and numerous publications—newspapers, magazines, comic journals, books, almanacs—and lectures as well helped carry the native humor to a growing number of people," wrote University of Chicago folklorist Walter Blair in 1931.[17]

In the twentieth century, Ring Lardner (1885–1933), H. L. Mencken (1880–1956), Max Schulman (1919–1988), Erma Bombeck (1927–1996), Garrison Keillor (b. 1942), and Steve Martin (b. 1945) are exemplary figures of an American style of humor. As a boy, my father introduced me to Garrison Keillor's *News from Lake Wobegon* series. The two of us were addicted to the show, and Keillor's homespun stories of life in northern Minnesota, a place where "all the women are strong, all the men are good looking, and all the children are above average." He would always begin his routine by saying, "Well, it's been a quiet week in Lake Wobegon," and then proceed to tell stories that had you riveted to the radio. Even as a teenager, I would be mesmerized listening to Garrison Keillor's heavy, baritone voice tell absorbing tales of ordinary folks doing ordinary things that were hilarious, heartbreaking, and everything in between. And my grandfather introduced me to Patrick Dennis's character Auntie Mame, the euphoric, sparkling, and sanguine title character played by Rosalind Russell in the 1958 movie who unforgettably exclaimed, "Life is a banquet, and most poor suckers are starving to death!"[18]

Unfortunately, many Americans of late are insisting on starving to death. They have forgotten so much that has animated their character, culture, and history. The sense of humor; the purposeful, aspiring optimism; the devotion to faith, family, and flag—all these are dropping away in the wake of identity politics on both left and right, along with hyperindividualism stirred by obsession with social media and submerged under a swirling sea of subjectivist sentimentalized epistemology animated by unmoored emotions and something nonsensical called "my truth." Americans are turning inward, and as they do so, they are turning against each other. We take offense as easily as previous generations laughed. Dennis Powell wrote, "Within the context of America losing its sense of humor, the woke cancel culture was born. It replaced humor with dogma—which is no laughing matter—and tried to erase anyone who disagreed."[19] In their preference for some abstract divine-right monarchy, grim Catholic integralists and glum magisterial Christian nationalists have given up on America. In the same way, the radical Left considers the American experiment in self-government really an experiment in depravity, and thus seeks to purge the memory of who we were from our minds by their blind iconoclasm. Perhaps the greatest tragedy in all this is how these ideas on the far left and right have taken hold of the imaginations of the younger generations. Youth is the period of life when you're supposed to be hopeful, but today's young people are more anxious and despairing than perhaps any young people in our history. We are losing our country, and many young American citizens shrug their shoulders as they bid good riddance to the inheritance of liberty handed down to them by their forebears.

C. S. Lewis is well known for having extolled the reading of old books. He wrote, "if [the ordinary reader] must read only the new or only the old, I would advise him to read the old."[20] Daniel Boorstin, former librarian of Congress (1975–1987) and University of Chicago consensus historian, is worth reading. At the risk of losing my historian friends who know well that consensus history, dominant in American historiography after World War II until the rise of the New Left in the mid-1960s, is itself history, I propose a reconsideration of some of Boorstin's thought. Boorstin was excoriated by historian Eric Foner in 1994 for allegedly embracing a simplistic view of an innocent and monolithic America that "was the sort of onward march of progress and freedom for the world."[21] My used, former library copy of Boorstin's 1953 *The Genius of American Politics* is stamped in black ink on its sides with the word "DISCARDED," indicative of how the historical profession has come to regard the author and his ideas. While we can acknowledge that consensus historiography in general, and Boorstin in particular, was often guilty of oversimplification in pressing the thesis that Americans have historically avoided domestic ideological conflicts, it does not follow that Boorstin should be dismissed entirely. Given the political and cultural climate of early twenty-first-century America, it is worth revisiting an important and influential thinker from another time who presented arguments about American history and identity that were based upon his veneration of rooted tradition and embrace of patriotism. It might actually be refreshing.

Boorstin's *The Genius of American Politics* is a collection of lectures he delivered at the University of Chicago in 1952. Central to his argument was that American democracy emerged from particular historical circumstances and geographical features unique to the United States. Those circumstances of history and features of geography were the sources of American culture and mores, or "values," as he called them. The context of his book was defined by the early years of the Cold War. In February and March of 1952, when Boorstin delivered the lectures that ended up in the book, the United States Senate was debating ratification of the Treaty of San Francisco, which established the terms for the formal end of World War II in the Pacific as well as collective security arrangements between the United States, Japan, the Philippines, Australia, New Zealand, and Great Britain. Those collective security arrangements were aimed at containing and deterring the Communists in the Soviet Union and China. The treaty was ratified by the Senate in early April 1952. Boorstin was speaking directly into that context as he said in his introduction: "The thesis of this book is that nothing could be more un-American than to urge other countries to imitate America."[22] Thus, Boorstin's book served as historical analysis, celebration of American character, and warning against overconfidence in that character. The book is, from some perspectives, outdated. Some of his conclusions, particularly about the Civil War being rooted in consensus around American constitutionalism, are stretched. But given these and other flaws, the book is remarkably prescient and applicable for our times, considering the contemporary collapse of confidence in traditionally held American values.

Eighteenth-century America, argued Boorstin, did not produce any original political theorists. There were no Hobbeses, Lockes, Molesworths, Smiths, or Pufendorfs among the American founders. The national founding did not emerge from the abstract thought of philosophers but was instead marked by what Boorstin described as "givenness."[23] By givenness, Boorstin meant that American political traditions at the national founding were already in place. No innovations were necessary because the framework for the order that came out of the 1787–1788 Constitutional Convention and ratification debates already, in Boorstin's words, "equipped our nation at its birth with a perfect and complete political theory, adequate to all our needs."[24] Thus, Boorstin understood givenness to be an inheritance from past experience and political consideration.

Not only did givenness refer to the inheritance of a past tradition. Boorstin argued that tradition continued to serve Americans in the present. While our values are "a gift of the *past*," they remain "a gift from the *present*" as Americans apply the constitutional tradition to contemporary questions and issues. Our present experience with republican democracy is animated and informed by the tradition of the past, so our traditions are not a dead letter but thoroughly relevant and practical for the challenges we meet with today.

Perhaps most controversial is Boorstin's third aspect of givenness, that is, "the *continuity* or homogeneity of our history . . . so that our past merges indistinguishably into our present."[25] American identity and history are more complex than that. Still, there is a great deal of truth in Boorstin's argument that Americans feel a sense of continuity with the founding such that we often see the founders as our "contemporaries."[26] More recently, historian Gordon Wood made a similar case for such continuity in American history because of the unique nature of the origin of American identity. He wrote, "No other major nation honors its past historical characters, especially characters who existed two centuries ago, in quite the manner we Americans do."[27] Why? American identity is not rooted in blood or soil, but in beliefs. Wood wrote, "We go back to the Revolution and the values and institutions that came out of it in order to refresh and reaffirm our nationhood."[28] Why else would contentious discussions about the founding; racial injustice; the applicability of the Constitution to war, religious expression, elections, and other issues be so animated by historical arguments today?

Boorstin acknowledged that Americans of his time were "hypersensitive" to their history, and that is still true of us. He pointed to Progressive historian Charles A. Beard's 1913 *An Economic Interpretation of the Constitution*, in which Beard argued that the framers were more committed to their financial interests than they were to the concepts of equality, rights, and liberties. Beard's book "scandalized respectable scholars," many of whom considered the book "a wholesale attack on the American creed."[29] A similar judgment could be made of a contemporary historian like Allen Guelzo after the publication of *The 1619 Project*. Guelzo described *The 1619 Project* as unhistorical, ignorant, cynical, and an illogical conspiracy theory. Furthermore, he said, "it is evangelism, but evangelism for a gospel of disenchantment whose ultimate purpose is the hollowing out of the meaning of freedom, so that every defense of freedom drops nervously from the hands of people who have been made too ashamed to defend it."[30]

American republican democracy has always been called an experiment. An experiment, by definition, is based on inductive reasoning and observation of how concrete elements behave in a controlled environment; designed to verify or falsify a general hypothesis; predicated on concrete experience in real time; dependent on evidence; and yielding probable conclusions. In these ways, an experiment differs from an abstract, *a priori* theory. In contrast to an experiment, *a priori* reasoning is based on deductive thought processes through syllogistic argumentation; designed to arrive at a particular conclusion that follows from prior statements that build one upon the other; predicated on propositions that require no instantiation in real time or place; dependent on validity; and yielding sure and certain conclusions, conditioned upon the soundness of the argument. The American experiment is a test of "whether that nation, or any nation so conceived and so dedicated, can long endure," in Abraham Lincoln's celebrated words of the Gettysburg Address. The experiment has been tested in the context of changing circumstances, and some tests were more forceful and concentrated than others. But the experiment itself remains unchanged—can the American people govern themselves with equal justice under law, predicated on God-given unalienable rights and individual liberties that are known and recognized by long experience? Unlike a valid abstract *a priori* deduction, an experiment *can really fail*. A deductive argument only exists in the mind, whereas an experiment involving concrete subjects exists in reality. Catholic integralism, magisterial Christian nationalism, and progressive utopianism (or nihilism) only exist in the mind, but the American constitutional order exists here and now, and is made up of actual people—dead, living, and yet to be born. If theories fall apart, who cares? If American liberty and republican democracy fall apart, especially from the irresistible application of forces emerging from some abstract theory, that would be a tragedy with unthinkable consequences to present and future generations alike.

Boorstin took the idea of the American experiment as evidence of givenness. Because American values have served as an inheritance received from the past, the American experiment has also been handed down from generation to generation from the national founding. The question of American self-government, asked in an eighteenth-century context in which no country possessed any tradition of republican democracy, was originally framed in the minds of the founding generation. Every generation of Americans since has asked the same question, albeit in differing contexts with unique challenges. Boorstin wrote that the American experiment is "the test or the proof of values supposed to have been clearly in the minds of the Founders," and thus "we have leaned heavily on history to clarify our image of ourselves."[31] The American experiment was, and continues to be, predicated upon a set of political theories that were articulated in the founding documents, and those founding documents remain the frame of reference for all our national political activity. As the experiment continues to be conducted by succeeding generations, the constitutional order flexes and evolves with the times, and that flexibility is a feature of the constitutional order as seen, for example, in the amendment process of Article V of the Constitution. To describe such flexibility, Boorstin used the metaphor of a lobster. Like a lobster, American society has an exoskeletal framework. This framework was developed in the Constitution—"we think of ourselves as growing *into* our skeleton, filling it out with the experience and resources of recent ages. But we always suppose that the outlines were rigidly drawn in the beginning."[32]

Even when Americans criticize themselves for hypocrisy, they do so within the framework of their shared past, especially the national founding. The ideals of the Declaration of Independence, as well as the rights and liberties that are contained therein, have been the inspiration for civil reform movements going back to when the ink was barely dry on the parchment itself. Lemuel Haynes (1753–1833), veteran of the Continental Army and the first African American to be ordained in a major Protestant denomination (Congregational church, 1785), called for the abolition of slavery on the basis of the Declaration just months after it was signed. He did so in an essay entitled "Liberty Further Extended," written on forty-six 3 ¾" x 6" pages. The first lines of the essay are direct quotations from the Declaration's preamble: "we hold these truths to be self-Evident, that all men are created Equal, and they are Endowed By their Creator with Ceartain unalienable rights, that among these are Life, Liberty, and the pursuit of happyness."[33] His central argument was that liberty was an unalienable right possessed not only by Whites but also by Blacks. Therefore, slavery was morally wrong. It was also against the stated policy of the Continental Congress, which had formally adopted the Declaration and all its affirmations on July 4, 1776, as the basis for the thirteen colonies' separation from Great Britain. "I think it not hyperbolic to affirm, that Even an affrican, has Equally as good a right to his Liberty in common with Englishmen," Haynes wrote.[34] From 1776 until today, Americans of every generation have looked to the ideals of the founding and called the nation to faithfulness to those ideals. Equality under law, rights, civil liberties, the pursuit of happiness, the advancement of the general welfare of the nation— these ideals were never abstract, but concrete in that Americans have purposed themselves to fulfill in real time and against long odds. Failures to fulfill those ideals have led to the greatest controversies in American history, but those failures are themselves evidence of Boorstin's thesis of givenness—American values were given as a complete theory at the founding and continue to serve as the shared frame of reference by Americans today. "We Americans are reared with a feeling for the unity of our history and an unprecedented belief in the normality of our kind of life to our place on earth," Boorstin wrote.[35]

Again, the reader should take caution not to go too far with Boorstin's thesis. We should not embrace the kind of American exceptionalism that features an innocent, divinely appointed nation central to a Hegelian world-historical movement. America is not God's chosen nation. And we should not misunderstand Boorstin's concept of givenness. Givenness does not entail some kind of American normativity for the whole world. Givenness simply refers to the idea that every generation of Americans has received a tradition from those preceding their own, and they have handed down that unique American tradition to their descendants. American civic values are thus transferable from parents to children because they consist of features that are broadly universal but simultaneously practical in specific historical contexts. Furthermore, America is made up of Americans, and Americans, as all human beings, are fallen and sinful. American history is a story of oppression, injustice, violence, and all kinds of offenses. Even considering these failures, America is a great nation with a noble history marked by durable commitments to preserving and extending liberty predicated upon the broadly Christian concept of human dignity. Notwithstanding its undeniable failures, America has been an exemplar of liberty and democracy to the whole world for its entire history. The history of immigration to the United States from the founding period to the present is an enduring testament to America's exemplarist role in human civilization. In a political and social sense, America truly is an exceptional nation, serving as a model for republican democracy consisting of a federal system of authority dedicated to the preservation and enjoyment of liberty under just law.

Tocqueville's classic work *Democracy in America* is the most important work on the subject ever written. Tocqueville is one of the most widely quoted, yet least understood, figures in American history. All Americans should read Tocqueville's writings, not only his famous *Democracy in America* but also his *The Ancien Regime and the French Revolution*. Tocqueville's penetrating insights serve as both historical artifacts and applicable principles for our own day. But first, some context.

The period from 1815 to 1848, from the Treaty of Ghent concluding the War of 1812 to the Treaty of Guadalupe Hidalgo ending the Mexican-American War, was a period of impressive economic, territorial, and demographic growth in American history.[36] Tocqueville's visit, from his arrival on May 9, 1831, through his departure on February 20, 1832, took place at the chronological center of this period of growth. Most Americans worked the land, and as Daniel Walker Howe wrote, "life in America in 1815 was dirty, smelly, laborious, and uncomfortable."[37] Recreation was rare, clothing was harsh, and most people hardly ever bathed. In 1832, a New England doctor reported that four out of five of his patients bathed less than once a year. Most households were crowded, heated by one fireplace, and everyone slept in the same bed.[38] Still, most people owned their own land, the entrepreneurial spirit was developing in earnest, and thanks to a booming economy (with the exceptions of the depressions occurring in 1819 and 1837), GDP (gross domestic product) averaged about 4 percent per year during this period.[39] Neologisms were coming into use, terms such as "self-made man," "businessman," "millionaire," and most importantly of all, "comfort." "Comfort" was a term denoting material well-being, an important idea in Tocqueville's writings. As Richard Swedberg said, "Tocqueville, who came from an aristocratic background, was quick to spot the new trend toward middle class comfort and to theorize it in terms of his scheme of aristocracy and democracy. What luxury was to aristocracy, comfort was to democracy."[40] It would be wrong to describe America as a classless society in the first half of the nineteenth century, but class was determined solely by possession of money, not by family name, title to land, hereditary privilege, or church authority as in feudal aristocracy.

Quite early in Alexis de Tocqueville's consideration of American democracy, a stark contrast formed in his mind between French and American society. The fundamental similarities between these two societies were, first, that both were seeing the permeation of equality of conditions, and second, that revolutions served to accelerate the spread of equality of conditions throughout their respective social, religious, and political institutions. But here the similarities between the two societies stopped. Revolutions in France yielded disruption, violence, chaos, degradation, and tyranny. Revolution in America resulted in comparative stability. America, Tocqueville said, "sees the results of the democratic revolution that is taking place among us, without having had the revolution itself."[41] In other words, the revolution of equality of conditions had brought peace and liberty to America, and America managed to avoid suffering the excesses of that revolution that France continued to experience during Tocqueville's lifetime.

For us, Tocqueville and the world he inhabited are both enormously foreign. For one thing, Tocqueville was born in 1805 into a truly ancient family. Many people in contemporary generations have trouble naming their own grandparents and great-grandparents (not a problem exclusive to our own times, but a problem with democratic societies, as Tocqueville noted). Tocqueville's family, by contrast, could follow its ancestry back almost a millennium. Also, Tocqueville was born into a specific position in the aristocratic hierarchy—and yet, while he occupied a position of privilege in a centuries-old feudal order that began its development at the fall of the Roman Empire, he was intrigued with the idea of equality of conditions—provided liberty was secured and preserved. And lastly, Tocqueville was a product of revolutionary France. His grandparents and parents were victims of the infamous Reign of Terror under Robespierre. He was born at the height of Napoleon's power. He was a minor judge at the time of the July Revolution of 1830. And he was a representative in the Chamber of Deputies during the 1848 revolutions, eleven years before the end of his life.

Tocqueville had a keen understanding of revolutions—what they were, how they got started, what they promised, how they unfolded, and the results they brought. For one thing, he carefully studied the history of the 1789 revolution in France. In 1856, he wrote *The Ancien Regime and the French Revolution*, in which he identified a great irony: the French revolutionaries sought to abolish the existing form of society, and the result was anarchy. He said, "Since the French Revolution had as its objective not simply to change the existing government but to abolish the existing form of society, it was obliged simultaneously to attack all established powers, to undermine all acknowledged influences, to efface traditions, to renew mores and customs, and somehow to rid the human mind of all the ideas on which respect and obedience had previously been founded. This accounts for its singularly anarchical character."[42]

Besides his historical and philosophical work, Tocqueville had direct experience of the revolution and its effects, both through his family and his own encounter with revolutions in his lifetime. The 1789 revolution cast the longest shadow over the Tocqueville family, a shadow that Alexis lived under all his life. His mother and father were victims of the horror of the French Revolution during the years 1793–1794. Tocqueville's father, Hervé de Tocqueville, married Louise Marie Peletier de Rosambo in 1793. Louise's grandfather, Lamoignon de Malesherbes, had served as defense attorney for Louis XVI before the National Convention just months before their wedding. But on January 21, 1793, the king was publicly beheaded at the guillotine set up in the Place de la Révolution (later, the Place de la Concorde). Later that year, Hervé and Louise were living at the Malesherbes chateau enjoying their first months as husband and wife when commissioners arrived to arrest and escort to prison the entire family represented by three generations. Their property was confiscated, and four members of the family were beheaded. The elderly Lamoignon was forced to watch as his daughter was guillotined before he himself was bound to the scaffold and beheaded. Hervé and Louise were scheduled to be executed, but they were freed from prison after Robespierre, in a delicious twist, himself went to the guillotine. Hervé was only twenty-one, but after ten months in prison and having witnessed the murder of his wife's grandfather, mother, uncle, and aunt, the stress he endured caused his hair to turn white.[43]

Louise never recovered from this experience. Some of young Alexis's earliest memories were of his mother's melancholia from the trauma of the revolution. He described a poignant family scene that gives us an idea of how profound the family's grief was:

> I remember today as if it were yesterday a certain evening in a chateau where my father then dwelt, and where a family celebration had gathered to us a large number of our near relatives. The domestics had been sent out; the whole family had collected about the hearth. My mother, who had a voice sweet and penetrating, began to sing an air which had been famous in our civil troubles, and whose words told of the misfortunes of Louis XVI and of his death. When she ceased, everyone was weeping; not over the many private misfortunes they had suffered, not even over the many relatives lost in the civil war and on the scaffold, but over the fate of this man who had died more than fifteen years before and whom most of those who were weeping over him had never seen. But this man had been the King.[44]

The French Revolution, Tocqueville wrote in *The Ancien Regime*, sought to destroy a core set of social and political realities, and when it did, everything else was also destroyed. One of the other realities that the revolution destroyed was a set of mores—or customs, manners, cultural habits—informed by tradition and religion, especially respect and proper obedience to legitimate authority.[45] Tocqueville admitted that many Christians betrayed its foundational commitment to human equality—that is, the idea that all people are equal in the sight of God. Too often in the days immediately preceding the revolution, religion had allied itself with tyranny. But not all Christians were guilty. Tocqueville wrote that Christians who served as champions of liberty during the revolution in France knew that Christianity served as the basis for liberty because Christianity formed the moral underpinnings of society. Tocqueville wrote in the introduction to *Democracy in America*, "you cannot establish the reign of liberty without that of mores, nor found mores without beliefs."[46] Later in the first volume, Tocqueville explained that

American society's mores—that is, society's "habits of the heart," "the ensemble of ideas from which the habits of the mind are formed," and "the whole moral and intellectual state of a people"—were more influential than anything else in fashioning the ethical assumptions of the culture.[47] The mores were more critical to the success or failure of liberty in America, more so even than the laws. Tocqueville observed that American democracy was maintained most generally by the cultivation of federalism, the fostering of township institutions, and the limiting of the power of the majority through the courts. But the mores were more influential than anything else, not only in the maintenance of democracy, but in the protection of liberty and the prevention of tyranny of the majority. And what informed the mores? In a word, it was *morality* informed by Christianity, supported and advanced through freedom of religion.

Tocqueville wrote *Democracy in America* so that his own countrymen in France could learn lessons from Americans who had experienced a revolution of their own and yet did not see the rise of tyranny that came with the extension of equality of conditions. "I sought there," Tocqueville wrote, "an image of democracy itself, its tendencies, its character, its prejudices, its passions; I wanted to know democracy if only to know at least what we must hope or fear from it."[48] Democratic societies, defined by equality of conditions, were marked by the social, economic, religious, and political mobility that resulted in the elimination of traditional hierarchies. Equality of conditions was the defining characteristic in America, Tocqueville observed. While he had some positive assessments regarding the spread of equality of conditions, he realized that tyranny was particularly threatening in an equal society, because he saw that people would abandon liberty more readily than equality because equality's benefits were easier to come by in comparison to those of liberty. But it was liberty, not equality, that led to human greatness. A free society ranked among the highest possible achievements for humankind. Reflecting on his travels, experiences, and the history of revolutions near the end of his life, Tocqueville wrote:

Only freedom can effectively combat the flaws natural to [democratic] societies and keep them from sliding down a slippery slope [to despotism]. Only freedom can rescue citizens from the isolation in which the very independence of their condition has mired them. Only freedom can compel them to come together and warm each other's spirits through mutual exchange and persuasion and join action in practical affairs. Only freedom can save them from the worship of Mammon and the petty vexations of their private business, enabling them to sense the constant presence of the nation above and alongside them. Only freedom can substitute higher, more powerful passions for the love of material comforts and supply ambition with goals more worthy than the acquisition of wealth. Only freedom, finally, can create the light by which it is possible to see and judge the vices and virtues of humankind.[49]

Liberty marked American society off from every other society in 1790. Historically, liberty has served as America's essential national attribute. Religion has generally served to promote liberty in America. There are notable exceptions, to be sure. Anti-Catholicism, anti-Mormonism, anti-Semitism, anti-Islamicism are among the most notorious violations of religious liberty in American history. These have been the exception rather than the rule. Disestablishment and free exercise of religion were built into the constitutional order from the beginning of the American experiment for citizens to flourish, both as individuals and as communities on the local, state, and national levels. Violations of religious liberty, no matter their basis, and regardless of when and where they occur, are always violations of the substance of the American constitutional tradition.

The challenge to the American experiment in the early decades of the twenty-first century is to defend the tradition of the harmony between the spirit of liberty and the spirit of religion. In defending America's two spirits, we defend what it means to be an American. The two spirits are not all that animates America. But the two spirits are essential to American values and American identity. Both the spirit of liberty and the spirit of religion require protection, cultivation, maintenance, and development from generation to generation. They require active citizenship predicated upon imagination, proper love of country, a realistic account of human nature that calls for ordered liberty, a virtuous and mature approach to history, and a humble submission to the eternal. Active citizenship does not happen by accident or pessimism, and a citizenry that is not aspirational will never be able to attain the blessings that come with active citizenship.

Who is in the best position to meet this challenge to the American experiment? My argument for this book is simple. American conservatives are in the best position to articulate and defend the best of the American character by receiving, venerating, applying, and handing down the tradition of harmony between the spirits of liberty and religion. The American conservative tradition is predominately based in the evolutionary, dispositional, humanistic, and aspirational conservatism of Edmund Burke. Burkean conservatism offers the clearest and most reliable understanding of liberty, grounded in eternal truths and in the American experience. Therefore, American conservatives living consistently within the Burkean tradition are in the best position to guard and advance the complementary spirits of liberty and religion as Tocqueville observed and articulated that complementarity nearly two centuries ago.

The book's argument will proceed through seven chapters. Chapter 1 will seek to answer the question, what is a conservative? It is a particularly fraught question, for conservatives are infamous for fighting each other over that very question. It is also a difficult question because, although Edmund Burke is the traditional founder of modern conservatism, Burke never used the term "conservative" to describe himself, nor did he intend on launching an intellectual movement by that or any other name. Nevertheless, conservatism can and should be defined in precise terms. And while there are many schools of thought in contemporary discourse on the right, I follow historian Peter Viereck in arguing that conservatism in American history has been articulated in two forms, one evolutionary and dispositional, and the other, reactionary and political.

Chapters 2 through 6 will consider conservatism and the imagination, the nation, ordered liberty, history, and religion. Imagination represents a humanistic part of conservatism, specifically, that part of conservatism that builds up and supports human dignity and worth. Human imagination is undermined by our modern aversion to boredom, resistance to religion, politicization of the humanities, tedium in ordinary tasks, and impatience. It is also undermined by an overreliance on technology, which results in dehumanization. Imagination helps to form the conscience by serving as inspiration toward the good, the true, and the beautiful. And imagination contributes to tradition by serving as a form of experience via the collected wisdom of previous generations.

A conservative understanding of the nation is predicated on differentiating three terms: "nationalism," "patriotism," and "nationality." Nationalism and patriotism are often contrasted with one another, but the concept of a nationality has evolved since the national founding. Every generation has asked and answered the question, what is an American? We continue to ask that question today. Patriotism is not something from which to shrink out of shame for past failures, because it involves sincere, yet ordered, love for country. Love for country takes the forms of both celebration and critique, because we know that all people, Americans included, are fallible.

Order precedes liberty. Liberty flourishes under order, which provides for just law. Liberty is a means to an end, not an end in itself. The end of liberty is happiness, in the sense that Jefferson intended when he drafted the Declaration. Happiness refers to private and public flourishing, which is the individual and corporate enjoyment of the good. The state's role is to create the conditions in which citizens may pursue their own flourishing justly in private and public life. The role of religious institutions, specifically, the church—not the state—is to point people to the highest good, which for Christians (my own religious tradition) is eternal life in Christ. Religious institutions *and* religious people must be free from state or cultural interference in publicly living out their faiths to fulfill their functions. If the freedom of religious institutions and people to live their faith out in public is stifled by external political or cultural pressures, then happiness and flourishing in the citizenry are not attainable. Apart from permanent things, liberty degrades into license and order degrades into authoritarianism. The nightmare of anarchy and tyranny is the sad result.

History and tradition are closely related, in that tradition is understood through the critical lens of history and a dedicated submission to virtue. History tells us what the present generation can morally retain in the tradition, and what traditions that may have held in the past no longer apply. History helps us make sense of the past, in order that we may have wisdom for living in the present. Rootless nostalgia and cynicism, which are prominent ways in which Americans interpret the past, both emerge from an ahistorical sense of despair. But history, when interpreted in light of permanent things, can be an antidote to despair. Unmoored from permanent things, history is a nightmare, but when universals such as virtue guide our interpretation of the past, history is redemptive.

Finally, religion defines what conservative thinker Russell Kirk called "permanent things." The permanent things refer to eternal truths that apply to everyone, everywhere, at all times. They are the basis for human interactions, thus, morality and law are directly related to religion. Religion tells us what is universal and unchanging. Religion gives us a standard by which we can judge those issues that are open for compromise, and which issues are not.

In conclusion, we will return to the theme of America's two spirits of liberty and religion. What does religious liberty mean, given our considerations of the Burkean conservative temperament concerning the imagination, nationality, ordered liberty, history, and religion? We will find that liberty and religion are not mutually exclusive categories. Religion is necessary to liberty, from philosophical and practical standpoints. Conservatives are in the best position to defend American liberty, because conservatives conserve the values and traditions handed down by previous generations. Those who want to remake American society along the lines of *a priori*, deductive, abstract theorizing, whether on the left or the right, are radical. We do not need to remake America. The constitutional order established by the founders in the eighteenth century has not become obsolete just because it is old. The America that our parents, grandparents, and great-grandparents fought for, often died for, and handed down to us is still worth defending. Conservatives conserve the American tradition of harmony between liberty and religion. Conservatives should be the ones standing for American liberty now as much as ever.

I write this book primarily to the younger generations. It is they who have the most to gain from a generous Western and American inheritance, and the most to lose if that inheritance is lost or squandered.

CHAPTER ONE

The Permanent beneath the Flux

Liberalism argues, conservatism simply *is*.

—Peter Viereck, *Conservatism*

In July 1603, James VI of Scotland was crowned King James I of England and Scotland. James had been king in Scotland since 1567, and when Elizabeth I died, the House of Tudor died with her. The illustrious dynasty of Henry VII, Henry VIII, Edward VI, poor Lady Jane Grey (who only reigned nine days and then was executed at the age of sixteen by her cousin who deposed her), Mary I, and Elizabeth I ended and was succeeded by the House of Stuart with the rise of James. Under Elizabeth's rule, Catholics were fined for not receiving the elements of communion in the Anglican church. Catholics were hopeful that James would lift the fine, and he did, but by early 1604, James banished Catholic priests. By the end of that year, James reinstated the fines. Many Catholics in England had quite enough of James barely a year after he took the throne because of his hostility to them.

By May 1605, a group of Catholic collaborators decided to do something about James. They concocted a plan to blow up the chamber in which the king, the lords, and the commons were assembled to open Parliament in the fall of 1605. They plotted to stuff a cellar under the Parliament building with gunpowder, to ignite it as the proceedings began, and to destroy the structure and kill the king, members of the royal family, and all members of Parliament who were in attendance. The leader of what became known as the Gunpowder Plot was Robert Catesby. Guy Fawkes, the name most famously associated with the conspiracy, was to guard the hoard of gunpowder in the cellar below the Parliament building.

The plot was discovered November 4, 1605, just a day before the Parliament was to open. The jurist Edward Coke led the prosecution of the conspirators, and eight were tortured and executed for treason on January 30, 1606. As the condemned were led to the scaffold to be "hanged to the brink of death, castrated, disemboweled, beheaded, and cut into quarters," they were forced through the crowds facing backwards as "a symbol of disorder, the world turned upside down," as historian Jonathan Healey described.[1]

Disorder, the world turning upside down: if there is one thing that conservatives set their minds to oppose, it is this. Conservatism as a body of social, religious, political, aesthetic, economic, historical, and diplomatic thought is committed to the right ordering of human activity, private and public, individual and communal, from birth to death in order to secure liberty. When thought and action are ordered rightly, peace and flourishing will prevail. When order metastasizes into cancerous disorder, the result is chaos and anarchy, tyranny and slavery, destruction and death. The Gunpowder Plot ended brutishly, but it is in every way illustrative of how even good ends never justify evil means, a cherished conservative principle based on order.

Just order does not come naturally to human persons. Persons are prone to selfishness, lust for power and wealth at the expense of others. Persons are marked by avarice, dishonesty, and violence. Jews and Christians have a word for moral error: sin. Jews and Christians, among the primary influencers of Western civilization, historically have held that all people are born with a sin nature, that human nature itself is fallen. But persons also have the capacity for good, and they have profound dignity because they are created in the image of God. Considering the paradox of fallen, yet dignified, human nature, conservatives seek to rightly order human relationships to God, to others, and to the self, recognizing that disorder is the default. Conservatives understand that disorder is, as the kids say, a feature, not a bug, of human nature.

At the outset of this exploration of conservatism and religious liberty, it is appropriate to try and work out what conservatism is, so we can have an understanding of what conservatives do. In this chapter, I will introduce two major postwar Burkean conservative figures, one well-known, the other largely overlooked. With certain awareness that I could bring many more voices into a chapter that introduces conservatism, the two figures I will analyze well represent postwar American conservatism. I will also introduce the Black conservative tradition and argue that while Black and White conservatism are distinct, they are still compatible, despite the oftentimes conflicted coexistence they share.

The word "conservative" is a deeply ambiguous term. Like all ambiguous terms, it can mean different things in different contexts, but it is also frequently used without any attempt at precise definition in a particular context. Among some individuals and groups, the term "conservative" has strong associations with racism, religious fanaticism, classism, pessimism, pedanticism, narrow-mindedness, and blind traditionalism. In today's discourse, many progressives even deploy the descriptor "fascist" to describe a conservative idea or person. Let's admit that if conservatism means any of these things, then it should be rejected out of hand. It would be beneficial neither to the individual nor to society as a whole, and it would not be worthy of historical, political, or aesthetic consideration. And the moniker "fascist," when used today for someone or something that is conservative, is meant purely for fear effect. Deployment of "fascist" is the result of an unfortunate reliance on the idiomatic logical fallacy *ad Hitlerum*, or the charge that someone is "literally Hitler" just because he exhibits skepticism on some progressive party line.

Thankfully, the American conservative tradition is not so easily reducible to the ugly characterizations of its hecklers. There have been many articulations of conservatism in America since the national founding. More recently, since the end of World War II, there have been numerous distinct categories of conservatism that have formed around the contours of specific events and issues emerging in the decades after 1945. Journalist Matthew Continetti identified a dozen of these postwar categories, some of which continue to thrive in contemporary times, while others have come and gone. Continetti's twelve categories for the Right are: (1) libertarianism, (2) majoritarianism, (3) Cold War conservatism, (4) southern agrarianism, (5) philosophical conservatism, (6) fusionism, (7) radical traditionalism, (8) neoconservatism, (9) religious conservatism, (10) New Right activism, (11) originalism, and (12) paleoconservatism.[2] I add a thirteenth category—Black conservatism, an old and varied conservative tradition in its own right, and distinct in many ways from White conservatism. These groups are quite often at odds with one another over what makes a true conservative. To make matters even more muddled, some members of these groups are uncomfortable being called conservative, such as many libertarians, Afrocentric Blacks, and many religious conservatives in the magisterial Christian nationalist camp.

There was once a time when the term "conservative" placed you in a particular orbit. From the mid-1960s to the late 1980s, conservatives were identified closely with the political trajectories of Barry Goldwater, Richard Nixon, and Ronald Reagan. Law and order, peace through strength, rendezvous with destiny, morning in America, Reagan Democrats—these notions and terms were popular among conservatives and set them clearly apart from colloquialisms associated with liberals during that period—tax and spend, Vietnam syndrome, misery index, nuclear freeze, and crisis of confidence. But younger Americans, those born after, say, 1990, have no frame of reference for the "Reagan Revolution" of the 1980s. They do not have personal recollections of growing up watching movies like *War Games*, *The Day After*, or *Red Dawn* (the real one from 1984, with

Patrick Swayze, not the absurd 2012 version with the laughable plot of North Koreans invading America) and wondering how they'd make it in a fallout shelter, or if they might face Soviet tanks massed on the plains of Europe in a real-life World War III. They do not remember the fall of the Berlin Wall, the freedom summer of 1989, Tiananmen Square, or Boris Yeltsin's 1991 coup that toppled Mikhail Gorbachev and shattered the Union of Soviet Socialist Republics into a much less ominous-sounding "Commonwealth of Independent States." For example, you can find on YouTube old films of Soviet soldiers marching in May Day parades to the dubbed Bee Gees hit "Stayin' Alive"—no doubt the product of some creative and witty techie. To many young people, it's all very cute, but to those who watched those May Day parade clips on the nightly news in the '70s and '80s, it was no joke.

Lest the reader take this as a "get off my lawn moment," the point is that the generations after Gen X see conservatism through a much more pedestrian and uninspiring frame of reference—George W. Bush's futile "Mission Accomplished," John McCain's hapless presidential campaign, Mitt Romney's weak conservatism lacking imagination or conviction—a conservatism that has ceded so much cultural, economic, and political ground to the Left since 2003 as to be unrecognizable from the stalwart examples set by luminaries like George Schultz the indomitable, Sam Nunn the wise, Ronald Reagan the magnanimous, Clare Booth Luce the stately, James Baker the prudent, Edwin Meese the fearless, or British prime minister Margaret Thatcher, the Iron Lady. Much of what passes as conservatism today has become pathetic and spineless to young people (what Thatcher would contemptuously refer to as "wet"). Sometimes today's conservatism is known by the insipid moniker "neoliberalism," and as C. S. Lewis might say, it almost deserves it. Today, if some think of conservatism as representing menace, others associate the term "conservative" with conspiracy theories, defeatism, MAGA, populism, America First, disruption, or kitschy Christian nationalism. "Conservatism" has become nothing but a political shibboleth for many born after 1990—trivial, doleful, desperate, weak, and lacking intellectual rigor, imaginative clarity, or depth of character.

What is needed is a new conservative inspiration among Americans, and especially young Americans. Conservative ideas are indeed inspiring, animating, and life-giving! Conservatism is so stirring because as an aspirational means of perspective it puts the focus on what could be based on what has been. In other words, we learn from our triumphs and our failures, and incorporate lessons learned from experience into our traditions for the good of persons. Conservatism reminds us how deeply satisfying it is to be made in God's image; to be placed in a world so beautiful, majestic, mysterious, and intricate; to be placed in America, the most liberty-loving nation in history, and the greatest example and defender of political, economic, and religious liberty in the world; to be placed in time, standing on the shoulders of the great imaginative and august men and women of the past; to be placed in a tradition in which ideas shape whole civilizations, and to think—we are a part of it! Conservatism as an aspirational starting point is predicated on the reality that when we think, speak, write, and stand for the good, the true, and the beautiful, we have the potential to reach far beyond our own temporal existence and bring meaning transcending our own times, even when we have to sacrifice to do so. And this sort of conservatism is not only dispositional, it is aspirational. No conservative is a "true" conservative. All conservatives are aspiring to conserve civilization, and since such a goal is never finally attainable, there will always be intramural debates among those on the right over who the true conservatives are. I argue that all conservatives are on the path to true conservatism, although none of us will ever truly get there. We aspire to true conservatism, in that we aspire to guard, extend, and hand down the best of Western and American civilization to our children. The kind of conservatism I want to espouse I call *aspirational conservatism*. Aspirational conservatives are committed to the effort of conserving the harmony between the spirit of liberty and the spirit of religion for the long haul.

I think of my grandfather Jasper N. Dorsey, a husband, father, soldier, educator, churchman, mentor, leader, writer, and public servant. His mother was his greatest inspiration, a woman of wit, wisdom, empathy, and strength. He has been dead now for many years, but his words, spoken and written, still ring in my ears. If I can be half the man he was, I would consider my life fulfilled. Conservatism is a standpoint looking up to the eternal, behind to the past, round about in the present, and ahead to the future—in that order—but always with the good of the human person at the forefront.

Conservatism is almost always considered political from start to finish. But aspirational conservatism is before politics; it is prepolitical. This conservatism is a temperament, an attitude, a disposition, and a way of life before it ever represents a political stratagem. For over two centuries, conservatism has been an aspirational disposition that aims for a higher moral destiny for human persons and societies, guided by the light of permanent things, tradition, and just order, while reckoning with the human condition marked by great dignity, but also limitation, imperfection, and change. The moral profit and ordered liberty of the person is the primary consideration of the conservative disposition. In this way, conservatism is humanistic. I do not use "humanistic" in the sense of the old saying that man is the measure of all things. No. We mortals dwell in what C. S. Lewis called the Shadowlands, and what Plato referred to as the Cave. Only the eternal is really real, and we are blind to the real when we shut our eyes to the unchanging and the divine. Conservatism is humanistic in that its first consideration is to bring the true, the good, and the beautiful to real people, sinful and flawed, born into a world of inevitable change yet possessed by an irrepressible yearning for, as Peter Viereck wrote in 1949, "the permanent beneath the flux."[3] Conservatism inspires us to resonate with the call of Jewel the Unicorn in Lewis's *The Last Battle*—"Come farther up, come farther in!"[4] To adapt another old saying—conservatism was made for man, not man for conservatism.

Continetti's astute rendering of the complexity of postwar conservatism is valuable in understanding the conservative movement, or what insiders call simply, "the movement." That complexity is good, because it demonstrates a variety and animation in a worldview that is too often misunderstood as being simple and obtuse. It is not my purpose to give detailed explanations of what Continetti's dozen categories entail. I leave that task to others. For my purposes, I wish to boil down this complexity in postwar American conservatism from many categories to just two: measured and extreme conservatism. Both measured and extreme conservatism are prepolitical. But the measured tradition is flexible and supple and can sift out what traditions to keep and what traditions to jettison based on interaction between timeless principles and time-specific considerations—the permanent beneath the flux. Extreme conservatism is inflexible and reactionary and accepts tradition uncritically. Continetti recognized that differentiating between these two broad categories of conservatism is the way to understand it in the past and the present. He wrote, "One way to think about the hundred-year war for the Right is to conceive of it as a battle between the forces of extremism and the conservatives who understood that mainstream acceptance of their ideas was the prerequisite for electoral success and lasting reform."[5] Measured, aspirational conservatism is the dominant form in American history and aims more truly at the true, the good, and the beautiful than its extreme distortion.

Conservatism is a rich and complex tradition that goes back to the eighteenth century in Europe, Britain, and America. Conservatives differ on issues concerning both first principles and practical politics, economics, religion, and society because conservatives are, after all, just people. The historical differences and debates between conservatives over the past two and a half centuries are part of what makes them so interesting. It is ignorant and obscurantist to think of conservatives in simplistic terms. And while the old description of conservatives attributed to John Stuart Mill—"the stupid party"— may make good progressives smile with self-satisfied pleasure, it is actually the height of stupidity either to take the quote attributed to Mill on its face or to write off all conservatives as a monolithic regressive bloc despising change in the name of self-preservation.[6]

Conservatism as a disposition—as an aspiration—is represented best, not through abstract aphorisms, but in the lives and examples of people. Let us now consider some representative figures in conservatism in our endeavor to understand it aright.

Russell Kirk (1918–1994) can be called the dean of postwar American conservatism without a hint of embarrassment. The author of the landmark book *The Conservative Mind: From Burke to Eliot* (1953), which has gone through seven editions, Kirk authored and edited another thirty-one nonfiction and fiction works over the course of his life. In 1960, he founded the *University Bookman*, a magazine dedicated to advancing the cause of liberal arts education and serving as a platform for the scholarly consideration of important yet neglected books. From 1962 until 1975, Kirk wrote a column entitled "To the Point" for the Los Angeles Times Syndicate, reaching over a hundred newspapers across the country, and a bimonthly column for *National Review* entitled "From the Academy" for twenty-five years. He also founded the journal *Modern Age*; it and *University Bookman* continue as leading conservative outlets today. In 1989, he received the Presidential Citizens Medal, awarded to him by President Reagan. He conducted all his writing and editing activities from his home and library (a converted toy factory and garage) at Piety Hill, the place he called his "ancestral acres" in the small town of Mecosta, Michigan, population 423.

Kirk was a thinker and prolific writer not only about conservatism. Kirk applied a conservative imagination to the writing of Gothic literature in the form of horror and ghostly stories (*Lord of the Hollow Dark* and *Ancestral Shadows: An Anthology of Ghostly Tales*, to name two) that remind the reader of the thin veil dividing the eternal from the temporal worlds. Kirk was also an inspiration to young people for many decades. Beginning in 1970, Russell and his wife, Annette, inaugurated the "Piety Hill Seminars" in partnership with the Intercollegiate Studies Institute (ISI). The seminars brought forty or fifty young scholars at a time to the Kirk library at Piety Hill to discuss, as Kirk described, "the large questions of morals, politics, economics, the questions of the soul, and moral imagination in an endeavor, and I think a successful endeavor, to rouse intellect and moral sense in the rising generation."[7] Ten years later, in 1980, the Kirks began the Wilbur Fellows Program in which scholars, writers, editors, and legal minds came to read, research, and write at Piety Hill for a few months or as long as two years at a time. The Wilbur Fellows Program continues to this day, hosting scholars in various writing and editing projects.

Russell Kirk has been a muse to many thousands of people through the legacy of his imaginative and intellectual writings, his steady and dependable example of the pursuit of the good life of the spirit and the mind, and his hospitality and personal friendship and mentorship to young people over the course of decades. What attracted so many to Piety Hill was Kirk's stress on the person, the sublime mystery of life in the here and the hereafter, his veneration of the moral and spiritual roots of Western and American civilization, and his unceasing work "to preserve those ancient edifices [of civilization], reinforce them, and reinvigorate the spirit which built them and hold back those forces of madness and despair which are threatening our whole culture," in Kirk's words.[8] Kirk embodied the prepolitical, aspirational conservative, and his life and legacy continue today through the thousands he inspired, and continues to inspire. Though dead, he still speaks.

Kirk was born in Plymouth, Michigan, the son of a train engineer and served as an enlisted man in World War II testing chemical and biological weapons. After the war, he went to Scotland and earned the doctor of letters degree from the University of St. Andrews in 1953. Kirk saw the world in sacramental terms, and wrote ghostly tales, not to send chills down children's spines, but to remind his audience that the world of the spiritual is more real than that of the material, and much closer to us than we perceive. Using a vivid metaphor to illustrate this point, Kirk wrote, "The limitations of our biological equipment may condemn us to the role of Peeping Toms at the keyhole of eternity. But at least let us take the stuffing out of the keyhole, which blocks even our limited view." Kirk said, "I aspire to help extract the stuffing out of the keyhole" because ghostly tales "may impart some arcane truths about good and evil."⁹

The Conservative Mind is Kirk's *magnum opus*. The work is an intellectual history of Anglo-American conservatism from the eighteenth to the twentieth century. Historian of conservatism Patrick Allitt said, "Kirk did more than any other writer at midcentury to devise a conservative family tree, over which his intellectual heirs have argued ever since."¹⁰ Kirk's obituary in the *New York Times* described the book as "the intellectual bible for the conservative movement."¹¹ And his obituary appearing in the *Los Angeles Times* quoted *Time* magazine's 1953 book review: "Kirk tells his story of the conservative stream with the warmth that belongs to it. Even Americans who do not agree may feel the warmth—and perhaps feel the *wonder* of conservative intuition and prophecy."¹² *The Conservative Mind* is a detailed and carefully crafted genealogy of the conservative disposition starting in the eighteenth century and remains a landmark text in American history of ideas.

Kirk opened the book with a chapter entitled "The Idea of Conservatism," in which he laid out the conservative disposition in spiritual terms. The essence of conservatism, for Kirk, was an interior impulse to preserve the ancient traditions of human moral life through a living respect and memory of the dead, namely, the ancestors of our civilization. Suspicious of those who would plow up and discard the past as so much recrement, the conservative is among those who "think society is a spiritual reality, possessing an eternal life but a delicate constitution."¹³ Following Abraham Lincoln, who asked in 1860, "What is conservatism? Is it not adherence to the old and tried, against the new and untried," Kirk proposed six mainstays, pillars—"canons"—that provide underpinnings for the conservative disposition. I will include this lengthy quotation from Kirk, in which he identified and developed his six canons:

> 1) Belief in a transcendent order, or body of natural law, which rules society as well as conscience. . . . 2) Affection for the prolif-

erating variety and mystery of human existence. . . . 3) Conviction that civilized society requires order and classes, as against the notion of a "classless society." . . . 4) Persuasion that freedom and property are closely linked. . . . 5) Faith in prescription. . . . Custom, convention, and old prescriptions are checks both upon man's anarchic impulse and upon the innovator's lust for power. 6) Recognition that change may not be salutary reform . . . a statesman must take Providence into his calculations, and a statesman's chief virtue . . . is prudence.[14]

Ultimately, a humanistic conservative like Kirk is concerned with the question, what is the proper understanding of liberty? Are people free when their actions are regulated by law? Does liberty consist in doing whatever one pleases, or whatever one has the power to do? Does rule of law secure liberty to the governed? How does liberty connect to law and justice? Because human nature is fallible, liberty cannot be understood as the doing of whatever one pleases. That would be better understood as license, not liberty. In the flow of thought consistent with the Western tradition, Kirk insisted that liberty without just authority is slavery.

Kirk argued that contrary to popular caricature, just authority is never arbitrary. It is known by long experience and the customs of a people. So, authority is not defined in conjectural and intangible terms. It is rather understood by considering what is consistent with eternal moral truth and what has stood the tests of time in real people living in real places under real circumstances. This is what Kirk called "prescription." By that, he meant "ancient custom and usage, and the rights which usage and custom have established."[15] Without just authority based on accepted prescription, it is impossible to maintain a free society. Authority is necessary to real liberty because authority restrains the human will, which naturally tends toward either anarchy or tyranny. To illustrate, Irving Babbitt, an important influence on Kirk, predicated his 1924 book *Democracy and Leadership* on "the most unpopular of all tasks—a defense of the veto power."[16] Babbitt pointed to the epistle of Paul to the Romans, in which Paul drew a distinction between the law of God and the law of the human members. "For the good that I want, I do not do, but I practice the very evil that I do not want," Paul wrote.[17] This tension is natural to persons, but the will to control oneself, to keep oneself from giving in to unrestrained passion, is a human desire with a divine source. "In general," Babbitt wrote, "the primacy accorded to will over intellect is Oriental. The idea of humility, the idea that man needs to defer to a higher will, came into Europe with an Oriental religion, Christianity."[18]

Consider for a moment, Kirk wrote, what it would be like to throw off traditional authority by prescription. Cast aside the authority prescribed through the tradition of religious mores and the American constitutional order, for example. Grant that the American Constitution was drafted and ratified as a proslavery document. Grant that the American experiment is an experiment in racist depravity. Further grant that Christianity, as an oppressive religion, has had too much influence on the customs and laws of the country. Throw off prescriptive authority handed down by "dead white men" based on custom, tradition, and experience because such authority is stained with sin. After all, human nature is basically good, and the chains that keep persons oppressed are those links of tradition, custom, and experience. "The tradition of all dead generations weighs like a nightmare on the brains of the living," Karl Marx wrote in 1852.[19] Can society then live without authority? Can anarchy bring real liberty now that all restraint has been cast aside? Perish the thought. Throw off one kind of authority, and another will take its place. You will either have slavery in anarchy, a Hobbesian state of nature in which might makes right and the only basis for right action is power. Or you will have tyranny of a truly arbitrary sort—divine right monarchy or totalitarian dictatorship. Kirk quoted his friend T. S. Eliot: "If you will not have God—and he is a jealous God—then you should pay your respects to Hitler or Stalin."[20]

Kirk contrasted his six canons of the conservative disposition with opposing canons of the Left. Since the French Revolution,

Kirk identified five schools of radical leftist thought—the secular rationalism of the French *philosophes*, who sought to elevate reason to the exclusion of divine revelation; the emancipatory Romanticism of Rousseau that sought to throw off restraint; utilitarianism inspired by English philosopher Jeremy Bentham (1748–1832); positivism, which elevated science and mathematics over and against divine revelation, particularly represented by French thinker Auguste Comte (1798–1857); and the materialism of Karl Marx (1818–1883), the economic, political, and historical philosophy from which emerged Communism.[21] These five schools of thought from the late eighteenth through the mid-nineteenth centuries are represented by four canons of the Left for Kirk. The first, the idea that human nature can be perfected by external means and that the moral and intellectual progress of the race is inevitable and limitless. Second, tradition should be rejected in favor of "reason, impulse, and materialistic determinism."[22] Third, absolute equality, or what our culture calls "equity," must replace any and all forms of hierarchy, even when hierarchy is measured by merit. Along with a commitment to equity is the tendency toward central planning. Finally, property rights must be swept aside in favor of the distribution of wealth. Property is an oppressive category. Kirk wrote, "collectivistic reformers hack at the institution of private property root and branch."[23]

The tensions between conservatism and progressivism can thus be summarized as follows. Is humanity inherently fallible with a tendency toward selfishness, or is human nature essentially good, and thus perfectible through purely autonomous human reason, will, or feelings? Should people in a society submit to rule prescribed by traditions and customs handed down to us by our forebears, or can people create a society anew, out of whole cloth, in which authority, law, custom, and tradition are noncompulsory? To illustrate, can we fashion a peaceable, greedless global society like in the fantasy world of *Star Trek*? This is the imaginary world of the distant future when persons finally abolish poverty, no longer use money, use technology that is beneficial in every way and has no filthy or harmful underbelly, live in perfect harmony, and no longer have any recourse to war (despite the irony that in the series, the Federation develops the largest and most powerful warship in the galaxy, the *Enterprise*, but never mind that). Is perfect equality possible among human beings, and should societies pursue perfect equality, by coercion if necessary? Or does equality have reference strictly to the law and to the doors of moral, economic, political, and intellectual opportunity as individual merit and circumstance dictate? And perhaps the most important question of all—can human individuals and societies pursue reform by changing the external realities in human institutions, or does true reform begin by change in the inner moral life of persons born with a sin nature? These issues are the first principles that will separate a conservative, who is oriented above to the transcendent, behind to the past, around about in the present, and then forward toward the future, from a progressive, who rejects the reality or authority of the transcendent, turns his back on the past, and rushes toward the future with the certainty that progress is inevitable.

A conservative's perspective on liberty is that it must be ordered rightly. Kirk wrote that the way to apprehend what right order looks like is to contemplate disorder. Consider again the Gunpowder Plot. If the plot had succeeded, and the government had been successfully decapitated in a spectacular explosion, would the conspirators have enjoyed the blessings of liberty and flourishing? In other words, what order would have been birthed out of disorder? What just and honorable system of rule would have emerged from chaos, death, and destruction? How can peace be the product of murder? Order, justice, and liberty must be cultivated, maintained, extended where necessary, and always guarded in the same way that a garden will be consumed by weeds and stripped by critters without similar cultivation, care, and vigilance. The default of human existence is disorder; right order is built over time with tools and materials that are tried in previous generations and circumstances. When certain methods are tried and they fail, then they are thrown out and replaced with other methods. Human slavery is an institution that goes back to the distant past, and the American colonies and later the nation were founded while slavery prevailed. But in the American experience of tragedy, death, and war, Americans came to reject slavery as unjust and immoral. The American experience of the injustice of slavery demonstrates this point that Kirk made—"If a society falls into general disorder, many of its members will cease to exist at all. And if the members of a society are disordered in spirit, the outward order of the commonwealth cannot endure."[24] Disorder reveals the essence of just order through contrast. Thus, the conservative will look for order before he will look to enjoy liberty. Where there is just order, governed by prescriptive authority, liberty and flourishing have the greatest chances of spreading broadly.

Like Kirk, historian and poet Peter Viereck (1916–2006) is one of the most insightful figures in postwar American conservatism. He is also one of the most compelling, even though he has largely been forgotten by many conservative scholars. For example, Continetti only has three brief references to him in his 418 pages of text in *The Right*. Patrick Allitt, in his 280 pages of text in *The Conservatives*, mentions him only twice. There is no mention of Viereck at all by Yoram Hazony in his *Conservatism: A Rediscovery*; nothing in Edmund Fawcett's *Conservatism*; and still nothing in Andrew Bacevich's *American Conservatism: Reclaiming the American Tradition*. There is also no mention of Viereck by George Will in his 539-page book, *The Conservative Sensibility*. Claes Ryn, Robert Lacey, Daniel McCarthy, and Lisa Bradford have researched Viereck recently,[25] but his thought deserves still more amplification.

Viereck joined the history department at Mt. Holyoke College in 1948 and taught there for nearly fifty years after earning his PhD at Harvard. Viereck wrote his doctoral dissertation on the intellectual roots of Nazism, which he located in the German Romantic thought of composer Wilhelm Richard Wagner. The Nazis, inspired by Romanticism, shook off the best traditions of Western civilization to take up the cause and identity of the German *Volk*, a mythological conception of an organic national identity based on racial purity.

He defined the contrast between the Western heritage and Nazism in this way: "loyalty to western civilization means loyalty not to one particular portion of geography—that would be nationalism—but to a universal civilization compounded of three separate heritages: rationalism, classicism, Christianity. Nazism stands for the opposite of each of these three heritages: for force against reason, for romanticism, for tribal paganism."[26]

Viereck's dissertation was published in the summer of 1941, just months before Germany declared war on the United States. In large respect, Viereck had his own father in mind as he wrote it. George Sylvester Viereck defended Imperial Germany during World War I, and then Nazi Germany in the years leading up to World War II. He was arrested and imprisoned for conspiring with the Nazis in September 1941. Peter did not speak to his father for the next sixteen years. He served as an enlisted man in the Psychological Warfare Branch of the US Army during the war, and his brother George Jr. was killed in combat fighting the Nazis in Italy. Peter finally reconciled with his father, and the elder Viereck read Peter's erudite and comprehensive historical critique of Nazism in the waning months of his life. Upon finishing the book, the old man was deeply moved—he who had once defended the kaiser, Hitler, and German nationalism said to his son, "Peter, you were right."[27]

Viereck defined and upheld the aspirational conservatism of the Irishman Edmund Burke (1729–1797) and the American John Adams (1735–1826) in several books he wrote during the 1950s and early 1960s. In addition to his historical work on conservatism, Viereck was also a poet. He won Guggenheim Fellowships in history and poetry as well as the Pulitzer Prize for Poetry in 1949 after the publication of *Terror and Decorum*. Viereck was his own man, however, and he ran afoul of movement conservatives like William F. Buckley, Willmore Kendall, Frank Meyer, and even the venerable Russell Kirk over differences surrounding issues of practical politics and some first principles of conservatism. Because of these differences, Viereck has been nearly forgotten as a postwar figure of conservative revitalization. Journalist Daniel J. McCarthy assessed Viereck as "an odd man out," but still, "conservatives need not agree with everything Viereck wrote to find much of value in his work, even in his criticisms of the Right. He was an insightful critic, if perhaps a premature one, of the forces that have lately sidelined traditional small-government, prudential conservatism: jingoistic nationalism, the politics of social resentment, and a politicized religiosity."[28] Political philosopher Claes Ryn wrote that Viereck's contribution to American conservatism was to write books "that challenge modern progressivism and attempt to define a modern conservatism that builds upon and develops the central insights of the classical and Christian traditions."[29]

Viereck broke from the movement conservative party line of the 1950s because he supported Adlai Stevenson's 1952 presidential candidacy, and he thought the New Deal should be reformed in order to shift the center of gravity to local jurisdictions from the top-down federal program it had been since the 1930s—but he did not support jettisoning it altogether. He wrote a negative review of William F. Buckley's *God and Man at Yale*, concluding that, while the book was valuable, "someday, being intelligent and earnest, Buckley may give us the hard-won wisdom of synthesis."[30] This won him exactly zero points with Buckley, who studiously did not ask him to join the team of writers and editors at *National Review* when Buckley launched that magazine in 1955. Senior *National Review* editor Frank Meyer charged Viereck with being a "counterfeit" conservative in a review he wrote of Viereck's 1956 book, *Conservatism: From John Adams to Churchill*.[31] Ryn rightly took Meyer's acidic reaction against Viereck to be sourced, not in a careful reading of Viereck, but in Meyer's zeal as a conservative neophyte—Meyer had come over to the Right after being a committed Communist, to the extent of having been "a member of the Soviet-directed underground 'cadre,'" in Ryn's words.[32] Dogmatic purity was what Meyer seemed to value, even though conservatism has never been a system of dogmata, but informed by a combination of transcendent and immanent realities.

Viereck alienated several high-profile conservative figures, but any careful consideration of Viereck's work will demonstrate him as a committed aspirational conservative in the school of Burke, Washington, Hamilton, and Adams. Viereck also has much more in common with his contemporaries than is often acknowledged, like Kirk, for example, who revered tradition as deeply as Viereck. Viereck understood the Western tradition as being informed by the Jews, Greeks, Romans, and Christians. He was a committed anti-Communist and a proponent of balance and harmony, and he held a deep understanding of the flawed state of human nature. He was a great critic of revolutionary leftism, represented especially by Jean-Jacques Rousseau, Thomas Paine, and Karl Marx. And like Kirk, the imagination was of primary importance to Viereck. Kirk was a brilliant fiction writer, and Viereck was a prolific poet. Yet one feature that sets Viereck apart from his contemporaries, and especially his conservative detractors, was that he had profound knowledge of authoritarian rightism from study and experience—in his scholarly treatment of the origins of Hitler's rise to power and in the fact that the Nazis wrecked his immediate family: they killed his brother and poisoned the mind of his father. Experience had moved Viereck to define conservatism in this way—"the conservative principles *par excellence* are proportion and measure; self-expression through self-restraint; preservation through reform; humanism and classical balance; a fruitful nostalgia for the permanent beneath the flux; and a fruitful obsession for unbroken historical continuity. These principles together create liberty, a liberty built not on the quicksand of adolescent defiance but on the bedrock of ethics and law."[33] It is a beautiful articulation of the conservative aspirational disposition.

Viereck was assuredly an eccentric. My favorite history professor while I was an undergraduate at Furman University, Marian Strobel, had him when she was a student at Mt. Holyoke for two history courses—Russian history and twentieth-century history. She described him as "an odd duck." He was always fifteen or so minutes late to class. He would address himself only to the light fixtures as he lectured; never took roll; never returned graded papers and never gave any feedback. He would run into things as he walked, being absorbed in thought. He wore a muffler around his neck all year, even during the warm seasons.

He forgot to request an office when he joined the faculty in 1948, and so he held no on-campus office and did not have office hours. But he was beloved and admired by his students, even though on one occasion a group of students invited him to Sunday dinner in the dormitory, but he showed up an hour late because he forgot about daylight savings time.[34] His eccentricities, bizarre as they were, reflected the emphasis he placed on the individual personality over mindless conformity, which is deeply important to the conservative disposition. In our own culture, which is too often obsessed with mindless conformity, a professor like Viereck probably would just be fired, and that would be that. Our times are blander and our skies greyer in the absence of such eccentric geniuses, people of personality. Alas, we are the poorer. While Viereck was rejected by many movement conservatives during the 1950s, his articulation of the meaning of conservatism is exquisitely delivered in and through his life and writings.

Viereck's is a helpful voice in sorting out specific features of measured and extreme conservatism. Viereck identified measured conservatism as evolutionary Burkean and extreme conservatism as reactionary Ottantottist. What did he mean?

Conservatism as a movement has its origins in the late eighteenth century, in the thought and writings of Edmund Burke, especially his book *Reflections on the Revolution in France* published on November 1, 1790. Within his critique of the radicalism of the French Revolution, Burke responded to the social contract theory of the eighteenth century that set natural rights ahead of social obligations. According to this view, the person is the basic unit of society and possesses the natural right to govern himself. But the individual is not a political animal designed to live in harmony with other individuals in society, as Aristotle argued in the *Nicomachean Ethics* and the *Politics* in the fourth century BC. English philosopher John Locke (1632–1704) posited that persons exist in a prepolitical "state of nature" prior to establishing government and civil laws, and in that state, the individual has sovereignty over himself. Locke wrote, "we must consider what estate all men are naturally in, and that is, a state

of perfect freedom to order their actions and dispose of their possessions and persons as they think fit, within the bounds of the law of
Nature, without asking leave or depending upon the will of any other
man."[35] Once the individual joins with other individuals to form a
civil society, he does not surrender that sovereignty, but as Francis
Canavan explained, "his natural right to govern himself became the
natural right to take part on equal terms with every other man in
the government of civil society."[36] Thus, a civil society is purely the
invention of individuals, as sovereign entities in and of themselves,
who come together to form a government in order to guard their
natural rights, chief of which was the right of property.

Social contract theory then, in the tradition of Thomas Hobbes
(1588–1679), Locke, and Jean-Jacques Rousseau (1712–1778), conceived of political society as consisting of the living only, but Burke
disagreed. He conceived of the social contract in concrete terms,
rather than the purely abstract. He wrote, "Society is indeed a contract . . . but the state ought not to be considered as nothing better
than a partnership agreement in a trade of pepper and coffee . . . or
some other such low concern, to be taken up for a little temporary
interest."[37] In other words, political society is not merely for material
ends in the immediate present. Furthermore, political societies are
not atomistic, but organic. The individual is important, but society
represents something beyond the mere sum of its individual parts.
And political society has importance going beyond the mere material
and temporal. Society, Burke wrote, "is a partnership in all science;
a partnership in all art; a partnership in all virtue, and in all perfection."[38] Thus, there is a mystery and majesty to political society,
made up as it is of individual persons, that inspires reverence. And
here is the essence of Burke's break from radical natural-rights ideology: "As the ends of such a partnership cannot be obtained in many
generations, *it becomes a partnership not only between those who are
living, but between those who are living, those who are dead, and those
who are to be born.*"[39] Political society is thus not imprisoned in the
present but is a continuing expression of a civilization across time.

Viereck argued that Burke's *Reflections* birthed conservatism in the same way that Karl Marx and Friedrich Engels birthed international Marxism through their *Communist Manifesto*. Central to Burke's view was the need to conserve tradition, particularly the tradition of ordered liberty. While Burke did not use the term "conservative," he did speak of conserving tradition in a time when the legitimacy of tradition was being questioned in the French Revolution, which began in July 1789. Viereck wrote that the Burkean tradition was evolutionary, and contrasted with the extreme, or counterrevolutionary, brand in the tradition of French thinker Joseph de Maistre (1753–1821). For Viereck, both the Burkean and the Maistrian strands of conservatism hold up tradition in the face of revolutionary change, but Burkeans stand for traditional liberties whereas Maistrians champion traditional authority. Viereck called the Maistrian tradition "ottantott," from the Italian word, *ottantotto*, meaning "eighty-eight." Viereck wrote, "A reactionary king of Piedmont-Sardinia became almost a figure of fun by wandering about mumbling pathetically the word 'ottantott.' . . . Thereby he meant to say: all problems would vanish if only the world turned its clock back to 1788, the year before the Revolution."[40]

Burkeans and Ottantotts differ on the way they understand the nature of change and how to respond to it. Burkeans see change as inevitable, and that it must be managed by honest deliberation based on constitutional procedure, tradition, and prudence. Ottantotts generally want to resist change, deploying nostalgia not for imaginative purposes but as a test for truth. According to Viereck, "the Ottantottist sometimes seems just as revolutionary against the existing present as the radical Jacobin or the Marxist, only in the opposite direction."[41] Ottantotts, since they are counterrevolutionary, seek disruption no less than leftist revolutionaries. They are utopian in the same way that revolutionaries are because the society they envision is predicated on obscurantist nostalgia, which is just as abstract as the leftist revolutionaries' dreams of a perfected society. The Burkean tradition—translated into American political culture through the thought of John Adams, Alexander Hamilton, John Jay,

James Madison, George Washington, John Quincy Adams, Alexis de Tocqueville, and Abraham Lincoln, to name a few figures—is the predominant conservative tradition in American history. The Ottantottist tradition, since it emerges from the thought of Maistre, is the predominant conservative tradition on the continent of Europe. It has made appearances in America, but as Viereck insisted, "Human beings are complex, inconsistent; many conservatives do not fully lend themselves to neat pigeon-holing in either category, but overlap."[42] Still, American conservatism since 1990 has demonstrated a turn toward Ottantottism, especially in its rising populist appeal due to the frustration among many Americans for its aimlessness in the opening decades of the twenty-first century.

Viereck was more pointed in his criticism of the Left than he was of those on his right. Viereck found the source of modern Leftism in Rousseau, particularly in *Emile* (1762) and *The Social Contract* (1762). Rousseau's estimation of human nature as essentially good is at the root of the leftist political philosophy. Rousseau famously began his *Social Contract* with the statement, "Man is born free, and everywhere he is in chains."[43] A catchy statement, but what did Rousseau's arresting metaphor signify? Rousseau's chains binding humankind consisted in "tradition, the past, the status quo—all now to be brushed aside by what he called the collective 'General Will' of the masses," Viereck wrote.[44] And while Rousseau was more influential in Europe, Thomas Paine (1737–1809), the celebrated American revolutionary author of *Common Sense* (1776) and *Rights of Man* (1791)—a direct rebuttal to Burke's *Reflections*—became the fountainhead of the leftist thought in America. Paine's progressive optimism and faith in human nature led him to reject the wisdom of tradition and custom. For Viereck, one's instinct to follow either Paine or Burke would indicate whether his disposition was liberal or conservative.

Liberalism and conservatism, to be sure, are both prepolitical because their first principles consist of ontological claims concerning the nature of the human person and the situation of the human being in time. Further critiquing leftism represented by Rousseau, Viereck fired, "'In chains, and so he ought to be,' replies the thoughtful conservative, defending the good and wise and necessary chains of rooted tradition and historic continuity."[45] While Rousseau considered rooted tradition to be the chains of imprisonment, Viereck believed that it was law rooted in tested custom and tradition that functioned as the necessary guardrail to keep humanity from careening over a moral cliff. Viereck insisted that "there is no freedom outside the law," and furthermore, "without the chaos-chaining, the Id-chaining heritage of rooted values, what is to keep man from becoming [Nazi SS officer and murderer] Eichmann or [Marxist revolutionary] Nechayev—what is to save freedom from 'freedom'?"[46] Abstract notions of liberty, rights, and progress, absent what Patrick Henry called "the lamp of experience,"[47] easily become the cryptograms of demagogues, tyrants, and misanthropes, particularly in a democracy, as Tocqueville argued. But the conservative disposition looks to concrete experience, actual articulations, examples, and instances of liberty, and liberty's opposite, slavery, in time and through the lives of real people in actual places in the past. In other words, a conservative knows that we do not understand liberty and rights by theorizing about them; we know them when we see them, and when we see what militates against them. Kirk richly brought this idea out in the lives of the American founders in his essay "The Framers: Not Philosophes, but Gentlemen." Kirk wrote, "the Americans were men of political experience; the French, men of political theory, and that theory untested."[48] The conservative disposition reveres the past, because the past yields the most convincing evidences of the whole human condition.

Through the lens of two important shapers of postwar conservatism, Kirk and Viereck, we have begun to consider the conservative disposition. There is a Black conservative tradition in America also, dating back to Jupiter Hammon (1711–1806), born into slavery on Long Island, New York. Hammon was the first Black literary figure, whose writings span from 1760 to 1781, and he is also the first

Black conservative. As such, he was a committed evangelical Christian who articulated with clarity the first unique ethic in the Black Protestant tradition. From Hammon in the eighteenth century to figures in the twentieth and twenty-first such as Robert Woodson, Anne Wortham, Zora Neale Hurston, Glenn Loury, Thomas Sowell, and Star Parker, Black conservatism has developed into a multilayered and sophisticated body of thought, yet distinct from White conservatism in this important respect—whereas White conservatism emerged from experiences with revolution, Black conservatism emerged from experiences with slavery and race prejudice. Because White and Black conservatism grew from different fields and soils, they should be considered distinct one from another. As political scientist Angela Lewis argued, "Scholars and pundits alike should not label the views of Black conservatives in the same vein as White conservatism."[49] Still, while acknowledging their distinct roots, the two traditions are compatible because they share many of the same essential aspirational characteristics. Because of this compatibility, the White and Black conservative traditions in America ought to be in conversation with one another as part of an emphatically American intellectual and imaginative heritage.

The category of *Black conservatism* is taken to be something of an oxymoron. For example, Lewis expressed skepticism that high-profile conservative Blacks such as Clarence Thomas, Thomas Sowell, and Condoleezza Rice represent the Black community, and that "a gulf exists between Black conservatives and the Black community."[50] She cited a number of scholars who concluded that Blacks are more politically liberal than Whites in general, and that Blacks also do not tend to vote for conservative Black candidates when they run for high office. And while the Republican Party has made concerted and organized efforts to tailor its message to Blacks, it has failed to persuade Blacks to vote Republican. Since the Black vote has been solidly Democratic since the 1930s and the New Deal, the very idea of a Black conservatism would appear to be a pipe dream at best. Lewis argued that one reason for this dynamic is the "linked fate or a feeling of closeness" that Blacks share within their population. The history of slavery and race prejudice leads Blacks to consider themselves to be sharing a uniquely mutual future in America. Thus, as Lewis argued, "race traitor and conservatism go hand in hand due to the idea of linked fate or the notion of a Black identity or Black consciousness."[51] Thinking of Black and White conservative traditions in conversation means thinking of how to build trust between members of the two traditions. As a start, Whites can acknowledge that their tradition has often been on the side advancing the cause of slavery and race prejudice, especially from the early nineteenth to the late twentieth century. Blacks can acknowledge that conservatism does not entail racial hierarchy, and that many White conservatives have been champions of liberty and equality for Blacks in America. Both can acknowledge the legitimacy of the idea of a shared fate among Blacks, while also acknowledging that the American constitutional tradition is one entailing ordered liberty for all, and ultimately excluding prejudice based on skin color.

What are the features of Black conservatism? Where do Black and White conservative traditions find common ground, and thus serve one another as conversation partners for the sake of conserving the American constitutional tradition and the harmony between religion and liberty? First, consider some unique features of Black conservatism. As Continetti identified twelve schools of thought in White conservatism, Lewis identified four among Black conservatives. She found conservatives divided into (1) the Black Right, (2) Afrocentric conservatives, (3) individualists, and (4) neoconservatives. Each of these schools has historically been shaped by racism, slavery, and Christianity, in that they all have historically responded to the challenge of racism and slavery while looking to Christianity in particular ways to make their responses. Each group has viewed local, state, and federal government institutions through the lens of responding to racism or slavery, or both. And each group developed from the starting point of the notion of a linked past, present, and future in the United States.[52] All four traditions have in common a rigorous critique of the Black community and Black culture. Their critiques of Black culture differ, as do their assessments of how much Whites are to blame or not to blame, and how much the government should be involved in economic improvement versus the free market. Self-help, education, and economic empowerment are priorities for all Black conservatives, in the context of the challenges presented by the history, and continued existence, of race prejudice in America.[53] These differences underscore the necessity of acknowledging that Black conservatism is not equal to White conservatism.

Still, there are points of essential agreement and compatibility between Black and White conservative schools of thought. The compatibility between Black and White conservatism has a great deal of potential in serving as a basis for lasting racial trust, especially because belief in a transcendent order is central to both traditions. First, Black conservatism, like White conservatism, is above all a dispositional, prepolitical worldview. Lee Walker used "conservative" as an adjective rather than a noun, because "the term is intended to describe a worldview and a culture, not a defined, partisan political tradition."[54] Walker stressed the importance of understanding conservatism as dispositional. "It is a state of mind and a type of character . . . a set of traditional principles and a philosophy centered on freedom and virtue."[55] Like Kirk and Viereck, Walker affirmed that the conservative disposition accepts change as inevitable but seeks to manage change by channeling its forces through the conduit of tradition, religion, restraint, procedure, and deliberation. An uncritical, unbounded faith in inevitable progress, the perfectibility of humanity, or the need for radical and rapid change is not in line with conservatism. Walker emphasized that the primary consideration in Black conservatism is liberty as expressed in the Declaration of Independence. In Kirkian fashion, Walker understood liberty through the lens of its opposite, slavery. "Being familiar with the long history in which freedom was denied to our ancestors, parents, and even to us in our own lives, we are especially sensitive to threats to it today. You might say that history has made blacks experts on reclaiming freedoms."[56]

Historian Peter Eisenstadt, in granting the dangers of generalizing about what Black conservatism represents, identified essential traits of the tradition. For Eisenstadt, the starting point of Black conservatism is a long-standing reverence for Western civilization and the American constitutional order. Within that order, and because of that order's development, Blacks can advance their interests in America through their own cultural and material resources. This is not to say that Black conservatives deny the reality of racism in contemporary America, nor does it imply that Black conservatives are against government intervention in the cause of civil rights for Blacks when necessary. "It is rather that black conservatives place their focus on individual achievement rather than on government action and redress."[57] Racism, while deeply problematic in American history and a continuing problem in America today, is foreign to the American ideal of liberty and opportunity for Black conservatives. Eisenstadt wrote that for Black conservatives, "racism tarnishes what America has been and can be, but what is valuable in America can and will be separated from its terrible legacy."[58]

Thus, Eisenstadt noted that Black conservatives are optimistic and positive about American civilization. They put the stress on the achievements of American Blacks despite the many hindrances and obstructions placed in their way since 1619. Even in assessing the sad years between the end of Reconstruction and the start of the Great Migration, for Black conservatives, "the glass is always half full. If later historians saw the period 1877 to 1915 as the 'nadir' of black history in the United States, conservatives such as [Booker T.] Washington always emphasized the tremendous progress former slaves made in the few short decades after emancipation."[59]

Black conservatives also know better than anyone the price paid for liberty and flourishing in America. In addition to the innumerable sacrifices Blacks have made in their struggles for the abolition of slavery, civil rights, economic opportunity, and personal safety over the course of the centuries, Blacks have fought, suffered, and died in defense of America and American ideals in every American war. The

American flag and all that flag stands for belongs to Black Americans as much as it belongs to Whites, for the simple truth that Blacks have spilled their blood in America's causes both at home and abroad. Eisenstadt wrote that "This is all the more reason not to throw away genuine achievements for illusory gains."[60] In this way, Black conservatism is the most aspirational of all traditions on the right.

Finally, for Black conservatives, Christianity is of prime importance to the coherence and efficacy of the disposition. Walker emphasized that the Black church is "the oldest and still most important conservative institution in black America."[61] The Black church has historically been the source of leaders, where the first schools were opened, and the first centers of community gathering for job training, economic improvement, and education. Eisenstadt argued that the moral grounding provided by Christianity was the basis for Black conservatism. "Black conservative thought has generally been highly moralistic, Christian, and deferential towards authority, both black and white."[62] Black conservatives, informed by religion, stress that rights are important, but much less so than duties.[63]

These features of Black conservatism represent striking points of compatibility. One other point of contact between Black and White conservatism is, ironically, race prejudice itself. While race prejudice is an important source for shared identity among Blacks and was too frequently an issue defended by powerful White conservatives like John C. Calhoun (1782–1850), race prejudice serves as irrefutable evidence for a fallible and sinful human nature. Whites and Blacks who embrace the conservative disposition can look to racism as a starting point—as evidence of a fallen human nature—in advocating together for the need to cultivate ordered liberty, to guard against threats to liberty and just order, and to critically sift tradition, keeping those elements that are consistent with the true, the good, and the beautiful, while dispensing with those elements that are not. There is no reason why Black and White conservatives cannot demonstrate durable and genuine racial trust based on prudence, religion, and a shared American identity rooted in history, tradition, and custom.

Human existence is a continuing tension between that which is permanent and those things which are changing. We see the tension in art, literature, history, science, politics, economics, and even theology. Conservatism is essentially about finding meaning in the permanent beneath the flux. Progressives are oriented toward the future, have little confidence in history and tradition, and understand human nature to be good and perfectible by human effort and the application of autonomous human reason. Thus, change is not only inevitable; change is good, because change equates to growth and progress. But the conservative does not see reality so. While the Ottantott may see change as inherently bad and something to be resisted, the measured, Burkean conservative—the conservative of the American tradition—sees change, while inexorable, through the lens of caution. Change is even necessary for human improvement, as both Burke and Kirk knew.

The permanent and the flux are both irresistible. Progressives err in minimizing or denying the permanent; Ottantotts err in vainly attempting to resist change. In erring in different directions, both give in to illusion—the progressive, to the illusion of utopia via inevitable progress, and the Ottantott, to a different utopia via epistemic nostalgia. But as Babbitt wrote, "Life does not give here an element of oneness and there an element of change. It gives a *oneness that is always changing*. The oneness and the change are inseparable."[64] And each human life is experiencing this paradox every moment. We are all in process of change as we get older, yet we are still the same person. Here we have a concrete example of Babbitt's oneness that is always changing. If we are to discern the real from the illusory, we will orient ourselves to the transcendent and the immanent with humility and wonder. This is an essential part of the aspirational conservative disposition.

Conservatism and the Imagination

The fight is for the private life.

—Peter Viereck, *The Unadjusted Man*

Between 1308 and 1321, the Florentine poet Dante Alighieri (1265–1321) composed one of the greatest works of the medieval period, *The Divine Comedy*. Dante narrated his imagined journey and exploration of the world beyond the tomb, from the nine circles of hell to the nine circles of purgatory, and thence to the nine spheres of paradise, ending with the abode of God in the Empyrean Heaven. He begins with an introductory canto (or section), then describes his travels through hell, purgatory, and heaven in 33 cantos each, for a total of 100—the number of perfection. Dante's journey serves as an allegory of the soul's ascent to God, beginning in the *Inferno* with a vision of sin as it really is, rather than what it falsely promises. The story transitions to the otherworldly penance of purgatory for the seven deadly sins (pride, envy, wrath, sloth, greed, gluttony, and lust) in the *Purgatorio*, and culminates in the Christian's pursuit of the beatific vision in the *Paradiso*. Thus, the work is a comedy, not a tragedy. For Dante, a medieval man indebted to the forms of Roman writers Seneca, Terence, and Horace, a tragedy would begin on a high note with a steady descent into death and destruction. Its opposite, a comedy, would begin on a somber note but ascend to a climax of hope and fulfillment of promise. As Dante wrote to his patron Can Grande Della Scalla, "And hence it is evident that the title of the present work is *the Comedy*.' For if we have respect to its content, at the beginning it is horrible and fetid, for it is hell; and in the end it is prosperous, desirable, and gracious, for it is Paradise."[1] So *Divine Comedy* was not meant to be funny, as a modern person might expect from the work's title. Instead, Dante meant to reflect the journey of the soul from aimlessly wandering in the sinister forest of castigation to its establishment and salvation in the eternal world of joy and exculpation.

The poem opens with the Augustan poet Virgil offering to guide Dante from the dark wood (representing his wandering in sin), in which he is stalked by a leopard, a lion, and a she-wolf. As Virgil introduces himself to Dante as the one who "sang the righteous son of Anchises who had come from Troy,"[2] he promises to help Dante out of the wood. Virgil warns Dante that he must first proceed through a place where he will hear "howls of desperation and see the ancient spirits in their pain, as each of them laments his second death."[3] From thence, Virgil would take him to the place of souls "content within the fire" but striving to attain to the home of "the blessed people," that is, the saints in heaven.[4] Virgil could not proceed with Dante to heaven since he, though virtuous, was a pagan, barred by "that Emperor who reigns above, since I have been rebellious to his law."[5] In his place, the mysteriously beautiful Beatrice would guide Dante through the celestial realms of Paradise to the eternal city of God.

The travelers begin their journey, proceeding through the horrible nine circles of hell, until finally reaching the Fourth Ring of the Ninth Circle. Here the teeth of the three-faced Satan grinds the writhing bodies of Judas Iscariot (betrayer of Jesus, the God-Man), Brutus, and Cassius (betrayers of Julius Caesar, the ruler of the noblest empire of man). Satan's red face gnaws Judas's body headfirst, while he flays the infamous betrayer's back with his terrible claws.

Satan's yellow/white face chews Cassius and his black face masticates Brutus, both from their legs as they writhe silently, like the living dead. After beholding this terrible scene and standing frozen with fear he cannot describe, Virgil leads Dante through the center of the earth to the antipode of Jerusalem in the Southern Hemisphere, where the mountain of Purgatory rises. To get there, they clamber down the hairy shoulder of the giant Satan, "tuft to tuft between the tangled hair and icy crusts" to his thigh, then turn upside down to climb up, as it were, his hairy leg to his foot. They then advance through rocky crags, up again through the bowels of the earth to its surface, where blinking stars greet them upon emerging. They find themselves on earth's opposite side from Jerusalem, under which have yawned the depths of hell since Satan fell from heaven.[6] Virgil proceeds to guide them to the island of Purgatory, the only land existing in the Southern Hemisphere since Satan's fall.

Prior to ascending the rising mountain of Purgatory proper, Virgil and Dante arrive on the shore of Ante-purgatory, in which they see an angel guiding a boat carrying baptized dead to their uncanny penance as they chant *In exitu Israel de Aegypto* (the first lines of Ps. 114). In Ante-purgatory, Dante finds those who were detained from Purgatory proper based on either having been excommunicated or having repented from sin at the last moment before a violent death, or from indolence, or from being distracted by worldly aims. In Canto VII of *Purgatorio*, Virgil leads Dante to the Valley of the Rulers, those of the late-repentant who were kings that turned their attention away from a noble, self-examining life to one given to trivial, shortsighted, and inferior ambitions. The Valley is so beautiful that the flowers and grass covering it exceed the glory of "gold and fine silver, cochineal, white lead, and Indian lychnite, highly polished, bright, fresh emerald at the moment it is dampened."[7] Spirits there sing *Salve Regina*, as one king enthroned sits silently. This king is Rudolph Habsburg, who was Holy Roman emperor from 1273 to 1291. In life, Rudolph was recognized as emperor by Pope Gregory X, provided he renounce all territorial claims in Italy, thus abandoning

Italians to the direct rule of the pope. Dante described Rudolph as having missed the opportunity to champion the lot of the Italians, turning his back on them instead for the sake of royal legitimacy north of the Alps. Dante sees "seated highest, with the look of one too lax in what he undertook—whose mouth, although the rest sing, does not move—was Emperor Rudolph, one who could have healed the wounds that were the death of Italy, so that another, later, must restore her."[8]

With the acknowledgment that this chapter is not meant to consist of a full summary of *Divine Comedy*, I will draw my attention to that illustrious piece of literature to a close. I have two purposes in mind in introducing Dante's poem. First and most simply, Dante's *Divine Comedy* is a capital example of imaginary literature central to the Western canon. It seems fitting to open a chapter on conservatism and the imagination by discussing the first parts of such an enduring work. Hopefully, my few lines of introduction to *Divine Comedy* might serve as an inspiration for you to take it up and read. In a more illustrative sense, a consideration of these sections from *Divine Comedy* serves as a morality tale for conservatives since World War II. The way Dante represents the emperor Rudolph seems sadly appropriate for the course that movement conservatives have charted for themselves since the 1960s.

Rudolph bartered the Italians away to secure his power in Germany. In similar fashion, conservatives after 1964 bartered away the opportunity of championing the interior life along with the potential gains in American culture that might have attended it for the sake of the short-term goal of attaining political power. More recently, conservatives were successful in national electoral contests in 1980, 1984, 1988, 1994, 2000, 2002, 2004, 2010, and 2016. As of this writing, conservatives possess, at least on paper, a 6–3 majority in the Supreme Court. But despite these electoral successes, conservatives have failed to advance much of their cultural and political agenda since Barry Goldwater's crushing defeat in the presidential race of 1964.[9] On top of that, conservatives have not prevented progressives from attaining to their cultural and political aims since then.[10] Enemies such as North Korea, Russia, Iran, and China are growing in power and influence and seek to undermine the post–World War II order built by America and the West.[11] The national debt has grown to a magnitude beyond the human ability to comprehend, and in this century our political leaders have lacked the will and courage to deal with it, making a catastrophic economic collapse more likely with every passing year.[12] Partisanship runs at all-time highs with no end in sight, to the extent that the prospect of political violence threatens our polity just as economic upheaval threatens our way of life.[13] The federal government has grown to an enormous size, especially by an unelected federal bureaucracy with massive power.[14] Much of higher education is yielded to critical theory, evidenced by young people seeing the world one-dimensionally through a lens of oppressors and oppressed. Many of these young people cheer for the massacre of Israelis by Hamas militants and have expressed sympathy for Osama bin Laden as he castigated America for its support of Israel after masterminding the murder of three thousand Americans on September 11, 2001.[15] Conservative values such as the sanctity of marriage, the sanctity of life, religious liberty, limited government, a strong middle class, love of country, localism, and ordered liberty have all suffered curtailment rather than advancement since Ronald Reagan's triumphant rise to the presidency in 1980. In the early twenty-first century, conservatism seems lost despite some GOP electoral success. Conservatives should guard against placing inordinate trust in power politics, a fickle weapon that can be effective in the short term, but ultimately turns out to be a deal with the devil.

What has happened to the dispositional conservatism of Russell Kirk and Peter Viereck? Their aspirational conservatism was prepolitical, dispositional. The rightism of contemporary times is populist, obsessed with politics, and fueled by social-media-inspired outrage in a similar style as their leftist counterparts. The American Right has thus far failed to conserve American ideals, Western civilization and culture, and religious values and liberty. In the words of Claes Ryn, this is "not just because of intellectual confusion but by advocating or accepting ideas and policies that a more mature intellectual conservative culture would have rejected."[16] The American conservative movement has become like Rudolph Habsburg as Dante saw him. Rudolph was not a forgotten outcast rotting in hell. He was enthroned in sublime beauty. But his mouth was shut in silence as he sat in glory, and his soul was detained in Ante-purgatory because he forfeited his chance to fight for the interior life, and instead gave in to the siren song of power politics. Like Rudolph, American conservatism holds some political power, but at the cost of sacrificing its soul.

A retrieval of a conservatism that aspires to conserve is necessary to stave off the implosion of Western and American civilization as we have known it since Washington's inauguration in 1789. How? Aspirational conservatism is formed by the imagination. And imagination determines a person's perspective on reality through worldview formulation. Before one can form moral and wise political positions on foreign and domestic issues, one must understand the relationship of the eternal to the temporal. Before one can wield power as a politician, one must exercise restraint as a statesman. Before one can hold the public trust, one must first be trustworthy. And before one can inspire confidence and optimism in an electorate, one must be courageously and convictionally animated by a vision that is just, moral, and worthy of a great and good nation.

Arriving at these ideals honestly does not happen on a lark. Moral vision and clarity; statesmanship; trustworthiness; the virtues of fortitude, temperance, justice, and wisdom—these traits that we find in the great political figures of the past emerged from years of moral formation and the catechizing of the imagination. Our first president is an example of this great truth. Washington's imagination was, from his boyhood, formed by his books, particularly his books on the discipline of meditation. Beginning in his teens, he found value in the discipline of religious meditation, but that spiritual discipline was transferable to any area of thought or activity that required devotion and care. He was shaped by eighteenth-century authors such as

Offspring Blackall, James Hervey, John Ray, Matthew Hale, Thomas Comber, Richard Allestree, as well as the ancient Roman stoic Seneca. Washington scholar Kevin J. Hayes observed that "As military commander, legislator, and president, Washington would establish a reputation for long, slow, judicious reasoning. The decision-making process he demonstrated as an adult hearkens back to the books he read in boyhood."[17]

What the American Right needs is to embrace aspirational conservatism by cultivating a well-developed, well-ordered, circumspect, and rousing imagination. In assessing the history of American postwar conservatism, Ryn observed that the movement shifted away from an internal philosophical foundation and toward an external pragmatism. Among conservatives, there has prevailed a "strong tendency for this pragmatism to become a general impatience with ideas or cultural-artistic phenomena that are not obviously and directly related to practical matters."[18] Acknowledging that the importance of politics in American life is deeply significant, and that American culture, law, and institutions cannot be shaped without political power, Ryn rightly stressed that politics cannot be the primary frame of reference for conservatives. When politics frames every issue for conservatives, then they become beholden to "the trends and fashions of the moment" and, consequentially, "drift and confusion then become the order of the day." Ryn argued that "if no sophisticated, overarching, and unifying vantage point exerts a magnetic pull, intellectual and other standards will not only be low but subject to trendy opinion."[19] Ryn's "road not taken" by conservatives refers to the pursuit of a life of the mind, a well-formed imagination, a philosophical framework to understand reality, both visible and invisible. Ryn's "road not taken" is Viereck's "fight for the private life."

The fight for the private life was, for Viereck, a struggle against conformity to the ever-changing whims of prevailing culture. We might describe the prevailing culture in terms of consumerism; obsession with political personalities and cults; psychological slavery to whatever is trending on social media; overdependence upon technology that dehumanizes; the thralldom of mass-produced and soulless art, music, literature, and film; and the commercial use of nature as a playground for overgrown adolescents. Philosopher Zena Hitz used the term "the world" to refer to the prevailing culture. She wrote, "the world . . . is governed by ambition, competition, and idle thrill seeking. It is a marketplace where everything can be bought and sold. . . . Human beings are primarily vehicles to achieve the ends of others."[20] Viereck wrote in 1956, "We can talk civil liberties, prosperity, democracy with the tongues of men and of angels, but it is merely a case of 'free from what?' and not 'free for what?' if we use this freedom for no other purpose than to commit television or go lusting after supermarkets."[21] The one immersed in and shaped by the prevailing culture, trivial and ephemeral as it is, is what Viereck called "the overadjusted man."[22] Such a person may have civil liberties but is not truly free. As philosopher L. Russ Bush wrote, "Those who do not ask or who do not care to ask the basic questions of life will never develop a perspective from which to determine the significance of their own activities and ideas."[23]

For Viereck, adjustment to the world pertains to one's attitude toward it, the extent one is being shaped and controlled by it. The person shaped by the world—the overadjusted person— has a weak interior life that cannot guard his mind and heart against its debasing force. One can be maladjusted to the world, too, being cut off from the world like a crotchety hermit imprecating at even the most innocent interloper, "get off my lawn!" Overadjustment and maladjustment both degrade the soul because one is completely of the world and the other is utterly cut off from the world. The unadjusted person resists being shaped by the world but nevertheless lives in the world and serves the world for its good.

Viereck used geographic metaphors to illustrate his concept of cultural adjustment: an island, a mainland, and a peninsula. The maladjusted, or never-adjusted, is on the island; the overadjusted is on the mainland; but the unadjusted is on the peninsula. The unadjusted person is not cut off from the culture but is not conformed to it either. He is, along the lines of Christ's High Priestly Prayer in John 17:14–19, in the world but not of the world.[24] Furthermore, in Viereck's words, he is a person of "adjustment to the ages, non-adjustment to the age," in that he is shaped by the collected wisdom of Western civilization but not shaped by the shifting sands of the prevailing culture.[25] Hitz put it like this: "Intellectual life is a way to recover one's real value when it is denied recognition by the power plays and careless judgments of social life. That is why it is a source of dignity."[26]

Conservatives missed an opportunity to fight for the private life, to take the road less traveled, and to cultivate an imagination and an inner life that led to true freedom from the spirit of the age. But it is not too late. Conservatives can come good, like the mutinous ship's carpenter Harry "Chippy" McNeish of Ernest Shackleton's famous Imperial Trans-Antarctic Expedition of 1914. After the *Endurance* sank and its crew was cast onto the ice of the Weddell Sea, a bitter McNeish declared he was no longer bound to follow orders since the ship had gone down. Shackleton suppressed this challenge to his authority, which could have metastasized into a real mutiny that would have resulted in the deaths of most, if not all, of the members of the expedition. Later, when the men were trapped on Elephant Island and Shackleton had the idea of sailing across the eight-hundred-mile Drake Passage to South Georgia Island in one of the lifeboats salvaged from the *Endurance*, it was McNeish with his unique carpentry skills that made the craft seaworthy for the perilous crossing of one of the most tempestuous seas in the world. McNeish, the surly crewman who challenged Shackleton's authority, ultimately came around and served as the one indispensable figure of the ill-fated expedition. Without his expertise and ingenuity, Shackleton's idea of sailing for South Georgia would have been nothing more than a pipe dream, and the entire crew would have starved or frozen to death on Elephant Island in 1916.[27] Like Chippy McNeish, conservatives in America can redeem themselves for their own sake, for the sake of their movement, and for the sake of the country.

Where to begin? How does one cultivate the imagination? What is the relationship between conservatism and the imagination that forms the inner life? There is likely more than one way to proceed, but in the remainder of this chapter, I will propose a strategy for the cultivation of the imagination for the conservative along the following lines. I have in mind those who desire to pursue an aspirational conservatism and who begin to consider religious liberty in theory and practice. And being a Christian myself, what I propose will be taken from Christianity as a religious starting point. One need not be a Christian to be an aspirational conservative, but being a Christian requires it to a significant degree, since Christianity is a faith system predicated on authority and tradition.

First, a definition for imagination: Kevin Vanhoozer presented a constructive clarification for the imagination, and I will employ his clarification in what follows. He wrote, "By imagination, I do not mean that mental faculty that produces fictions (things that are not real) but rather the mental capacity that enables us to see more of reality than what we can perceive with our eyes or other physical senses."[28] Following Vanhoozer's understanding, we can say that a conservative imagination begins with the consideration first of reality, then of truth, then of morals, and then of aesthetics. We will start with being, then move to truth, on to ethics, and finally, to worthy art, music, literature, and film to roughly follow the pattern of the Transcendentals: truth, goodness, and beauty. As my proposal proceeds, notice that I will draw on the Western tradition, most especially Augustine of Hippo (354–430). As Robert Maynard Hutchins wrote in 1951, "The tradition of the West is embodied in the Great Conversation that began in the dawn of history and continues to the present day. . . . We should not reject the help of the sages of former times. We need all the help we can get."[29] It is a conservative belief that no problem of the human condition is essentially new. Every question we ask in the present has been asked in various ways by the people of the past, thus tradition is ever relevant for living generations. Drawing on the Western tradition for wisdom will demonstrate that for the conservative, that tradition serves not only as a symbol of the past but as a constructive resource for the present.

Augustine was born in the Roman town of Thagaste in the province of Numidia, what is now the city of Souk Ahras in Algeria. His father, Patricius, was a Roman administrator in Thagaste, and his mother, Monica, was the most important Christian influence of his early life. The young Augustine was torn between a profound draw to sensuality and an equally profound desire for truth. "I had been extremely miserable in adolescence, miserable from its very onset," Augustine wrote in *Confessions*, "and as I prayed to you for the gift of chastity I had even pleaded, 'Give me chastity and self-control, but please not yet.' I was afraid that you might hear me immediately and heal me forthwith of the morbid lust which I was more anxious to satisfy than to snuff out."[30] While he became convinced that the meaning of life was bound up in attaining to the knowledge of God, still, his sensual inclinations and practices clouded and stymied his search. Thus, Augustine came to grips with a war of wills within him, one inclined toward the self, the other inclined toward God. He wrote, "A new will had begun to emerge in me, the will to worship you disinterestedly and enjoy you, O God, our only sure felicity; but it was not yet capable of surmounting that earlier will strengthened by inveterate custom. And so the two wills fought it out—the old and the new, the one carnal, the other spiritual—and in their struggle tore my soul apart."[31]

Seeking for truth, the young Augustine was attracted to a variety of systems of thought that might satisfy him. Early on, he rejected Christianity because he thought it too simplistic, and not sufficient to answer the problem of evil and suffering. For nearly a decade, he found an intellectual home in Manichaeism, the belief that cosmic good and evil endlessly contended with one another. Augustine eagerly sought out the Manichaean prophet Faustus while he taught rhetoric at Carthage and met him in about 383. But he found out that sometimes it is better not to meet your heroes—Faustus turned out to be a dullard.

After going to Milan to teach rhetoric in 384, Augustine came to meet a superior teacher in the person of Ambrose, the bishop of Milan. Ambrose was well-known for his powerful connections, and Augustine initially wanted to hear him because of his reputation. Augustine was intrigued as he observed Ambrose reading silently, a rare practice in antiquity. After hearing Ambrose preach Sunday after Sunday, Augustine's intellectual and spiritual frustrations began to find resolution. Augustine concluded he had misunderstood Christianity, and Ambrose's preaching opened the door to a new understanding of the faith. "I had been all the more foolhardy and impious in my readiness to rant and denounce where I ought to have inquired and sought to learn," wrote Augustine.[32] Exploring the writings of Neoplatonists such as Porphyry and Plotinus, the mystery of the problem of evil became clear when he came to the conclusion that evil did not have an essence of its own, but was rather the absence of good. Moving from the Neoplatonists, Augustine turned to the New Testament, particularly the writings of the apostle Paul. Augustine found in Paul the same war of wills (Rom. 7:22–23) that he found in himself, but he had not yet had a breakthrough. Reading Paul, he became full of fear because he could see no way out of his condemnation under rebellion against God. Until one day, while meditating upon his sinful life in a small garden adjacent to the house in which he was staying, he heard what sounded like the voice of a child coming from a neighboring house near his. The voice repeatedly chanted, "Pick it up and read, pick it up and read."[33] Finding a copy of the book of Romans that he had earlier placed in the garden, Augustine wrote, "I snatched it up, opened it and read in silence the passage on which my eyes first lighted: *Not in dissipation and drunkenness, nor in debauchery and lewdness, nor in arguing and jealousy; but put on the Lord Jesus Christ, and make no provision for the flesh or the gratification of your desires.*" No sooner as he read those words, Augustine's mind and heart were flooded with "the light of certainty."[34]

Augustine's conversion story is one of the most compelling narratives of spiritual metamorphosis in the Western canon. His *Confes-*

sions marks one of the greatest literary innovations in human history, being the first autobiography. The author's sincere introspective nature on display in the work, as well as its acute philosophical insights, makes *Confessions* an indispensable resource for the formation of the human imagination.

Augustine's conversion occurred in 386, and he was baptized the next year. In 391, he was ordained a priest in the Catholic Church, and in 396, he was made bishop of the Roman Numidian city of Hippo-Regius. In his role as bishop, Augustine thought deeply about the nature of the church and Christian theology. He was engaged in intense controversies with the Donatists (a group we may describe today as ultraconservative) and the Pelagians (another group we may describe as ultraliberal), and through those controversies, his theological instincts and insights were strengthened. Augustine's thought had no peer in the Western mind for the next eight centuries until Thomas Aquinas came upon the scene in the thirteenth century. During the Reformation, Augustine's thought would experience a renaissance through Protestant Scholasticism initiated by John Calvin (1509–1564). Astoundingly, Augustine remains among the most important theological and philosophical thinkers in the Western tradition to this day, 1,600 years after his death.

Augustine ordered his philosophy starting with God as the ground of all being. This starting point is relevant for the conservative since belief in the transcendent is primary in conservative thought. In other words, the conservative knows that the individual is not the ultimate reality. Rather, the individual is a finite part of a whole, situated in space and time, and contingent upon moral, physical, intellectual, and spiritual forces over and above him. As Kirk wrote, "political problems, at bottom, are religious and moral problems" and "true politics is the art of apprehending and applying the Justice which ought to prevail in a community of souls."[35] To begin with God in worldview formulation, and especially God as the ground of all being, is eminently appropriate in aspirational conservatism.

For Augustine, God is Spirit, absolutely good and absolutely real. Without God, there can be nothing, for God is the Creator of all things. Creation is good, inasmuch as God is the source of all created things and evil is the absence of both the good and the creative activity of God (God did not create evil). So far as the world is truly real, the world is good, but the actual world is not quite real because of the Fall, which occurred in the garden of Eden. God alone possesses the attribute of perfection, and God is the ultimate expression of the Good. He is transcendent, that is, he is over and above time, and his consciousness is an eternal present, since he himself is changeless. Time and change belong to the created world, and with the entrance of sin into the world, the world as it is cannot be perfect. But the world, albeit groaning under the weight of sin, is still good because God is immanent, that is, he is continuously active in the world, accomplishing his good will.

The upshot of God as the ground of all being is that all of reality has a coherence and a meaning. Nothing in the created order, no matter how great or small, is random, pointless, irrelevant, out of place, or lacking significance. Augustine based his concept of God as the ground of all being on his understanding of how God created the universe. In contrast to the ancient Greeks, who believed that creation was constructed from elements that had already existed, Augustine argued that God created all that exists from nothing. This is the doctrine of creation ex nihilo.

In his exposition of the Apostles' Creed, "On Faith and the Creed," Augustine disputed the Greek view of creation, writing that the ancients based their argument that the gods formed the world using preexisting materials on their experience of observing "craftsmen and house-builders, and artisans of all descriptions, who have no power to make good the effect of their own art unless they get the help of materials already prepared."[36] No, Augustine said. God is not dependent upon previously existing materials from which to instantiate his intended space-time-matter order of things. Rather, he said, "granting that he is almighty, there cannot exist anything of which he should not be the Creator." Even in creating humanity, although he fashioned Adam "of dust from the ground,"[37] Augustine made it clear that "the earth from which the clay comes he had made out of nothing."[38] Certainly God made all things in the universe from nothing, even those things that are invisible to us. Thus, all things are dependent on God, not only for their actual existence but also for whatever potential forms they may take in future time—"the same Being who imparts form to objects, also imparts the capability of being formed."[39] What must follow for everything God made is that all creation displays the good, the true, and the beautiful either in its actual or potential existence. Consider this amazing statement: "For of him and in him is the fairest figure of all things, unchangeable; and therefore he himself is One, who communicates to everything its possibilities, not only that it be beautiful actually, but also that it be capable of being beautiful. For which reason we do most right to believe that God made all things of nothing."[40]

Augustine wanted his reader to understand that creation itself, determined as it is by the creative will of a good and wise God, bears something of God's characteristics within it. We can see God in the things in the created order, from looking through a microscope, to observing our surroundings, to peering through a telescope, to gazing in a mirror. Creation is not God, but creation does reflect God because God instantiated what had previously existed only in his mind, but now exists in reality. Do you want to find truth? Then find God. Do you want to know goodness? Then know God. Do you seek to behold the beautiful? Then behold God. If God is the ground of all being, then all that is good, true, and beautiful must be found in God.

Consider how Augustine resolved the problem of evil after years of grappling with this challenging conundrum. He had been a Manichaean for nine years, and during that time he thought of good and evil as having equal and independent essences that were in perpetual and irreconcilable conflict with one another. As he became convinced of the truth of Christianity, he came to a new understanding of the meaning of the good and the evil. Augustine saw pure reality as consisting in God alone, since he alone did not change. Also, because God was unchanging, God was fully real and fully good. Thus, the Good was eternally more significant and enduring than the evil. Moreover, all things that God made were contingent, that is, completely dependent on God for their existence and sustenance. All created things were temporal, so while they were good on account of having been created by God, they were temporal and changing, thus they were not fully real. For Augustine, created things "do not in the fullest sense exist, nor yet are they completely non-beings; they are real because they are from you, but unreal inasmuch as they are not what you are. For that alone truly is, which abides unchangingly."[41] So all things, by their essence, reflect God's goodness and reality to a limited extent, but because they are mutable and temporal, they lack what only God by his essence possesses.

From this it follows that all things in creation are good, but they are not, in Augustine's words, "supremely good." Created things are not only mutable, they are also destructible. When a thing is destroyed, it loses its goodness, and thus it loses its existence. If a thing exists, it is good, even if it is not supremely good. Augustine's consideration of creation as good led him to his thought on evil. Since all that exists is good, then evil itself cannot have an independent essence. If it did, then it would be good at least in part. Augustine wrote, "I saw, then, for it was made clear to me, that you have made all good things, and that there are absolutely no substances that you have not made." Furthermore, all things by their collective existence are all very good, because God declared all creation to be so as recorded in Genesis 1:31. In contrast, that which is evil has no essence, and therefore, no existence. Augustine wrote, "For you evil has no being at all, and this is true not of yourself only but of everything you have created, since apart from you there is nothing that could burst in and disrupt the order you have imposed on it."[42] Thus, God is completely good, and everything God has made is good, including the order of creation. When we experience evil, we are experiencing the effects of the privation of good that Augustine understood as the definition of evil.

Disorder and corruption emerge from the privation of good, and human sin is the source of moral evil. From whence does moral evil emerge? From a fallen will. The misery that follows evil choices occurs because persons "have forsaken him who supremely is, and have turned to themselves who have no such essence," or, in other words, are not unchangeable and supremely good.[43] Persons forsake God because their will is corrupted by the Fall. Thus, their will is not essentially evil, but the corruption of their will is "because it is contrary to the order of nature, and an abandonment of that which has supreme being for that which has less."[44] For instance, luxury is not evil in itself, but because the human heart longs for luxury more than moderation, unfettered pursuit of luxury is disordered, and the effects of this disorder bring miserable results. "Pride, too, is not the fault of him who delegates power, nor of power itself, but of the soul that is inordinately enamored of its own power, and despises the more just dominion of a higher authority."[45] So for Augustine, all things that exist are good, though they are inferior to the God who created them; and God himself is the highest good, the author of good, and if one finds the good in its proper ordering, then he has found God. The same holds for the true. Augustine wrote, "you hold all things in your Truth as though in your hand; and all of them are true insofar as they exist, and nothing whatever is a deceit unless it is thought to be what it is not."[46] As with the good and the true, Augustine found God as the standard of beauty. He wrote, "the beautiful designs that are born to our minds and find expression through clever hands derive from that Beauty which transcends all minds, the Beauty to which my own mind aspires day and night."[47]

For Augustine, God epitomized truth and beauty in his being. In a famous passage of *Confessions*, he considered the being of God as that which he loved, and proceeded to ask what the object of his supreme love was. When he thought of his love for God, it was a love not for anything of this created world, although his love for God was not altogether unlike the beautiful things of the world. God, unlike created beautiful things, could never be taken away, could never die, and never loses his beauty. Considering the truth and beauty of God, the source of all truth and beauty and the ground of all being, Augustine put his thought to poetry:

> This is what I love, when I love my God. And what
>   is this?
> I put my question to the earth, and it replied, "I am
>   not he";
> I questioned everything it held, and they confessed
>   the same.
> I questioned the sea and the great deep,
> And the teeming live creatures that crawl, and
>   they replied,
> "We are not God; seek higher."
> I questioned the gusty winds,
> And every breeze with all its flying creatures told me,
> "Anaximenes was wrong: I am not God."
> To the sky I put my question, to sun, moon, stars,
> But they denied me: "We are not the God you seek."
> And to all things which stood around the portals of my
>   flesh I said,
> "Tell me of my God.
> You are not he, but tell me something of him."
> Then they lifted up their mighty voices and cried,
> "He made us."
> My questioning was my attentive spirit,
> And their reply, their beauty.[48]

So in Augustine's ordering of thought, God serves as the starting point, and ontology, or the study of being, was at the foundation of his interpretation of reality. Second after ontology in Augustine's ordering of thought was epistemology, the nature of truth and knowledge and especially the relationship between faith and reason. For Augustine, faith and reason ought not to be seen as separate and distinct kinds of truth. Such a conception of faith and reason emerged in early modernity. Beginning with the rise of the universities in the twelfth and thirteenth centuries and culminating in the writings of Descartes (1596–1650) at the beginning of the Enlightenment, faith and reason became seen by Western thinkers as two separate kinds of truth that had little or no relevance to the other. By the nineteenth century, with the diffusion of Charles Darwin's evolutionary theories, faith and reason began to be seen by philosophers and scientists[49] as against one another. By the beginning of the twentieth century, with the triumph of modernism over fundamentalism, not only were faith and reason understood to be in conflict, but faith must always yield to reason and science.[50]

For Augustine, faith and reason, while distinct, were complementary. He never conceived of faith and reason as two completely different kinds of truth having no relevance to the other, nor did he think of them as being at war with one another. Augustine saw faith and reason as being in conversation with one another as each clarified truth, as grounded in God. Augustine knew Christianity as a revealed religion. Thus, Augustine believed that the Bible served as special revelation from God in which God speaks truth that cannot be known by reason alone. The created world disclosed general revelation, in that one can know that God exists and know of his excellent quality through nature.[51] Reason apprehended general revelation, but knowledge of general revelation was not enough for salvation. Special revelation, God's disclosure of himself through his word, was necessary for a person to understand the doctrines of the faith, such as the way of salvation. Augustine understood that faith and reason were distinct; nevertheless, both served as knowledge. The source of all truth, whether it was from special or general revelation, was God. Faith and reason both yielded knowledge of God's truth, although both fulfilled different functions. When it came to knowledge of special revelation, faith came before reason.

If one seeks to live the good life, one must begin with right faith. Augustine taught that the world of the temporal, while good, was not fully real. The real was in God, and our lives on earth were preparing us for eternal life in heaven. Thus, for Augustine, "the starting point of a good life . . . is right faith."[52] The essence of faith was to believe what one cannot see, and faith was a gift of God, just as all our existence was a work of God's grace. When God created humankind, he gave him being, life, sensation, and, most importantly, reason. Sticks and stones had being. Shrubs and vines had life. Animals had senses. But only human beings had reason, and furthermore, only human beings had dominion over the earth. So for Augustine, reason and dominion were the two distinguishing features of humankind, and these were what demonstrated them to be made in the image of God. But understanding was another important category for Augustine, and he distinguished between reason and understanding in observing that even though persons had reason by nature, they often did not have understanding. Augustine said, "he has already got reason before he understands. After all, that's why he wants to understand, because he surpasses other animals in reason."[53] Understanding had to do with right conduct—it was the right use of reason, which belonged to persons by nature.

Going further, Augustine clarified the distinction between understanding, which referred to right conduct, and faith, which led to eternal life. It may be intuitive to ask how to use reason to get understanding in order that one could then believe to attain eternal life. For Augustine, faith was necessary to attain the full truth, but reason can be employed to deepen understanding of that truth that faith apprehends. "Understand, in order to believe; believe, in order to understand. I'll put it in a nutshell, how we can accept both without argument: Understand, in order to believe, my word; believe, in order to understand, the word of God."[54] In this way we see how faith and reason were complementary to one another in Augustine's epistemology. Pope Benedict XVI explained Augustine's view of the harmony of faith and reason in this way: *crede ut intelligas* ('I believe in order to understand')—believing paves the way to crossing the threshold of truth—but also, and inseparably, *intellige ut credas*

('I understand, the better to believe'), the believer scrutinizes the truth to be able to find God and to believe."[55]

For Augustine, reason was necessary for right knowledge, but reason was not sufficient on its own to have knowledge of God that led to salvation. Not everyone who used their reason would arrive at right reason leading to virtue. And reason, even though it provided sight, could not by its own compulsion direct the eyes to a vision of God by itself. For this to happen, faith was necessary. Blind faith would not do, nor would faith for the sake of faith. True faith had Christ as the object, and when the person placed faith in Christ, he would receive the blessing of knowing God in his fullness. Attended by hope and charity, which granted certainty and enjoyment, the vision of God attained by faith was complete. Virtue, which was the state of blessedness, was thus within reach once faith was employed, because once a person had a vision of God, there would be no vision higher than that which he had attained. Faith gave sight to the one who was looking for God, in a similar way that reason gave sight to the one who was looking for knowledge of the world. Thus, *crede ut intelligas*, that famous formulation that Augustine derived from Isaiah 7:9, was consistent with these beautiful lines from the first book of his *Soliloquies*:

When therefore the mind has come to have sound eyes, what next? That she look. The mind's act of looking is Reason; but because it does not follow that everyone who looks sees, a right and perfect act of looking, that is, one followed by vision, is called Virtue; for Virtue is either right or perfect Reason. But even the power of vision, though the eyes be now healed, has not force to turn them to the light, unless these three things abide. Faith, whereby the soul believes that thing, to which she is asked to turn her gaze, is of such sort, that being seen it will give blessedness; Hope, whereby the mind judges that if she looks attentively, she will see; Charity, whereby she desires to see and to be filled with the enjoyment of the sight. The attentive view is now followed by the very vision

of God, which is the end of looking; not because the power of
beholding ceases, but because it has nothing further to which it
can turn itself: and this is the truly perfect virtue, Virtue arriving
at its end, which is followed by the life of blessedness. Now this
vision itself is that apprehension which is in the soul, compounded
of the apprehending subject and of that which is apprehended: as
in like manner seeing with the eyes results from the conjunction of
the sense and the object of sense, either of which being withdrawn,
seeing becomes impossible.[56]

Augustine's epistemology, framed in a complementary view of
faith and reason, led him to see both the material and spiritual world
through the lens of grace and gratitude. His right ordering of interpreting reality, by starting with God and proceeding to knowledge,
helped him to have an imagination that reflected truth.

In Augustine's thought, epistemology followed ontology and
ethics followed epistemology. Whereas ontology asked what is the
nature of being, and epistemology asked what is the nature of truth
and knowledge, ethics asked (to borrow from Francis Schaeffer),
how should we then live? Ethics necessarily follows ontology and
epistemology because the practical was the application of the philosophical. Ethics was circumscribed by limitations placed upon it
by the nature of our being and of what and how we know as finite
creatures. For Augustine, ethics followed from his understanding of
human nature as being fallen in sin, which has important implica-
tions for free will.

Augustine argued that human beings possessed free will. Augustine observed that God's commands would be completely futile if
it were impossible for persons to choose to obey those commands.
Moreover, the fact that the apostle Paul wrote that persons were without excuse due to the testimony given by nature as to God's existence
and his excellencies offered further evidence that persons possessed
liberty to choose. God required of persons that they obey his commands, so, as Augustine put it, "How does he make this requisition

if there is no free will? What means 'the happy man,' of whom the Psalmist says that 'his will has been the law of the Lord'? Does he not clearly enough show that a man by his own will takes his stand in the law of God?"[57] And when a person did wrong, he would have no one to blame but himself. He could not blame God, and he could not plead ignorance. The grace of God was necessary to renew the will so that a person could lead a righteous life that led to salvation. "But the grace of God is always good; and by it, it comes to pass that a man is of a good will, though he was before of an evil one."[58]

Augustine's ordering of the imagination, from ontology to epistemology to ethics, puts all creation in its proper place before its Creator. In this way, humanity is dignified with the acknowledgment of real liberty and responsibility. Humanity also knows its place, that it has the highest place of honor in creation as bearing the image of God and at the same time has the highest responsibility given the task of exercising just dominion using reason and authority. Persons can recognize, know, and take part in the good, the true, and the beautiful to enjoy them and pass them down to their children and children's children. All that makes life worth living is available to the person because the Creator of all things has bestowed on persons the ability to participate in himself and in his bounty. A rightly ordered worldview sees the actuality and potentiality in the reality of which we are a part, without delusions and without despair. Delusion and despair come with the disordering of imagination.

Allow me to illustrate the power of a rightly ordered worldview starting with God as the ground of all being, moving to truth and knowledge as also grounded in God, and finally settling on ethics, or the living out of a set of moral standards established by, and with reference to, God.

I have one hobby. Some folks have a lot of hobbies, but I have one: orienteering. Orienteering is a sport played in a variety of ways, but my application of orienteering is in the context of hiking and backpacking. I love orienteering, and if I could do it and make a living off it, that is what I would be doing all the time. I learned hiking and backpacking from my father from a very young age, and I learned orienteering in my early twenties as a single man with a lot of time (and not much money) on my hands. Orienteering is great fun no matter the weather conditions, and the greatest challenge (in my opinion) is orienteering at night. I was told by a friend who served as an air force pilot that night orienteering is a lot like flying by instrument rather than by sight. You must rely entirely on your instruments, the map and compass, since you do not have the wide visual perspective on the terrain and your surroundings that you have in daylight conditions. For years, I have taken students, friends, and family members on night-orienteering excursions, and the most wonderful part of those trips is seeing someone with no prior experience take point, successfully lead the group to a waypoint by map and compass, and immediately get hooked on the sport herself.

Night orienteering requires three essential tools: a reliable, working lensatic or baseplate compass, an accurate topographical map of the area, and a light source, preferably a headlight. Hiking on a trail at night is fun, but none of these tools is necessary to enjoy a night hike. To go off the trail, navigate to a particular waypoint or series of waypoints, and return to the jumping-off point requires a compass, a map, and a headlight. And for a point of indispensable clarification: phones and other GPS devices count for squat in orienteering. Skillful orienteering relies not on fickle gimmicks and gadgets.

Where does one go when night orienteering, and why? Orienteering frees you from being bound to places and sights someone else thought you should visit and see. When you orienteer off-trail, you can truly explore the terrain, see the way streams and rivers progress from their sources, understand the rise and decline of ridgelines and undulations in the terrain, and climb lonely mountain summits untrammeled by other people. There are waterfalls, pools, vistas, rock formations, whole sectors of forest that are untouched by trails, trash, campsites, and other signs of human activity. Wildlife stirs in the recesses of the forest away from trails, so it is possible and even likely that you will encounter signs and sights of animals you would not see on the trail. The experience of orienteering at night deepens the mystery of the forest, accentuates its solitude, and heightens your senses.

Navigating by compass and map at night is immensely freeing since the only limits placed on where and how far you go are determined by the topography itself and the limits of your own endurance. The compass is your primary tool for navigation. By it, you can set your course direction and stay on course no matter the obstacles. By following the compass, you can proceed in a straight line through all kinds of terrain, and provided you follow the compass carefully, you can always know your position at any given time on the map, how far you have traveled, and how far you have to go. The map shows you all the details of the terrain you must traverse, in addition to revealing places off the trail to which you may want to navigate. The map and compass, when used properly in coordination with one another, ensure that you know your current position, what to expect from the changes in the terrain ahead of you, how far you must travel, and the distance and time it will take to make your trip. And your headlight gives you the ability to see your compass and map hands-free as you navigate, as well as your surroundings, depending on the thickness of the forest. If the moon is out, you will be able discern the contours of hills, ridges, and mountains in the distance to help you with your bearings, but your reliance is going to be on your map and compass.

Orienteering by night with compass, map, and headlight is analogous to living by an imagination ordered first by ontology, second by epistemology, and third by ethics. In night orienteering, the compass is your vital instrument, without which you have no ability to set or maintain a course. You can navigate with a compass and no map, but you cannot navigate with a map but no compass. Even with a detailed topographical map, attempting to navigate at night without a compass is not realistic, because you would not be able to set an accurate course and maintain it with the help of the stars alone. Having a light and a map would make no difference in your ability to navigate without a compass. If you try to navigate without a compass, even with a detailed map and strong headlight, eventually you will be swallowed up by the forest.

Think of the compass in night orienteering as you would think about God in the imagination, the map as you would think of truth and knowledge, and the headlight as you would think of ethics. Just as the compass is the one thing needful for accurate navigation in a dark forest, belief in God as the source of all reality, truth, and standards of justice is necessary for navigating through life and its challenges. Take God and God's necessity out of the equation, and you will be lost. You cannot build an imagination on a theory of truth without God as the standard of truth. Without God as the standard of truth, one can only grope blindly along. In the same way, it is not possible to start with a theory of right and wrong to the exclusion of God as the moral standard. Without God as authority and standard of justice, all theories of right and wrong come down to individual whim and desire. Once again, stumbling around in the darkness blindly is the only alternative to having God as your lodestar. With God at the center of the imagination, it is possible to build an interpretation of reality that is coherent and harmonious. When we recognize God as the ground of all goodness, truth, and beauty, then faith, reason, and justice work in harmony resulting in true human flourishing. Just as in navigating through a dark wilderness at night with no path, road, or trail to guide you, the compass, the map, and the headlight all work together in harmony to ensure not only a definite way forward but one that is enjoyable and exhilarating for its adventure and challenge.

An imagination formed by a right ordering of ontology, epistemology, and ethics prepares the person to discern and revel in good art, music, literature, and film. Goodness, truth, and beauty are no longer "in the eye of the beholder," subject to individual taste, preference, or circumstances. The Transcendentals have meaning when the imagination is founded on a rightly ordered philosophical framework. Take as an example Pieter Bruegel the Elder's (1525/1530–1569) painting *The Return of the Hunters* (1565). Here is a winter scene from a collection of paintings depicting the months of the year. Bruegel's scene shows a group of hunters with their dogs emerging from a forest and coming into town. The landscape is bleak but still possesses a wintry beauty that is attractive in spite of the snow-covered hills, the frozen ponds, the skeletal trees, and the grey skies. Spend enough time with this piece, and you can almost feel your feet, cold and wet in your boots, as you come over the rise and view home in the distance. To the far left is a group of people gathered around a fire, and the wood smoke hanging in the distant air conjures up memories of the smell of wood smoke on a winter evening. The natural landscape is the setting for the painting, not an afterthought, and there is irony in the forbidding and inviting features that swell the scene.

Consider the oratorio *Saul* (1739) of George F. Handel (1685–1759), which dramatically sets to music the events surrounding the deteriorating relationship between Saul and David as recorded in the First Book of Samuel, chapters 15 to 31. Handel invented the English oratorio as a new genre by emphasizing the role of the chorus. His combined experience with Lutheran choral music, heavily influenced by the theology of the Reformation and the musical innovation of Johann Sebastian Bach (1685–1750), and English choral music led him to give the chorus a central part in the outworking of the drama in a way that Italian oratorios did not. "Handel was a dramatist, a master of effects,"[59] as J. Peter Burkholder, Donald Jay Grout, and Claude V. Palisca argued in their *History of Western Music*. Listen to the "Dead March" in *Saul*, and you will understand their meaning. The "Dead March" is an inimitably moving piece of music, with a strange but thrilling irony that mixes sorrow with wonder. It was considered fitting for the funeral procession for one of England's most cherished heroes, Lord Horatio Nelson, from Westminster Abbey to St. Paul's Cathedral in 1806. It is difficult to find a grander and more measured musical piece in three hundred years of musical history.

When it comes to great literature, there are, of course, the masters: Shakespeare, Milton, Dickens, Dumas, Carroll, Tolkien, Lewis, and many others. I love reading Russell Kirk's ghostly tales, a genre for which he is less known beside his philosophical works. Kirk wrote an essay entitled "A Cautionary Note on the Ghostly Tale," which serves as an epilogue to his collection of short stories, *Ancestral Shadows*. Kirk's word of caution was to remind his audience that the veil between the material and the spiritual worlds was thin, and that everyone should carefully prepare themselves for the world to which we shall all go in the hereafter. Kirk's ghostly tales were his "experiments in the moral imagination," each one having "for its kernel some clear premise about the character of human existence."[60] One of Kirk's aims in writing horror stories was to remind his readers that the edifice of the physical and spiritual world is supported and held together by a moral structural support. He observed that Irish Gothic writer Joseph Thomas Sheridan Le Fanu (1814–1873) "is believed to have died of fright. He knew that his creations were not his inventions merely, but glimpses of the abyss."[61] Kirk was a famous night owl, often taking walks in the middle of the night to clear his mind. He closed his essay with these memorable words: "These lines are written at the hour of three, the witching hour, when most men's energies are at ebb, 'in the silent croaking night,' a cricket for company. 'The small creatures chirp thinly through the dust, through the night.' Pray for us scribbling sinners now and at the hour of our death."[62] I remember reading these lines for the first time in Kirk's library at about two in the morning (I am also a night owl), just feet away from where the old bending author used to occupy his desk. As I read those lines, I remember the sound of a lone cricket chirping outside the window in the darkness. The lonely chirp of that cricket in the stillness of the night was as loud as a train horn to my ears as I read those words, and Kirk's moral presence filled the room.

Film can be a wonderful art form that exhibits the Transcendentals of goodness, truth, and beauty. I taught history in a baccalaureate program for inmates in a maximum-security prison for six years and found that none of my references to movies in my lectures were known to my students. Believing that their lives were poorer for their ignorance of great films, I created what I dubbed "The

Wilsey Re-education Program" (WREP). On Saturdays and during breaks between semesters, I brought in movies to show to the men, all of whom were serving life sentences. We watched classics like *The Cowboys*, with John Wayne; *The Scarlet Pimpernel*, with Anthony Andrews and Jane Seymour; *Glory*, with Matthew Broderick and Morgan Freeman; *Zulu Dawn*, with Peter O'Toole and Burt Lancaster; *Patton*, with George C. Scott; and many others. They loved them. Many of these men, who had been hardened criminals, were moved to tears during and after each film. When my children came of age, we expanded the WREP to include about fifty films. These films all carry with them great moral truths and demonstrate the meaning of the heroic in the human character. I want my students and my children to adopt heroes for themselves, great men and women to emulate even though they are flawed sinners. In our culture, where so many great figures of Western and American history have been canceled, it can be an act of rebellion to even have heroes. The heroic figures, the inspiring tales, the beautiful art and music, the soaring architecture, the storied history of our civilization ought to be a source for cultivating our imaginations, rightly ordered beginning with God, truth, and justice.

The conservative imagination, so constructed, is an act of rebellion also against a world that is becoming ever more dominated by technology. Technology at its best is a great good, making life more efficient and contributing to real flourishing for people everywhere in the world. Technology at its worst exercises a tyranny over humanity. Henry David Thoreau wrote in 1854, "We do not ride on the railroad; it rides upon us,"[63] and over a century later, Peter Viereck observed, "we need to be freed from what freed us."[64] If we are not careful, our imagination will be completely subsumed under the influence of technology as it pours images, information, and all kinds of stimulation into our minds without any basis in the good, the true, or the beautiful. American politics in the twenty-first century, unmoored as it is from an imagination grounded in an ordered philosophical framework, suffers from this defect. But the impulse to conserve that which is best in Western and American civilization can still recover an imagination that makes us fully human, even amid the cultural threats that would take away those things that are worth living for, either through active cancellation or simply letting them die in the fading shadows of forgetfulness.

Conservatism and Nationality

This lovely land, this glorious liberty, these benign institutions, the
dear purchase of our fathers, are ours; ours to enjoy, ours to preserve,
ours to transmit. Generations past and generations to come hold us
responsible for this sacred trust.

—Daniel Webster, *Adams and Jefferson*

I was a nationalist; but I was not a patriot.

—Adolf Hitler, quoted in John Lukacs,
The End of the Twentieth Century and the End of the Modern Age

---

O ne of the most remarkable and uncanny events in American
history took place on July 4, 1826, the fiftieth anniversary of the
adoption of the Declaration of Independence by the Second Continental Congress. At about 12:50 in the afternoon that day, Thomas
Jefferson (1743–1826), third president of the United States, died in
his home at Monticello in Albemarle County, Virginia, at the age of
eighty-three. Later that afternoon in Quincy, Massachusetts, at about
six o'clock, John Adams (1735–1826), the second American president
and successor to George Washington, died at the age of ninety. The

two men had a decades-long friendship, and their careers intersected from the 1770s to 1801. Jefferson and Adams had both served on the Committee of Five (with Roger Sherman of Connecticut, Benjamin Franklin of Pennsylvania, and Robert Livingston of New York), commissioned by the Congress to draft the Declaration of Independence in June 1776. They were both diplomats, Adams having represented the United States to France, the Dutch Republic, and Great Britain between 1778 and 1788, and Jefferson holding the position of Minister to France from 1785 to 1789. They both occupied the office of vice president: Adams under Washington from 1789 to 1797, and Jefferson under Adams from 1797 to 1801. They were bitter opponents in one of the most partisan and ugly presidential elections in American history, the election of 1800, in which Jefferson narrowly defeated Adams and went on to serve two terms as president until 1809. The two were so bitterly alienated from one another after 1801 that they did not speak again until 1812, although Jefferson continued to correspond with Abigail Adams throughout this period. But the two men renewed their friendship through written correspondence thanks to the mediation of their mutual friend, Benjamin Rush.[1] The story of the friendship between Jefferson and both John and Abigail Adams is a great American story, simultaneously inspiring and poignant.

The deaths of two of the most celebrated men of their generation on such an illustrious anniversary was regarded as much more than a coincidence by the people then living. Boston authorities asked then-US representative Daniel Webster of Massachusetts (1782–1852) to offer a eulogy of the two men, and he presented his tribute on August 2 at Faneuil Hall. He noted that the renowned venue had never been draped in black for mourning in its history. "These walls," said Webster, "which were consecrated, so long ago, to the cause of American liberty, which witnessed her infant struggles, and rung with the shouts of its earliest victories, proclaim now, that distinguished friends and champions of that great cause have fallen."[2] But it was fitting that Faneuil Hall should bear the "badges of mourning" because the occasion for his oration was not only poignant, it was providential. The two men "took their flight together to the world of spirits," said Webster.[3] It was arresting evidence of God's favor on the young nation that these two men, whose careers had paralleled one another in so many noteworthy ways, should take their leave of earthly life not only on the same day, but on the fiftieth birthday of the nation they helped to quicken. Webster said, "It cannot but seem striking and extraordinary, that these two should live to see the fiftieth year from the date of [Independence]; that they should complete that year; and that then, on the day which had fast linked forever their own fame with their country's glory, the heavens should open to receive them both at once."[4] Webster captured the mood of early America, in which it was generally believed that God's providence was easily discernible, when he ascribed the uniqueness of the occasion to the work of God. "As their lives themselves were the gift of Providence, who is not willing to recognize in their happy termination, as well as in their long continuance, proofs that our country and its benefactors are objects of His care?"[5]

Perhaps most consequentially, Webster situated the passing of Adams and Jefferson on July 4, 1826, as significant for generations of Americans past, present, and future. In the spirit of Edmund Burke, Webster saw American society as a contract between the dead, the living, and the yet to be born. The generation of Adams and Jefferson had bequeathed the trust of American nationality to Webster's generation, and it was the solemn responsibility of those living to pass that trust on to the generations yet to come. As historian Paul Nagel wrote, "Americans thought about their nationality as a Trust and themselves as Stewards."[6] An aspirational conservative understanding of proper love of country is consistent with Nagel's statement. Our American nationality is a gift, an inheritance, or a trust handed down to us by our ancestors. As Americans, it is our duty to preserve our nationality like responsible stewards, with an eye toward handing it down as a trust to our children, grandchildren, and all those who come after us.

Now, however, there is broad confusion over American nationality.[7] Over the past several years, there has been much talk of something called "Christian nationalism." Michelle Goldberg first employed this term in her 2006 book entitled *Kingdom Coming: The Rise of Christian Nationalism*, and since 2017 a cottage industry has developed around "Christian nationalism." My interest in the intersection between American identity and theology began in 2006 when I began researching and writing my PhD dissertation on the Christian America thesis, the idea espoused by many on the Christian right beginning in the 1970s that America was founded as a Christian nation. Since then, I have written on the themes of American patriotism, nationalism, and exceptionalism through biography and intellectual history.[8] In all that time, I rarely saw the term "Christian nationalism" used except in Goldberg's book and maybe one or two others. Then after Donald Trump's presidency commenced in 2017, "Christian nationalism" took off. Numerous books appeared, especially since 2019, that explore the phenomenon historically, theologically, sociologically, and even psychologically.[9] Most of these books tell us how "Christian nationalism" is racist, sexist, homophobic, exclusively right wing, harmful, violent, and even heretical. Andrew Whitehead and Samuel Perry even go so far as to argue that having certain traditional views about religious liberty, marriage, sanctity of life, or biblical authority make a person a "Christian nationalist." For example, if you are a Christian who understands that religious liberty means that you have the constitutional right to exercise your faith in the public square, it follows that you are a "Christian nationalist" out to exclude or marginalize anyone who holds to a non-Christian religion and seeks to live out their conscience in the public square.[10] Also, if you hold to traditional gender identities and roles and the traditional view of marriage as between a man and a woman, then you are a "Christian nationalist."[11] Thus, according to many critics of Christian nationalism on the left, if you are an aspirational conservative, you are likely to be a "Christian nationalist," which supposedly is an inherent threat to democracy. Our national conversation about this thing called "Christian nationalism" became mainstream as a response to the so-called Age of Trump. As a result, many are taciturn about embracing patriotism because they do not want to be tagged a nationalist and an enemy of democracy. This is deeply problematic. Without a proper love of country, it is not possible for the United States to cohere as a nation predicated on the ideals and institutions that historically have identified it to itself and to the world. One of the problems with the trend of classifying anyone who embraces tradition or patriotism as a "Christian nationalist" is that there often occurs a conflation of *nationalism* with *nationality*. Nagel's study of how American national identity developed in the nineteenth century is helpful here. He defined nationalism as "a deliberate effort to glory in the spirit, fact, or endeavor of a polity."[12] Furthermore, nationalism refers to "a doctrine or a specific form of consciousness conveying superiority or prestige."[13] In contrast, Nagel wrote that nationality "refers to what it means to be a nation. This word encompasses both the matter of citizenship and the ideology arising from belonging to a polity."[14] Nationalism and nationality should not be thought of as opposites, however. Nationality is a broad category to which the narrower terms like "nationalism" and "patriotism" pertain. Critics of "Christian nationalism" are often correct when they caution against making an idol of the nation, arbitrarily defining groups as superior or inferior, or jingoism based on specious theological wiles. Not everyone who embraces ideas, institutions, and practices that are identifiably American engages in nationalism of this sort. Every stage in every process of nationality creation in the American tradition has involved some sort of civil religion, which entails mythos, symbol, ritual, and liturgy based on text, tradition, and collective memory, lived out through active expression, and embraced with devotion and loyalty. Nationalism scholar Anthony D. Smith made this point when he wrote, "we must go beneath the official positions, and even the popular practices, of modern nationalisms to discover the deeper cultural resources and sacred foundations of national identities; and that in turn means grasping the significance of the nation as a form of communion that binds its members through ritual and symbolic practices."[15]

The United States began its career as an independent federal republic constitutionally based upon rule of law and liberal political, economic, and religious propositions. The founding documents—the Declaration of Independence, the Constitution, and the Bill of Rights—articulate these propositions in terms of natural equality under God, natural and prescriptive rights, sovereignty resting with the people (not the states or any branch of government), and the Contract Clause of the Constitution, to name a few examples. Additionally, race and ethnicity were ever-present features in the American colonial and national foundings. Any account of American nationality can candidly recognize this reality, without the need for crafting new origin narratives like *The 1619 Project*. Racial considerations in nationality formation over time through the regulation of slavery, immigration policies, territorial expansion, and *de jure* segregation have been important in the development of American nationality. Religion, especially Christianity, has historically exerted great influence on American culture. Americans have looked to make sense of their nationality through the lens of providence and moral norms as defined by the Bible since before the national founding. So while fashioning their identity, Americans often have embraced various models of nationality over time, and some of these models have carried exclusivist and imperialist manifestations. Still, not every form of American nationality has been nationalistic. I have differentiated between these two kinds of nationalities referring to the former as closed American exceptionalism and the latter as open American exceptionalism. Nationalism, or closed exceptionalism, entails an essentially disordered devotion to country, informed by the application of certain Christian theological doctrines, in which country comes above every other consideration. Patriotism, as a rightly ordered love for country, is predicated on a belief in open exceptionalism, or a celebration of American ideals and institutions that contribute broadly to human liberty and flourishing from local to national community. Political scientist Steven B. Smith wrote that "patriotism is a species of loyalty" that he regarded as "the first virtue of social institutions."[16]

As loyalty, patriotism entails "affirmation of what we care about" and consists within "a structure of loyalties. . . . What we care about defines the kind of person we are, or wish to be."[17] Tocqueville defined patriotism as an "instinctive love" that "is mingled with the taste for ancient customs, with respect for ancestors, and the memory of the past."[18] Patriots consider their native country in terms of the familiar, according to Tocqueville, thus patriots would "cherish their country as one loves the paternal home."[19]

The process of creating American nationality occurs in every generation, and every American nationality gets constructed along the contours of immediate historical context and circumstance as time progresses. This process is nothing new, nor can it be understood as one simple and unchanging dynamic over the span of four centuries. It is multifaceted, emerges from diverse ideologies, and changes over time. It is also manifested in both political and religio-philosophical terms. Sometimes, the process of nationality creation has brought forth nationalistic, closed exceptionalist expressions. At other times, more open exceptionalist nationalities have emerged with time and circumstance. The point is, since the colonial founding, Americans have participated in creating complex and contested nationalities. Americans have been divided, often bitterly so, in their visions for the nation, represented at times by loyalists against patriots, Hamiltonians against Jeffersonians, Unionists against secessionists, assimilationists against those espousing "hyphenated Americanism,"[20] and segregationists against integrationists. In their processes of nationality creation, they have been perennially challenged by revolutions in technology, communications, religion, politics, economics, society, diplomacy, territorial growth, and events beyond their shores. Still today, we find competing groups in our continuing efforts at nationality creation on the political/social/religious/economic left and right. Why should we be surprised? This process of national identity creation is ongoing and complex, not a simple matter of pointing the finger at those who would allegedly threaten democracy simply because being an American matters to them.

American history is a demonstration of the complexity of nationality. In all the social media hot takes from the left on "Christian nationalism," it is easy to miss how nuanced nationality creation has been in the American experience. The project of the Revolution and the Constitution was to forge a nation out of distinct parts: former colonies that called themselves "states" starting in 1776. The process of early republican political and cultural consolidation, territorial expansion, organization of newly acquired territories—not to mention diplomacy—was a nationalistic process in that the United States was in process of becoming a modern nation-state. Americans steadily developed national identity through various forms of political and social nationalities and advanced westward thanks to a commercial and transportation revolution after the War of 1812.[21] So, the America of 1844 was not exactly the America of 1866, which was not the same as the America of 1890—and so on.

The first English colonists, particularly the New England Puritans, began the American tradition of creating a nationality. George McKenna, in his 2007 book, *The Puritan Origins of American Patriotism*, argued convincingly that the tradition of American patriotism "dates back to seventeenth century Puritanism, yet it has adapted itself to all the modifications in Puritan-derived Protestantism over the past three centuries."[22] While McKenna distinguished between nationalism and patriotism, Americans[23] began their nationalistic conviction of chosenness and mission, themes they drew from Protestant theology, in the context of seventeenth-century Puritan New England. And this conviction is an example of the potency of the combination of theology and national identity.

American nationality has always been three-dimensional. That is, the people who have developed it over the generations have cast a vision of America in space (as in, the land, the people, and its place in the world), in time (as in, orientation toward the past, present, future, and eternity), and in spirit (as in, its ideas, mores, and aesthetics). Since the colonial period, Americans have frequently deployed closed exceptionalist themes that carry theological weight, such as a sacred land, a pure origin, the millennial kingdom, providence, divine favor, and a sacred mission. In crafting national identity, figures such as Thomas Jefferson used philosophical ideas derived from sources like the Enlightenment (inevitable progress and equality); others such as Thomas Cole and John C. Calhoun have employed ideas related to Romanticism (the sublime and scientific racism), and even German idealism (Hegelian dialectic) in the case of historian George Bancroft. The tradition of nationality development in America is old, continuous, and culturally salient, and therefore knotty. Great care and thought should be employed in trying to understand it in the past and in the present.

Tocqueville captured this complexity well in just a couple of pages in volume 1 of *Democracy in America*. Of American patriotism, he wrote, "often this love of country is intensified even more by religious zeal" and that "there is nothing more annoying in the experience of life than this irritable patriotism of the Americans."[24] Tocqueville observed that Americans of the 1830s possessed a blend of both healthy and unhealthy attitudes in their patriotism, but were so convinced of their moral purity that they would not abide any criticism of their culture, ideas, or institutions. Because they *defined* their national identity in normative terms, their expressions of *devotion* to the nation were limited to praise and adulation. But he also observed that American patriotism could be expressed through quiet reverence for tradition, attachment to family and place, and devotion to the law and to the exercise of rights.[25] Patriotism also could be diminished when people cease to cherish their ancestral customs, their religion, and their laws. When the people "no longer see the country except in a weak and doubtful light," patriotism goes the way of the passenger pigeon.[26] Once that happens, Tocqueville wrote, the people "have neither the instinctive patriotism of monarchy, nor the thoughtful patriotism of the republic; but they have stopped between the two, in the middle of confusion and misery."[27] Once patriotism ebbs away, what rationale is there among citizens to maintain a particular nationality? And if nationality is not cultivated as a trust with careful stewardship in order that it be handed down to future generations, then what is to become of American ideals, institutions, memories, places, traditions, families, and liberties? Many critics of "Christian nationalism" miss the point of the basic fact of human nature that Tocqueville identified in Americans. Namely, American nationality formation is an uneven business, and patriotism is an ideal to which we imperfectly aspire. True, selfish ambition communicated in closed exceptionalist terms taints the picture of what the American nation should be, but such chauvinistic accounts of the nation are not inherent to nationality formation or patriotism.

To help give substance to the historical picture, let us consider six examples of nationalities since 1630: Puritan millennialism, Christian republicanism, Manifest Destiny, Lincolnian unionism, Wilsonian idealism, and Christian America. Each of these nationalities bears marks of both closed and open exceptionalism and may be studied accordingly. That is beyond the scope of our subject here. The point of the following paragraphs is to illustrate the complexity of American nationality formation and to argue that, in a broad sense, patriotism does not have to be scary. Most Americans embrace their nationality, in that they are, and have always been, interested in crafting a national identity for the benefit of themselves and their children.

At the establishment of the New England colonies, the Puritans saw their project in terms of a covenant with God. They believed they were fulfilling theological types introduced in the Old Testament. John Winthrop (1588–1649), the first governor of Massachusetts Bay Colony, famously articulated this vision in one of the most famous sermons in American history, his "Model of Christian Charity." Faithfulness to the covenant meant that God would "please to heare us, and bring us in peace to the place wee desire."[28] If the people were unfaithful, then God would "surely breake out in wrathe against us, be revenged of such a perjured people and make us know the price of the breache of such a Covenant." Samuel Danforth (1626–1674), pastor of the First Church in Roxbury, preached a sermon on Matthew 11:7–9, in which he saw Massachusetts as fulfilling the biblical type of Israel, going into the wilderness to hold a feast to the Lord after escaping Pharaoh's wrath. The colonists thought there was eternal significance to their "errand in the wilderness."[29] Cotton Mather, in his massive history of New England from 1620 to 1698 entitled *Magnalia Christi Americana*, saw New England in the strongest providential terms. He opened with an introduction to his history by referring to the Pilgrims settling at Plymouth in 1620, in which he wrote, "Tis possible, that our Lord Jesus Christ carried some Thousands of *Reformers* into the Retirements of an *American Desart*, on purpose, that, with an opportunity granted to many of his Faithful Servants, to enjoy the precious *Liberty* of their *Ministry*, tho' in the midst of many *Temptations* all their days, He might there, *To* them first, and then *By* them, give a *Specimen* of many Good Things, which He would have His churches elsewhere aspire and arise unto."[30]

The New England Puritans saw the discovery of America, the Reformation, and their colonizing project as evidence that God was bringing near the millennial kingdom of Christ, not in allegorical but in historical terms. Historian Ernest Lee Tuveson argued that the Puritans replaced the traditional amillennialism of medieval Europe with a progressive postmillennialism that was much more active and optimistic for the future. Augustine posited a view of history that was essentially static, that persons should accept the fallen world as it is: cursed under the weight of sin. The Puritans read the book of Revelation and came away with a view that God was working through his people to effect progress that culminated in the breaking forth of God's kingdom. The Reformation, they believed, was the beginning of the end for this fallen world.[31]

From the 1630s to the 1750s, this Puritan millennialism was the predominant expression of the intersection between theology and nationalism. As historical circumstances changed, theology continued to inform national identity, but it did so in ways unique to those changing circumstances. By the time of the American Revolution in the late eighteenth century, Americans were forming a new nation. American colonists saw the English triumph over the French in the

Seven Years' War in 1763 as the triumph of true religion over the forces of antichrist.[32] After 1763, revolutionary ideas drew inspiration from the Bible, English common law tradition, classical antiquity, the Enlightenment, and radical Whig ideology, those liberal ideas emerging from the English Civil War (1642–1649) and the Glorious Revolution (1688).[33] Historians Bernard Bailyn and Pauline Maier argued that radical Whig ideology brought together those disparate sources of revolutionary thought into a coherent whole.[34] Mark Noll observed that colonial preaching baptized this ideology into the language of Puritan exegesis and theology that produced "Christian republicanism."[35] Christian republicanism was the earliest expression of an American nationality after the close of the colonial period.

The blending of biblical language with English liberalism is clear in another famous sermon in American history, this one by Jonathan Mayhew. In his sermon based on Romans 13:1–8, "Discourse on Unlimited Submission" (1750), Mayhew said of a people oppressed by a tyrant: "For a nation thus abused to arise unanimously, and to resist their prince, even to dethroning him, is not a criminal; but a reasonable use of the means, and the only means which God has put in their power, for mutual and self-defence."[36] Mayhew believed that a nation ruled by a tyrant had a righteous duty to overthrow that tyrant because the ruler served God as the minister of good. When the ruler no longer served that divine purpose, the people were justified in overthrowing him.

Mayhew's sermon, influenced by radical Whig ideology, interpreted Romans 13 by the principle of consent of the governed. Seeing liberal political theory as consistent with the precepts of Scripture became commonplace during the struggle for independence. Samuel Sherwood preached a sermon in 1776 based on Revelation 12:14–17 entitled "The Church's Flight into the Wilderness," in which he saw the American colonies in similar terms as the church. Following the tradition of the Puritans, Sherwood used typology to depict the tyrannical George III and the Church of England as the persecutors of the American colonies. For Sherwood, King George was the anti-typological depiction of the dragon, and the colonies were that of the woman in the Revelation passage.[37] Connecticut preacher Nicholas Street, in his 1777 sermon, "The American States Acting over the Part of the Children of Israel in the Wilderness," similarly saw the colonists in the role of the Israelites of the exodus, the revolutionary leaders as Moses and Aaron, Britain as Egypt, King George III as Pharaoh, the Red Sea as the military struggle, and victory in the war as the land of Canaan.[38]

Such a blending of biblical motifs with revolutionary ideas gave a strong sense of national purpose and strengthened the idea that God had chosen America and blessed the states with great responsibility. Two generations later, John L. O'Sullivan, founding editor of the Jacksonian periodical *United States Magazine and Democratic Review*, coined one of the most recognizable terms in American history, "manifest destiny," in 1845. In the context of the American annexation of Texas, O'Sullivan wrote that Europe aimed at "limiting our greatness and checking the fulfillment of our manifest destiny to overspread the continent allotted by Providence for the free development of our yearly multiplying millions."[39] Along with a Christian concept of providence, manifest destiny also employed Christian-inspired themes of innocence, mission, and millennialism. Thus, there was a divine inevitability to American expansion. O'Sullivan's conception of manifest destiny was an important justification for the Mexican-American War (1846–1848). It was important also in the Spanish-American War of 1898, and America's acquisition of overseas colonies.[40]

O'Sullivan was an important figure in the years prior to the Civil War—a prominent editor, but also a member of the diplomatic corps, having served as minister to Portugal from 1853 to 1857 under the administration of Franklin Pierce. As an editorialist, he gave voice to the form of closed exceptionalism that prevailed in the context of American westward expansion. He thought of the Christian gospel in thoroughly American terms, presenting "a secular version of millennial 'political religion'" that cast "nationalism as a new *ersatz* and heterodox religion," in Anthony Smith's words.[41] He was convinced it was the will of God for America to overspread the North American continent, and because of this, America's rise to continental dominance was inevitable. Since America was the providential nation, it was morally pure. It was also in the vanguard of human progress. "All history has to be re-written; political science and the whole scope of all moral truth have to be considered and illustrated in light of the democratic principle" that America embodied, as O'Sullivan wrote in 1837.[42] Furthermore, America was chosen by God to spread liberty to the world—"freedom of conscience, freedom of person, freedom of trade and business pursuits, universality of freedom and equality. . . . For this blessed mission to the nations of the world, which are shut out from the life-giving light of truth, has America been chosen; and her high example shall smite unto death the tyranny of kings, hierarchs, and oligarchs, and carry the glad tidings of peace and good will where myriads now endure an existence scarcely more enviable than that of the beasts of the field," O'Sullivan wrote in 1839.[43]

We see the continuation of Puritan millennialism and Christian republicanism in O'Sullivan's manifest destiny but articulated in a new context. We also see O'Sullivan's racial prejudice inform his concept of nationality, in that he saw the Anglo-Americans as superior to indigenous people, Blacks, and Mexicans. Thus, manifest destiny is an example of closed exceptionalism. In contrast to O'Sullivan's providential certainty and racial chauvinism, Abraham Lincoln's open exceptionalist idea of the nation was benevolent, generous, and exemplary while retaining its debt to theology. Lincoln was committed to preserving the Union, and by 1862, he knew that it was impossible to save the Union as it was. By 1865 the Union, what Lincoln had called "the last best hope of earth" in 1862,[44] rested in God's hands. In his Second Inaugural Address, Lincoln noted that "Both [sides] read the same Bible, and pray to the same God; and each invokes His aid against the other."[45] In Lincoln's view, God was judging all America, North and South, for its 250-year embrace of slavery, and Americans had to change their conception of their relationship with

God. God, Lincoln contended, should not be described as taking the side of either belligerent. Americans should care more about whether they were on God's side, and to be on God's side was to be on the side of right.[46] This national vision was confirmed in the Union victory, and sacralized after Lincoln's assassination, as evidenced especially in the construction and 1922 dedication of the Lincoln Memorial in Washington. The memorial was dedicated in a carved dictum over the awesome statue of Lincoln as a "temple," and it has served as a symbol of Lincolnian justice merged with American nationality for over a century.

The Gettysburg Address may illustrate Lincolnian unionism better than any single document that Lincoln wrote. Lincoln conceived of the Civil War as a great testing of whether the American experiment in just self-government could survive. That experiment, which Lincoln described as "a new nation, conceived in liberty, and dedicated to the proposition that all men are created equal,"[47] was in stark contrast to the European monarchies that were not conceived as national experiments and remained dedicated to the principle of natural hierarchy and some to rule by divine right. What was required now, said Lincoln, was a renewal of dedication on the part of the living to carry the experiment forward. Such a rededication should take the form of a "new birth of freedom."[48] Allen Guelzo likened this to a "religious revival," the success of which would guarantee the success and spread of liberal democracy.[49] Guelzo observed that Lincoln placed the ongoing strife of the Civil War into a "world historical context."[50] In doing so, Lincoln normativized the American nation as the paragon of righteous government for all time, but minus the racial chauvinism of O'Sullivan. Lincolnian unionism was an open exceptionalist, religiously informed nationality that cast America as an exemplar to the world, manifesting hope and flourishing through liberty and equality under God.

Woodrow Wilson, the twenty-eighth president, led the American war effort in World War I beginning in 1917. He believed God had commissioned America to lead the world into Christian civilization through the defeat of the Central Powers and the establishment of the League of Nations. Historian Milan Babík connected Wilson's vision to Puritan millennialism: "the old Puritan dream of returning to the old world from the transatlantic refuge in order to spread the American millennium worldwide seemed to him on the verge of fulfillment."[51] Wilson's dream of an international order of Christian civilization, led by the United States, animated American interventionist foreign policy during most of the twentieth century. John Foster Dulles, who was a student of Wilson's at Princeton and who had attended the 1919 Versailles Conference under Wilson's leadership, was deeply impressed with Wilson's vision for American global leadership. As secretary of state under Eisenhower, Dulles said in 1955, "Our people have always been endowed with a sense of mission in the world. They have believed that it was their duty to help men everywhere to get the opportunity to be and to do what God designed."[52] That sense of divine mission and of solemn duty undergirded American actions, from the early years of the Cold War to the War on Terror in the early twenty-first century.

Dulles represents Wilsonian idealism as a religiously informed nationality better than Wilson because he was more successful at applying Wilson's vision to foreign affairs after World War II. Where Wilson's efforts at achieving a lasting peace at Versailles failed, Dulles's efforts at forging peace in the Pacific were successful with the ratification of the Treaty of San Francisco in 1952, a treaty involving forty-nine nations that he led in crafting and finalizing. Whereas Wilson died before he could see America face down the Nazis to "make the world safe for democracy," Dulles became the most powerful diplomat in the world during the early years of the Cold War, as the United States and its allies confronted the Soviet threat in the spirit of Wilsonian idealism.

Dulles repeatedly reminded Americans that theirs was a Christian nation, founded on Christian principles, and the most powerful champion of civilization. America had both a unique capacity and a solemn duty to stand for human liberty against the great foe of human liberty, the Soviet Union. If America retreated into itself, the whole world would fall to Communist tyranny. Dulles conceived of the world in Manichaean terms, seeing the United States as the champion of light and justice and the Communists as the purveyors of darkness and wickedness. Wilsonian idealism represented a continuation of a tradition in American nationality development in which, as historian Richard Gamble argued, Americans "have seen themselves as a progressive, redemptive force, waging war in the ranks of Christ's army . . . liberating those in bondage and healing the afflicted."[53]

After the rise of the New Left in the late 1960s, a book appeared in 1977 that launched the Christian America movement, a movement that continues to prevail in some conservative evangelical circles today. *The Light and the Glory*, by Peter Marshall and David Manuel, sold hundreds of thousands of copies. Marshall and Manuel argued that America was God's new Israel, chosen to be "a new Jerusalem, a model of the Kingdom of Christ upon earth."[54] In America, Marshall and Manuel argued, "God was making His most significant attempt since ancient Israel to create a new Israel of people living in obedience to the laws of God, through faith in Jesus Christ."[55] The book served as a path forward for the nation to recover its Christian origins and calling after rejecting its natal heritage with the radical student movement, second-wave feminism, the disgrace of Watergate, and military/diplomatic failure in Vietnam. The Christian America thesis—the argument that America was founded as a Christian nation—is based on a historiographical model known as a declension narrative. Advocates of the Christian America thesis all have agreed that the nation has fallen from its glorious Christian past and must recover what had been lost. Figures like Tim LaHaye, Jerry Falwell Sr., David Barton, John Eidsmoe, and others produced books, pamphlets, curricula, and multimedia to advance the Christian America thesis from the late 1970s into the twenty-first century.

The Christian America thesis can be understood in terms of three categories: historical, theological, and philosophical. Historically, advocates of Christian America have argued that the founders were Christians, the Great Awakening set the stage for the Revolution, and the founding documents were inspired from Christian sources. Theologically, they argued from a providential view of history that American exceptionalism was evidence of God's unique blessing on the nation, which was the chosen nation of God. Philosophically, the original intent of the founders as recorded in the Constitution, for ex- ample, may be discerned using the same hermeneutical methods used to interpret Scripture. Furthermore, they argued that the founders intended to build Christian principles into the fabric of the nation. The Christian America thesis is distinguished from previous national- ities in that its proponents orient the nation toward the past. They are concerned with the faith of the founders, the Christian origins of the nation, and returning America to a golden age. Nostalgia plays a crucial role in this brand of nationalism. Prior to about 1965, every generation of Americans took for granted that America was a Christian nation. With the slow dissolution of an American Protestant consensus be- tween 1790 and 1970, this is no longer broadly assumed. Advocates of Christian America are now trying to *recover* a Christian nationality.

The Christian America thesis remains animated today, and it seems that most of the criticism leveled at "Christian nationalism" has the Christian America thesis as the intended target. But even the Christian America thesis is complex, since, for example, its advocates often have not agreed with one another on basic principles, such as a clear understanding of what kind of Christian nation America was supposed to be at the founding. This thorny problem of complex- ity is also evident when trying to figure out exactly what "Christian nationalism" is. There is no single satisfying definition, but the term is almost always treated as if there were one prevailing, clear, and recognizable idea of "Christian nationalism" to assail. The problem is not that "Christian nationalism" does not exist. The problem is that "Christian nationalism" takes different forms for different reasons to serve various purposes, and each separate expression must be taken in historical context to fully understand its dynamics.

That said, one form of Christian nationalism is clearly defined and defended by Stephen Wolfe in his 2021 book, *The Case for Christian Nationalism*. I will treat this book in greater detail below. For now, let us regard this magisterial brand of Christian nationalism as something different from anything appearing before it. Wolfe's project does not entail the formation of an American nationality as such. It rather casts a vision for the purpose of the state in general, and the American state in particular. Wolfe's vision departs from the American tradition of republicanism in crucial ways pertinent to religion and ordered liberty. Wolfe is the exception to the rule that most understandings of Christian nationalism are ambiguous.

One thing we can say for sure is that nationality creation is necessarily historical. All nationalistic paradigms orient the nation in time, but not all in the same way. Puritan millennialism, Christian republicanism, manifest destiny, Lincolnian unionism, and Wilsonian idealism were oriented toward the future. Puritan millennialism looked ahead to the thousand-year reign of Christ. Christian republicanism and manifest destiny saw America turning its back on the past and turning toward the future. Lincoln cast America as being in the throes of a national death but also experiencing "a new birth of freedom" as "the last, best hope of earth." Wilson and Dulles looked forward to an international order with America as the indispensable nation, guaranteeing free trade and world cooperation under the aegis of benevolent American power. Each of these nationalities was committed to the idea of inevitable progress. They were progressive in that they situated America as the nation of the future. And Wilsonian idealism, as a progressive nationality, directly sprang from the political and religious left—not the right. The fact that nationality creation is necessarily historical is deeply important. Those who comment, reflect, disparage, or praise it must understand the historical complexities inherent in nationality and nationalism. Both progressives and conservatives have forged nationalities at different points in American history. At times, these nationalities were closed exceptionalist, and at other times they were open exceptionalist. At still other times, they were a mixture of both.

Enter the dynamic of religion in thinking historically about American nationality—how has religion shaped the way Americans have identified themselves in relation to God, to other nations, and even to themselves? How religious have Americans tended to be over the generations? How has religious affiliation changed in America since the eighteenth century? Is religion as important to Americans in the present as it was in the past? These questions, and others like it, are significant in addressing the changing ways that Americans have thought about themselves as the United States grew from independence to continental supremacy, world power, and superpower in a bipolar world, and later, in a multipolar world.

America was founded upon transcendent ideas, as in the Declaration of Independence: "all men are created equal" and "they are endowed by their Creator with certain inalienable rights, that among these are life, liberty, and the pursuit of happiness." During the Civil War, it was refounded upon other transcendent propositions, such as Lincoln's words in his Second Inaugural Address: "with malice toward none, with charity for all, with firmness in the right as God gives us to see the right let us strive on to . . . do all which may achieve and cherish a just and lasting peace among ourselves and with all nations."[56] Since America is a nation predicated on ideas that are essential, above and beyond space and time and applicable morally and ontologically to all generations, religion plays a unique role in American national identity. Without religion, the ideas that are necessary to the American project are meaningless. Thus, an American nationality devoid of religion or religious presuppositions is inconceivable. In American nationality development, Tocqueville's observation on the harmony of the spirit of religion and the spirit of liberty is on full display.

In such a nation as the United States, founded as it is on transcendent moral ideas, we can count on controversy and contest in the way Americans think of the application of those ideas. We can be certain that religion will be, just as it has been, abused and perverted to suit particular national interests, and some of those means and interests will be unjust and contradictory to the very ideas expressed in the founding documents. But aberrations such as these cannot justify the jettisoning of religion in American national identity, or of patriotic devotion to the trust of American nationality handed down to us by those who went before us.

All Americans this side of lawfulness and sanity embrace American nationality as we recognize the nation as the normative polity in which we live, move, and have our being. If we abide by the laws; acknowledge the supremacy of the Constitution; enjoy the blessings that America offers; appeal to American ideals; acknowledge the blessing of God on our security, prosperity, and liberty; and contend for justice in the name of the United States both domestically and internationally, we subscribe to a religious American nationality in broad terms. To throw out the baby of a national identity informed by religion is to throw the bathwater of America out with it.

We should think carefully about American history, nationality, and the interplay of religion with American identity. And we should stand against expressions that twist and debauch religion and nationalism to ends that militate against American ideals that many of our forefathers and foremothers gave their lives to defend and extend. As we do so, we may think of our loyalties along the lines of Augustine's ordering of loves. As Augustine wrote in *City of God*, "When the miser prefers his gold to justice, it is through no fault of the gold, but of the man; and so with every created thing. For though it be good, it may be loved with an evil as well as with a good love; it is loved rightly when it is loved ordinately; evilly, when inordinately."[57] This is where the distinction between patriotism and nationalism becomes necessary to explain clearly.

Aspirational conservatives take the many nuances inherent in American identity seriously. The term "Christian nationalism" can serve as a useful category. Christian nationalisms, to be sure, have often been articulated in ways that pervert Christianity's message.

Conservatives work to understand those nationalisms, and critiques of them must take precise and measured forms. For example, racism is part of closed exceptionalism, and as such, it is a corruption of American ideals and opposed to American identity. Religious bigotry contradicts the constitutional guarantee of disestablishment and liberty of conscience, and liberty of conscience cannot be appealed to in the name of bigotry. Christ's kingdom is not of this world, but we do live in the world. Christians do not contradict themselves when they express ordered love for Christ's kingdom first, and the nation subsequently. Americans must recognize that we all inherit something from nationality, whether political or religious, because American nationality is a trust handed down from our ancestors. Most importantly, we cannot allow critics on the left of "Christian nationalism" to use the concept to further undermine the necessary place of religion and religious people in the public square without answering them using reasonable and historical arguments. Religion must always have a place in the public square, and patriotism as devotion to the national idea is a good thing, provided it is rightly ordered and conceived. Historical and philosophical precision is needed to pinpoint whatever kind of religio-philosophical nationality is at hand, so that we may intelligently separate the precious from the worthless.

Historian John Lukacs described the difference between patriotism and nationalism. He said, "Patriotism is traditionalist, deeply rooted, introverted and defensive; nationalism is populist, extroverted, aggressive and ideological."[58] This is an apt contrast that everyone claiming to be a conservative or a progressive should heed.

It is not difficult to find examples of worthy expressions of patriotic devotion. In the predawn hours of May 15, 1918, Private Henry Johnson was pulling sentry duty with Private Needham Roberts in a French trench that faced the German line just west of the Argonne Forest. Johnson and Roberts were members of the 369th Infantry Regiment from New York.[59] The 369th, the "Harlem Hellfighters," was an African American regiment, and one of the first regiments led by Black officers and NCOs in the US Army. The regiment had joined the French line as replacements, and its soldiers were given French equipment to face German frontline veterans of four years of trench warfare.

At 2 a.m., Johnson and Roberts heard German trench raiders clipping wire, preparing to surprise the Allied troops, spread mayhem, and seize prisoners in hopes of gathering intelligence. Johnson started throwing grenades into the darkness toward the sound of the Germans, while Roberts ran back to the main line to alert the French. In the melee that followed, Johnson expended all of his grenades and grappled with the Germans in hand-to-hand combat, armed with a heavy bolo knife. He killed four Germans, plunging his knife into the head of one of them, and wounded twenty more, while sustaining over twenty gunshot wounds. He saved the severely wounded Roberts from capture, and the 369th subsequently never lost a man captured, spent the longest amount of uninterrupted time in combat of any American regiment in the war, and was the first regiment to reach the Rhine. Johnson and Roberts were also the first American privates to receive the Croix de Guerre from the French government in World War I.[60]

But when Johnson returned home to Jim Crow America after the war, his discharge papers did not mention anything about his combat record. He received no disability pay and was unable to return to his prewar work as a railroad porter. He died in 1929 at thirty-two years of age, largely forgotten. But in 1996, President Clinton awarded him the Purple Heart. In 2001, he was awarded the Distinguished Service Cross. And in 2015, President Obama bestowed on him the Congressional Medal of Honor.[61]

Johnson's biography, as well as the righting of the injustice of his remarkable service having been forgotten, stands as a testament to the uniqueness of American patriotism. One of the salient features of American patriots is that they reflect on the nation's glories as well as its failures. As Steven Smith wrote, "Patriotism can be self-critical. Consider the belated recognition of war heroes who had been overlooked due to their race, but were then awarded the Congressional Medal of Honor decades after their actions. What does this demonstrate, other than an enlarged conception of who belongs in the American family?"[62] American patriotism, according to Smith, should be distinguished from three extremes: national self-hatred, a cosmopolitanism that naively universalizes humanity, and a nationalism that breeds dangerous divisiveness and suspicion. Patriotism, unlike these intemperate attitudes, is found in a blend of reason and love. As Smith defined it, patriotism "is an expression of our highest ideals and commitments, not only to what we are, but also to what we might be."[63]

In a cultural moment marked by divisions cleaved by issues surrounding race, class, sexuality, gender identity, religion, economic disparities, and a host of other challenges, Smith's book on patriotism is profoundly appropriate. How can a nation like the United States cohere without a set of fundamentally shared ideals, hopes, symbols, texts, and mores? How can Americans avoid the lure of retreating into bunker mentalities defined by various "identities" and "communities" that see themselves as pure and others as wicked? What are we to do with the intuitive tendency to ignore our faults and exaggerate our triumphs? How do we balance the demands made upon us by our country, while at the same time championing universal human rights and seeking to care for the environment—both of which are global responsibilities, transcending national boundaries? These questions, and many others like it, demand our attention and serious thought as Americans. The partisanship and rancor that have divided Americans so bitterly over the past decades are a threat to our existence as a nation, a threat as serious as any of the foreign foes that have arrayed themselves against us in wars past as well as any existential crisis that has vexed our people in the troubled times of our forefathers and foremothers. National identity was once a concept from which Americans could find strength and comfort in times of stress because that identity was predicated on an agreed notion of American greatness and exceptionalism. When I wrote my 2015 book on American exceptionalism, I was concerned that conservatives and Christians were going too far in idolizing the nation. Now I am concerned that there has been a massive overcorrection among Americans on both the left and the right, by repudiating the nation and its greatness, by seeing America as a failed project in republicanism and liberty, or simply through a thoughtless and thankless apathy.

American patriotism is a loyalty that emerges from two methods of situating the nation in time. I argued above that patriots on the political right tend to stress the past, such as the original intent of the founders. Patriots on the left have historically been oriented toward the future, imagining what America can become when and if it will be true to its ideals. Both postures have value, but both can lead to harmful thinking—conservatives can nostalgically deify the nation, while progressives can cynically repudiate its legitimacy. Patriotism calls the citizen to a loyalty that Smith frequently analogized with that among family members. We love our family members, we prefer them to others, but that love does not necessitate hatred for, or apathy toward, members of other families. We think of our country, as we do our families in neither idealistic nor fatalistic terms. Our nation, just like our family, has its assets, its defects, and everything in between. But our nation, as our family, is made up of our people. We have a history that must be made sense of for contemporary times, and we have a future in which our collective hopes are rooted. As Smith described it, "Patriotism is rooted in a rudimentary, even primordial love of one's own; the customs, habits, manners, and traditions that make us who and what we are."[64]

Interestingly, ours is not the only generation that has needed voices to guide us into what healthy patriotism (or enlightened patriotism, as Smith put it) entails. Americans in all times have looked to examples and guides—Jefferson, Tocqueville, Lincoln, Anthony, Douglass, Parks, and King, for example. Smith looked to Lincoln as the quintessential enlightened patriot and rightly set his patriotism up as an example to follow. The features of Lincoln's patriotism—magnanimity, aspirationalism, and devotion to American ideals—are timeless. They are also necessary to the survival, establishment, and extension of American values that have served us so well in the past two and a half centuries. In this way, enlightened patriotism needs an orientation both to the past and to the future. This dual orientation fosters the kind of loyalty necessary for patriotism—"loyalty is an affirmation of what we care about, and our cares are not momentary whims or desires but a structure of loyalties," Smith argued.[65]

To what are we loyal, and how do we express loyalty to our nation? Smith described patriotism as "constitutional loyalty."[66] We feel and express loyalty to both the people of the United States as our own people and to the constitutional democracy under which our society and government are ordered. The result is a combination of heart and mind directed toward love for the nation, and an actively cultivated habit of engagement with one another through political and civic associating together. When we engage our hearts and minds in love and loyalty to the nation, we find ourselves taking joy and pleasure in the nation's achievements, but we also do not shy away from its failures. We are ashamed of them, but we work to correct them. Smith reminded us, "We are not shamed about things to which we have no emotional connection. Pride and shame are the two sides of loyalty, and patriotism is inconceivable without them."[67]

Take the example of Henry Johnson. There are lessons we can learn about Smith's enlightened patriotism in the example he set through his actions. There is also instruction from the years after Johnson returned to the United States when the war was over, and in the years after his death. Johnson went to fight for a nation that classified him as a second-class citizen, persecuting him based on his skin color. He was willing to die for that country and its ideals, considering them his own. It is reasonable to believe that he considered Americans he had never met "his people," but he fought alongside his fellow soldiers in the 369th and saved their lives by offering his own in their place. This is loyalty of the highest order. Johnson's country did not requite that loyalty upon his return. It continued to classify him as a second-class citizen and neglected him in his suffering after the war.

It would be easy to point to the example of Henry Johnson as evidence that America is irredeemable, that its faults and flaws were unforgiveable, and that its ideals were nothing more than rank lip service. How perfect an episode to demonstrate for all time that America's promise is reserved only for White people. But Johnson's own son was surprised to learn that his father's body had not been kicked into a pauper's grave in 1929. In fact, after Johnson died, the army buried him with full honors at Arlington Cemetery. And while condemning the injustice of neglecting his service and sacrifice is absolutely warranted, it is essential to observe that Americans came around to doing what they could to correct those injustices appropriately. Now, the posthumous recipient of the Congressional Medal of Honor, Henry Johnson, is memorialized in the Hall of Heroes at the Pentagon.

Should Johnson have received the honors due him in 1920 rather than in 2015? Assuredly, yes. But American patriotism is morally aspirational, self-reflective, and self-correcting. Patriots recognize their flaws and sins and resolve to learn from those sins. They do not overcorrect, nor do they abandon hope in the ideals established in the founding documents, those ideals that define the essential nature of the republic. Gratitude is at the heart of patriotism, and as Smith rightly stated: "Anyone who shares hope for America and faith in America may participate."[68] Patriotism takes vigilance, but patriotism ultimately yields blessings that are reflected in the nation's hopes and aspirations.

If what Burke said was true, that society is a contract between the dead, the living, and the yet to be born, then enlightened patriotism is eminently appropriate and necessary to the American project. It is especially necessary for the preservation of all forms of liberty, including religious liberty. The harmony between the spirit of religion and the spirit of liberty can only exist in a nation that is, first, at peace with itself, and second, grateful for the trust handed down to it by earlier generations. For the nation to be at peace with itself, it must acknowledge the mistakes it has made in the past and work to mitigate their deleterious effects in the present. But this does not entail national self-hatred. Gratitude ensures against the corroding force of national self-flagellation. We can be grateful for the fact that our founding ideals offer a stark relief to national injustices. And we can be grateful for patriots like Henry Johnson and Needham Roberts who actively preserved those ideals, even when they were barred from enjoying them to their fullest extent. How easy it is to find fault, but how humane it is to recognize real fault and yet demonstrate love and loyalty nonetheless. Without those human impulses of love and gratitude, with honesty, all we can expect in future days is national confusion and misery.

Conservatism and Ordered Liberty

Is it because liberty in the abstract may be classed amongst the blessings of mankind, that I am seriously to felicitate a madman, who has escaped from the protecting restraint and wholesome darkness of his cell, on his restoration to the enjoyment of light and liberty? Am I to congratulate an highwayman and murderer, who has broke prison, upon the recovery of his natural rights?

—Edmund Burke, *Reflections on the Revolution in France*

E arlier in the book, I mentioned that several years ago I compiled a list of movies and affectionately christened it "The Wilsey Re-education Program" (WREP). As I said, I originally devised it out of concern for my students whose exposure to great film was sorely lacking (for understandable reasons). My children also, growing up during the 2000s and 2010s, in what I am personally convinced is a dark age of film, cry out for exposure to classics that teach virtue and humanity (that may be a slight exaggeration, but someone should cry out on their behalf!).

One of the titles in the WREP is *Fail Safe*, a 1964 film starring Henry Fonda, Walter Matthau, and Larry Hagman. *Fail Safe* is a critique of a prevailing overconfidence in and overreliance on computer technology for managing nuclear-armed bomber and strategic missile protocols. Such moral failure is exhibited by both the American and Soviet militaries in the high-stakes nuclear tensions in the immediate wake of the 1962 Cuban missile crisis and the 1963 Kennedy assassination during the middle of the Cold War. The film warns against such overconfidence and offers a poignant statement on human liberty and moral responsibility.

Reacting to an unidentified plane flying over Canada toward Detroit, which turns out to be a passenger liner off course, a group of six American bombers flies to its predetermined fail-safe point in northern Alaska, to circle briefly there in preparation for a run into Russia to drop its nuclear payload in the event of a Soviet attack. The emergency is resolved in short order, but the bombers in "Group Six" receive coded orders, due to a computer glitch, to commence their attack run to Moscow and drop their bombs. At the same time, the Soviets use an innovative and as-yet-unknown radio jamming device against the Americans, altogether preventing communications between the group commander and Strategic Air Command, communications that would have corrected the situation entirely. The president (played by Henry Fonda) is compelled by the circumstances to order American fighters to intercept the bombers to shoot them down, but they fail. As the bombers cross into Russian territory, the president works to convince the Soviet premier and his generals that the whole affair was a mistake. To demonstrate his good faith, the president promises that if the bombers do not turn back or are not destroyed by Soviet air defenses, and Moscow is destroyed by hydrogen bombs, then he would order American bombers to destroy New York City. The Soviet premier expresses forlorn satisfaction with this proposal.

There is a powerful exchange between the American president and the Soviet premier that underscores the simultaneous realities of human liberty and human responsibility. The exchange occurs toward the end of the film, right before its climactic moment. The Soviet premier calls the president on the Moscow-Washington hotline as the last US bomber in "Group Six" to survive Soviet air defenses closes on its target.

SOVIET PREMIER: Mr. President, I have ordered our long-range missiles to stand down from their alert. Only that part of our defense that has a chance of shooting down your bomber is still active. We do not think we have much of a chance.

AMERICAN PRESIDENT: I know.

SOVIET PREMIER: And yet, this was nobody's fault.

AMERICAN PRESIDENT: I don't agree.

SOVIET PREMIER: No human being did wrong, no one is to be blamed.

AMERICAN PRESIDENT: We're to blame, both of us. We let our machines get out of hand.

SOVIET PREMIER: Still, it was an accident.

AMERICAN PRESIDENT: Two great cities may be destroyed, millions of innocent people killed, what do we say to them, Mr. Chairman? Accidents will happen? I won't accept that!

SOVIET PREMIER: All I know is that as long as we have weapons—

AMERICAN PRESIDENT: All I know is that men are responsible, we're responsible for what happens to us! Today we had a taste of the future. Do we learn from it, or do we go on the way we have? What do we do, Mr. Chairman? What do we say to the dead?

SOVIET PREMIER: I think if we are men, we must say that this will not happen again. But do you think it possible, with all that stands between us?

AMERICAN PRESIDENT: We put it there, Mr. Chairman, we are not helpless. What we put between us we can remove.[1]

The moral of this story is that in the final analysis, we as human beings cannot abrogate our moral responsibility when our free choices go awry. Even when our intentions are noble and even when evil unintended consequences prevail, those consequences are ours to own because they spring from our free decisions. We cannot hide behind fate, chance, or impersonal technologies when things go wrong. Liberty and moral responsibility are often in tension with our flawed moral and intellectual senses, but this tension is inescapable and essential to the human condition. We can also learn wisdom from our past mistakes, and while our free choices can lead to disaster, they can also redeem good out of evil. The aspirational conservative is awake to those realities and holds to the proposition that human liberty is not absolute. It must be ordered by justice. Too much order results in tyranny, and too much liberty results in anarchy. Balance between order and liberty must be maintained for a society to flourish.

What is ordered liberty? To get at that question, we must start with a consideration of human nature. To be sure, whole books have been written that explore the deep intricacies of the relation between human nature and human liberty, and what follows merely sets the context for a broad understanding of ordered liberty.[2] In the Western tradition going back to antiquity, philosophers and theologians have worked to identify the basic elements of human nature. Obviously, there exists no simple assessment of human nature in Western thought, and the thinkers diverge from one another not only on the issue itself but on methodologies used to arrive at conclusions about the issue. Still, despite great complexities, distinctions, and debates, there remains a recognizable convention within the long-term trend of Western thought concerning human nature. At least four features of that convention are thus identifiable: human nature is rational, fraternal, dignified, and yet fallible. From rationality and fraternity proceed the human consciousness, articulation, and practice of liberty in the context of observing the balance between privileges to be enjoyed and duties to perform on behalf of others. From human dignity proceeds knowledge of the inherent value of the person and the person's liberty. And from human fallibility appears the need for order. Taking a realistic accounting of human nature and from a measured and mature reflection on human history, an aspirational conservative confidently claims that true liberty can only be known through restraints placed on human passions by just law, thus setting the conditions for striking a balance between order and liberty.

Let us begin with a reflection on one specific practical manifestation of the interaction between human liberty and moral responsibility. Since we inherently possess rationality and knowledge of the good, we are free to choose between right and wrong. Aristotle (384–322 BC) observed in his *Nicomachean Ethics* that a tension exists in the person between a principle of rationality and irrationality, and these two war against each other in the soul.[3] Similarly, the apostle Paul (ca. AD 5–ca. 65) wrote that a conflict existed in the person between two laws, or principles, one of evil and one of righteousness.[4] William Shakespeare (1564–1616) illustrated the tension between the rationality and irrationality in Hamlet's frustration with himself as he wavered over whether he should avenge his father's murder at the hands of his uncle, King Claudius. In Hamlet's case, his struggle was between the principles of wisdom and courage, of decision motivated by honor and indecision springing from fear or indolence. In act 4, scene 4 of *Hamlet, Prince of Denmark*, Shakespeare had Hamlet acknowledge that God created persons with "capability and god-like reason"[5] and that he had "cause and will and strength and means to do't,"[6] that is, take action in the name of his dead father and injured mother. Haunted by the fact that his father's blood cried out for justice while he watches thousands of Norwegian soldiers march against the Poles to give their lives for nothing but the sake of honor, Hamlet realizes he had wasted time in pointless overthinking. He concludes that perhaps his thought process consisted of "one part wisdom and ever three parts coward,"[7] but nevertheless, "from this time forth, my thoughts be bloody, or be nothing worth!"[8] Hamlet thus steeled himself to be decisive, to take the path of revenge.

Through Aristotle's reflection, Paul's testimony of inner turmoil, and Shakespeare's imagination, we see the reality of human liberty on display. Liberty comes with responsibility. Human liberty is not absolute, but contingent on propensity to selfishness and wickedness. Some choices bring forth good consequences, and we enjoy the effects of positive responsibility in those cases. At other times, choices we make bring about bad consequences, and we must then endure heavy responsibility. Still, Thomas Aquinas (1225–1274) argued that, despite the conflict in us between rationality and irrationality, righteousness and sin, and virtue and vice, persons always possess free will. "Otherwise," Aquinas wrote, "counsels, exhortations, commands, prohibitions, rewards and punishments would be in vain."[9] Persons act, according to Aquinas, from the standpoint of judgment, but the judgment persons employ emerges not from instinct but from reason. Since reason is the source of human judgment, that judgment can tend toward one direction or another and is not foreordained or predetermined. Therefore, Aquinas wrote, "since man is rational man must have free choice."[10] And such liberty brings human dignity into stark relief. Our exercising of liberty matters because we matter. If the good of the individual and the good of society is our aim, we must have guardrails in place to channel our free choices in the proper direction.

Going back to Aristotle, he observed that law was prerequisite to justice in any community. He understood justice to prevail when every individual receives what he is due. Injustice consists in "assigning too much to oneself of things good in themselves and too little of things evil in themselves."[11] This is why it is improper for a person to rule other free persons justly, "because a man," Aristotle wrote, "behaves thus in his own interests and becomes a tyrant."[12] Instead of arbitrary rule by men, Aristotle argued that men must rule by "rational principle."[13] Furthermore, since "man is a political animal" and by nature "desire to live together," the primary goal of government is to attain "well-being," "happiness," or the "good of the governed."[14] Thus, the only form of just government over free persons is the one restrained by just law. Aristotle wrote, "governments which have a regard to the common interest are constituted in accordance with strict principles of justice, and are therefore true forms; but those which regard only the interests of the rulers are all defective and perverted forms, for they are despotic, whereas a state is a community of free men."[15]

Modern thinkers like John Locke and Montesquieu (1689–1755) articulated liberty along similar lines as the ancient Greek philosopher Aristotle. Locke denied that liberty ought to be understood as simply the doing of what one pleases. Instead, he argued that liberty consists only under law that holds everyone responsible for their actions, including the ruling class. "Freedom of men under government is to have a standing rule to live by, common to every one in that society, and made by the legislative power erected in it."[16] Just law (to be distinguished from arbitrary law), wrote Locke, was not designed to limit freedom but to define it and even extend it, or as he said, "preserve and enlarge freedom."[17] He went on to say that "where there is no law there is no freedom" because freedom without restraint inexorably results in wanton violence.[18] Similarly, Montesquieu in his *The Spirit of Laws* acknowledged that liberty may appear to be unfettered by law, especially in a democracy where the people directly rule themselves. This is wrong. "In governments . . . directed by laws, liberty can consist only in the power of doing what we ought to will, and in not being constrained to do what we ought not to will."[19] Furthermore, liberty properly understood can only exist in governments that are designed with structures in place that prevent them from abusing power. "Power should be a check to power," Montesquieu stated, and thus began his development of the idea of separation of powers through an analysis of the English constitution.[20]

Since the American founding, the idea that liberty must be restrained by lawful order was articulated in some of the most important early documents. Alexander Hamilton said in *Federalist* 1 that "the vigour of government is essential to the security of liberty."[21] James Madison in *Federalist* 37 wrote that the just laws of an active government that exists by consent of the governed were essential to guard liberty from within and without. He said, "Energy in government is essential to that security against external and internal danger, and to that prompt and salutary execution of the laws which enter into the very definition of good government."[22] Also, he argued that stable government ensures liberty because the people place their confidence in it, whereas a government that is constantly changing causes discontent and insecurity.[23] In *Federalist* 57, Madison argued against the idea that the federal legislature could make arbitrary laws favoring only the ruling class by appealing to the nature of the whole Constitution as serving as the basis of just law guarding liberty. The Constitution, and the "vigilant, and manly spirit which actuates the people of America—a spirit which nourishes freedom, and in return is nourished by it."[24] In other words, the just order established by the Constitution and the public spirit and patriotism of the people are the best guards of liberty against tyranny.

In American history, the Constitution established the conditions for the preservation of ordered liberty. We should revere the Constitution of the United States, recognizing that the American constitutional model, which bears both national and federal characteristics, rightly defines the end of government and has the potential to do what it claims to do in the preamble: "to secure the blessings of liberty for ourselves and our posterity."

In *Federalist* 51, James Madison argued that the purpose of republican government was to protect the civil and religious rights of the people. "Justice is the end of government. It is the end of civil society."[25] Madison did not fear diversity but embraced it as a great potential guarantor of security for rights. He believed that the more diversity a republic has, the greater security for both civil and religious rights.

John Locke championed the idea that government's chief end was the security of rights, especially the right of property. "The great and chief end, therefore, of men uniting into commonwealths, and putting themselves under government, is the preservation of their property."[26] The civil laws do not prescribe the good, but they protect against sinful and selfish people who would deprive citizens of their property.

Madison, Hamilton, and John Jay were in accord with Locke's understanding of the purpose of government. They did not articulate it in quite the same way, but they did, like Locke, limit government to the protection of rights in the interest of the promotion of the good, not the defining and enforcing of a particular conception of the good. They believed that the republic ordered along the lines of the Constitution was the best plan—not a perfect plan—in establishing a just government. "We may define a republic to be . . . a government which derives all its powers directly or indirectly from the great body of the people," Madison wrote in *Federalist* 39.[27] Some aspects of the federal government were to be directly democratic, like the selection of representatives that would serve two-year terms. Other aspects of the government were to be indirectly democratic, such as the selection of the senators, the president, and the justices of the Supreme Court. Titles of nobility would be forbidden, and the states would be guaranteed to have republican governments. It would be the people, not the states, that would ratify the Constitution so that it would go into effect.[28]

The Constitution would create a republic that not only had some direct and some indirect elements of democracy (since the sovereignty ultimately lay with the people). It also bore some national elements, and some federal. Since the House of Representatives would be selected directly, this was a national element. The selection of the senators would be a federal element. The selection of the president would be a mixture of both federal and national, since the citizens of the states would cast votes for candidates for the office, but the Electoral College would make the final selection. Thus, Madison argued, the Constitution could not be called a purely national document; nor could it be called a purely federal one. Madison said, "the proposed constitution therefore, even when tested by the rules laid down by its antagonists, is in strictness neither a national nor a federal constitution; but a composition of both."[29] Such a balance between national and federal elements puts the interests of the people of the nation and the interests of the states in competition with one another, so that neither the people nor the states would be able to concentrate and abuse power. Power would be set against power, thus helping to secure liberty for the citizens.

Regarding the relationship between church and state, the Constitution guarantees disestablishment as well as free exercise of religion.

The two are logically entailed in one another—no consideration of disestablishment is possible without free exercise, and vice versa. It is true that, originally conceived, the First Amendment did not apply to the states but to the Congress, which is why we see states having established churches as late as 1833 (Massachusetts). But historical events change things—since 1868, we have the Fourteenth Amendment that applies the Bill of Rights to the states. The Fourteenth Amendment had the Civil War for a cause. I would argue that the application of the Bill of Rights to the individual citizens is a net positive.

Suffice to say that religious liberty entails disestablishment and free exercise. It also means that magistrates do not have to meet a religious requirement to qualify for federal office. In *Federalist* 52, Madison said, "the door of this part of the federal government is open to the merit of every description . . . without regard to . . . any particular profession of religious faith."[30] In *Federalist* 57, Madison argued, "No qualification of wealth, birth, of religious faith, or of civil profession, is permitted to fetter the judgment or disappoint the inclination of the people."[31] This is a profoundly republican statement—religious qualifications are placed alongside aristocratic qualifications of birth and wealth as being out of bounds for consideration of public office. It also pertains to the end of civil government—government is not competent to define the highest good of the people, but it is competent to secure the common goods of citizens as they pertain to liberty and order in society. Government is to provide for ordered liberty, and the churches will then define the heavenly good through their ministry of proclamation and mercy.

Furthermore, Madison argued for separation of powers in *Federalist* 10, 38, 51, and 66. Hamilton did so in 73 and 79. Separation of powers was an idea predicated on a realistic view of fallible human nature. If human nature is indeed fallible, then governments that are stewarded by persons cannot be competent to know, dictate, prescribe, enforce, will, and do the good in every circumstance. The problem with purely conceptual models of government that are detached from history and concrete experience is that every plan, no matter how logical, no matter how many objections can be answered, will always collide with a human nature that seeks power over all. The American tradition, as seen especially in the *Federalist*, gives us the blueprint we need to preserve ordered liberty.

In chapter 3, on conservatism and nationality, I made the argument that critics of Christian nationalism conflate nationalism with nationality. I also argued that trying to define "Christian nationalism" is very difficult because it has taken so many forms over time that often have been mutually exclusive. One exception to that rule emerged in 2021 with the publication of Stephen Wolfe's book *The Case for Christian Nationalism*.[32] In that book, Wolfe established a careful definition for Christian nationalism and offered a sophisticated defense of his conception. Wolfe's Christian nationalism is an example of how order and liberty can be out of balance, with too much emphasis placed on order to the exclusion of liberty. Wolfe's argument is important to engage in detail, because his argument for a magisterial Christian state emanates from, and resonates with, the contemporary Ottantottist Right.

Wolfe argued that the way to combat immoral and tyrannical cultural forces is to confront them directly. Rather than cowering before them or being distracted by laziness or apathy ("lose the dad bod," he counsels in the epilogue, and be "men of power"),[33] Christian men should embrace a vision of the nation that is centered on greatness. Such greatness is not a mere abstract concept for Wolfe. Greatness should be personified in one great man, the "Christian prince." This Christian prince is the head of the Christian state, the legal expression of the self-conscious Christian nation. It is the Christian prince that champions the people of the nation. Wolfe saw the answer to our flabby, immoral, cowardly, trivial culture in a form of Christian nationalism that is predicated on the political thought of the Protestant scholastics of the sixteenth through the eighteenth centuries. The Christian nation, headed by the Christian prince, has the power to ensure that citizens attain to their heavenly good. "Our time," Wolfe writes, "calls for a man who can wield formal civil power to great effect and shape the public imagination by means of charisma, gravitas, and personality."[34] Such a man, a divinely ordained *Epiphanes* at the center of Christian nationalism, is the only real solution to what he describes as pagan nationalism.

Essential to Wolfe's case is that our options are limited to only two choices: pagan or Christian nationalism.[35] We are in a pagan nationalistic situation, "but we do not have to live like this," Wolfe writes.[36] Christian nationalism provides the political, religious, and cultural solution to the perversity of our age.

In ten chapters, with an introduction and an epilogue, Wolfe built his case for magisterial Christian nationalism. Wolfe did not use the term "magisterial" as a descriptor of the Christian nationalism he conceived, but this is an apt term to describe it. Wolfe insisted on making a purely rational argument, not historical, for Christian nationalism: "I do not appeal to historical examples of nationalism, nor do I waste time repudiating 'fascist nationalism.'"[37] This conceptual and logical methodology of Wolfe's is one of the unique innovations he introduced into the conversation about Christian nationalism. The Christian prince—a figure that Wolfe presented in *a priori* terms—is at the heart of his *a priori* model of the Christian nation.

Wolfe began his "conceptual defense"[38] of Christian nationalism with two chapters on anthropology, specifically, the impact of creation-fall-redemption on man and human nature. Man's natural end was the fulfillment of the dominion mandate, and obedience to natural law is the outward display of man's dominion over nature. Even if Adam had not fallen into sin, man would have formed nations with distinct cultures and governments, for these were all part of human nature and the created order. Adam's fall necessitated government be "augmented" in order to "suppress sin,"[39] but governments, nations, and cultures were not themselves a part of the curse of sin.

Grace in redemption restores man to his prelapsarian state. Man has been given eternal life through Christ, and this entails sanctification in Christ. The people of God are restored to God's original intention for mankind by grace, and so in a state of grace, the people of God orient the temporal to the eternal through the institution of the church.

The argument continued with a consideration of nation and nationalism. To clarify the meaning and substance of the nation, Wolfe started with specific "fundamental relations of people and place" of our experience in ordinary life, such as customs, language, geography, and cultural norms.[40] He also pointed to the family as the basis of the nation, arguing that the basic unit of a nation is the family. From there, he showed how our loves are ordered, that we favor those who are closest to us. Favoring one's own nation over another is not immoral but natural and good. Transitioning from nationalism to Christian nationalism, Wolfe asserted that Christianity perfects the nation. The perfected nation—the Christian nation—orients its people to their "earthly and heavenly good" and "true religion."[41] When it does so, it is fulfilling what God intended government to do, that is, relate the secular and the sacred spheres in their proper order.

It follows that the national culture should reflect the true faith. Thus, Wolfe provided a defense in the fifth chapter of "cultural Christianity."[42] Cultural Christianity is "a mode of religion"[43] complementary to the Christian faith, providing a touchpoint for a unified identity for the nation as well as a coherent array of mores that is informed by Christianity. These mores direct people to the saving Christian faith, even if they do not hold legal or exegetical authority per se.

Wolfe went on to situate the role of civil law in the nation. Civil law is the legal expression of natural law, or the moral order God built into the universe at creation. The civil magistracy mediates between natural law and divine law to provide a civil legal framework that is consistent with the Christian faith. Furthermore, the spheres of life have authorities unique to the nature of each sphere. In the sphere of civil life, the civil magistrate is the authority. But civil law, while efficacious in the realm of the external life of the nation, is not pertinent to the inner life of the individual conscience.

In the seventh chapter, Wolfe laid out his theory of the Christian prince. The Christian prince is marked by the attribute of greatness, serving as an inspiration to the people and striking terror in the hearts of the enemies of the nation. Following the contours of the two kingdoms, the Christian prince is the chief magistrate of the nation, but the church is not under his jurisdiction. The Christian prince is the prime instrument for Wolfe's "great renewal" of Christian nationalism.[44]

Chapter 8 dealt with Wolfe's conception of the right of the people to conduct violent revolution (when prudent), particularly when true religion is threatened or when the good of the people is threatened. And chapter 9 addressed the issue of the liberty of conscience. Wolfe based his conception of liberty of conscience on the premise that the conscience is free, but civil magistrates still retain the right to enact and enforce civil laws that direct the people to the highest, heavenly good.

While Wolfe did not base his case for Christian nationalism on historical experience, he did include a chapter-length historical consideration of the relationship between church and state in the colonial and early republican period of the seventeenth, eighteenth, and early nineteenth century. To demonstrate that negative religious liberty, disestablishment, and a neutral state are modern innovations, Wolfe pointed to the experience of New England and the period of American history prior to the Civil War. Wolfe concluded the book with a variety of practical considerations with regard to politics and culture in the twenty-first century.

The book's overall argument is coherent. It is based on a theological tradition that is often misunderstood, misapplied, and overlooked. Wolfe's considerations on the edifying influence of cultural Christianity are well conceived. My own synonymous term for cultural Christianity is civil religion, and I am on record as endorsing civil religion, provided it is consistent with theistic premises and does not serve to make the nation into an idol. It seems to me that Wolfe's defense of cultural Christianity is a needed one. When it comes to the role of civil law as pertaining to the good of the citizens, I am also with Wolfe, albeit only up a point. Specifically, civil law ought to comport with the second table of the Ten Commandments but ought not to seek to enforce the first table. The synergy between a body of civil law consistent with the second table and a civil religion (or cultural Christianity) that promotes mores that correspond with and aim toward the Christian faith is something I desire to see, especially in the context of a world that seems to be going completely crazy.

Wolfe was also right to reject the gaslighting tactics often employed by the political and social Left, especially from figures like Samuel Perry, Andrew Whitehead, or Philip Gorski. As I stated previously, they see anyone who embraces pro-life arguments, complementarianism, and biblical sexual ethics as being a Christian nationalist.[45] I find Wolfe's rejection of such ill-informed and blatantly partisan intimidation maneuvers to be refreshing and inspiring. And if holding to biblical inerrancy, free exercise of religion, and traditional Christian moral norms makes me a Christian nationalist, then button that Christian/American flag lapel pin on me.

The central issue Wolfe raised in his case for Christian nationalism is the purpose of the state for human flourishing. Is it the purpose of the state to secure, through civil law, the highest good of the citizens? Or is the purpose of the state to secure the citizens' rights, namely, the rights of life, liberty, and the pursuit of happiness? What is the ultimate end of the state? How does the state assist in the pursuit of the highest good? In whatever way the question is answered, it will have necessary entailments having to do with other issues, such as the relationship between church and state, the legitimacy of magisterial authority, the structure of government, the relationship of citizens to their rulers, and the role of voluntary associations outside of the government—as well as a host of other issues.

One of the strengths of the book is that Wolfe scrupulously provided precise definitions as he made his overall argument. For example, his definition for Christian nationalism proceeded in this way:

"Christian nationalism is a totality of national action, consisting of civil laws and social customs, conducted by a Christian nation as a Christian nation, in order to procure for itself both earthly and heavenly good in Christ."[46] He defined civil law as "an ordering of reason, enacted and promulgated by a legitimate civil authority, that commands public action for the common good of civil communities."[47] Such precision in Wolfe's use of terms is necessary to the coherence of the argument, and we are left with no ambiguities, even if we are not in agreement on all points.

Consistently throughout the book, Wolfe's understanding of the end of the Christian national state was to secure the highest good of the people. I understand this to be the central issue of the book. I part ways with Wolfe because his model is contra-American, that is, it is closer to Hegelian state theory than to the American constitutional tradition of federalism and ordered liberty.

True, Wolfe nowhere relied explicitly on the writings of G. W. F. Hegel (1770–1831). He built his argument on Reformed scholastic thought. But Wolfe's model adopted, intentionally or unintentionally, the substance of Hegel's theory of the state and refracted it through a Reformed Protestant lens. The effect is to render his Christian nationalism totalitarian. Wolfe's magisterial Christian nationalism is simply incompatible with the American political tradition.

This seems to be Wolfe's point exactly. For him, the classical liberal political tradition has gotten us to the pagan nationalism of today. Classical liberalism does not orient a nation to its highest good, in part because the individual citizens are not competent to determine what the good is and how to pursue it. They need the civil magistrate to orient them to the highest good, otherwise they will descend into license and harm. The upshot of the failure of classical liberalism is that we only have two real options before us—pagan nationalism or Christian nationalism.

This is a false choice. Wolfe sought a "great renewal" of the nation through the Christian prince, but I contend that the renewal that we need is a renewal of tradition, reverence for the Constitution and adherence to American ideals and institutions. From its founding, the United States was conceived on the idea that the government of the nation is to secure the rights of the people, and in doing so, to "secure the blessings of liberty." These blessings would abound for the citizens of the living generations, as well as those yet to be born. Government's role was to set the conditions for the citizens to rightly order and pursue goods under just law, disestablishment, free exercise of religion, and the right to pursue happiness, described by C. Bradley Thompson as "the foundation of moral action and therewith of civilization."[48] In the American tradition, the role of government is not to define and orient the people to the highest good. The role of government is to protect natural rights of the citizens and thus, secure their liberties. In so doing, government fosters the conditions for a virtuous society in which citizens may act on their long-term interest, balancing individual goods with the goods of society. Entailed in such a conception is that the common good is best pursued in a society of ordered liberty in which religious people, through their institutions like churches and synagogues, which are disestablished, define the highest good and not the state.

For our purposes, we will examine Hegel's theory of the state in *Philosophy of Right*, published in 1821, and *Philosophy of History*, published posthumously in 1858. These works emerged from Hegel's thought while he was professor of philosophy at the University of Berlin until his death in 1831. As we walk through Hegel's theory, the comparisons with Wolfe will become apparent.

Hegel's definition of the state is difficult to put in plain terms, but essentially, he thought of the state as the actualization of the good, which is the final end of human existence. The state emerges first from the family, specifically the feeling of family devotion. This feeling leads to ethical behavior, which is feeling directed to the good. Finally, devotion to family and ethical behavior develop into "political virtue," which comes about through the willing of the final end, that is, the good. This transition from that which is feeling to willing represents the shift from the subjective to the objective, the particular to the universal, and the abstract to the concrete. The state grows from the root of the family, and it comes into being by the joining together of individuals into the universal whole.

For Hegel, the state is "the actuality of the ethical Idea." The state is the merging together of the "ethical mind" and the will of the universal whole. The state has a consciousness of itself, it knows and thinks of itself and expresses itself through an active will, which Hegel understood to be manifested in the laws of the state. The state's universal consciousness stems from the self-consciousness of individuals as they combine to form the whole. Hegel's definition of the state is worth quoting at length:

> The state is the actuality of the ethical Idea. It is ethical mind *qua* the substantial will manifest and revealed to itself, knowing and thinking itself, accomplishing what it knows and in so far as it knows it. The state exists immediately in custom, mediately in individual self-consciousness, knowledge and activity, while self-consciously in virtue of its sentiment towards the state finds in the state, as its essence and the end and product of its activity, its substantive freedom. . . .
>
> The state is absolutely rational inasmuch as it is the actuality of the substantial will which it possesses in the particular self-consciousness once that consciousness has been raised to consciousness of its universality. This substantial unity is an absolute unmoved end in itself, in which freedom comes into its supreme right. On the other hand this final end has supreme right against the individual, whose supreme duty is to be a member of the state.[49]

Thus, the state is the supreme expression of the ethical ideal, in that it consists of the merging of particulars into the universal whole. The unity of the particular with the universal results in the objectivity of the state and the basis for the self-determining action of the state through its laws.

What is the highest good, that which the state embodies? According to Hegel, the good is the state itself, when the will of the particular, that is, the individual person or family, unites with the universal whole of the nation. When the particular will is united to the universal will, the good obtains. The expression of the good is freedom. Hegel wrote, "The good is the Idea as the unity of the concept of the will with the particular will. . . . The good is thus freedom realized, the absolute end and aim of the world."[50]

We have thus far the idea of the state as the unity of the particular to the universal, the actuality of the ethical Ideal, which has its primitive root in the family. The state is essentially active, in that its being is expressed in the will of the whole, which is seen in the laws of the state. The state possesses self-consciousness of itself, so it knows itself as the ethical ideal. The universal self-consciousness is rooted in the individual self-consciousness of the particular, merged together to form the whole. The state is an end in itself, and the state fulfills the absolute end of human civilization and human history, which is the realization of complete freedom, which is the highest good.

What did Hegel mean by freedom? There are two kinds. He wrote, "Rationality, concrete in the state, consists (*a*) so far as its content is concerned, in the unity of objective freedom (i.e. freedom of the universal or substantial will) and subjective freedom (i.e. freedom of everyone in his knowing and in his volition of particular ends); and consequently, (*b*) so far as its form is concerned, in self-determining action on laws and principles which are thoughts and so universal."[51] So, freedom emerges from rationality, and rationality is entailed in the state as the state is the unity of the particulars with the universal.

When the unity of the universal and the particular is achieved, rationality is achieved, and thus objective freedom. Objective freedom Hegel understood as the will of the universal. Objective freedom is to be distinguished from subjective freedom. Subjective freedom pertains to the particular. Every individual, or particular person, has self-consciousness as a particular and also knows and wills his particular rights, desires, and purposes. What we might call individual liberties, in the Lockean sense—rights to life, liberty, and the pursuit of happiness, for example—Hegel refers to as subjective freedom. Hegel was dismissive of such freedom. Subjective freedom dissipates, as it were, when the particular unites with the universal. The state is the universal, and the final state of the becoming of the ethical ideal. Perfect freedom is birthed in the universal, when the state is perfected through its becoming universal. When the state is perfected, freedom is no longer subjective, that is, it is no longer defined by the individual. The individual is now united with the universal, fulfilling his destiny. So, freedom is objectivized in the universal. The will of the universal is expressed in the law. Perfect freedom, objective freedom, as the absolute end of the world and the highest good, we can thus understand as, in Bertrand Russell's description, "the right to obey the law."[52]

Freedom, the good, is realized only through the state. Individuals do not lose their particularity or their identity when they unite with the universal. They also do not surrender their individual freedoms. But subjective freedom is inferior to the objective freedom of the universal. And the universal is predicated on the unity of the particulars as they form the whole. But the individuals relinquish their particular ends and freedoms in the interest of the whole, and the will of the individuals is merged into one universal whole, which has a single self-consciousness of itself and a single will of its own as expressed through the law. Such is perfect freedom, the highest good of the world. Hegel said this:

> Personal individuality and its particular interests not only achieve their complete development and gain explicit recognition for their right (as they do in the sphere of the family and civil society) but, for one thing, they also pass over of their own accord into the interest of the universal, and, for another thing, they know and will the universal. . . . The result is that the universal does not prevail or achieve completion except along with particular interests and

through the cooperation of particular knowing and willing; and individuals likewise do not live as private persons for their own ends alone, but in the very act of willing these they will the universal in the light of the universal and their activity is consciously aimed at none but the universal end.[53]

This conception of the state as the culmination of perfect freedom in the universal has this direct implication—the state, Hegel said, is the divine will. By that he meant that the state is Mind moving toward a world *telos*. "The state is the divine will, in the sense that it is mind present on earth, unfolding itself to be the actual shape and organization of the world."[54] Hegel did not conceive of the divine in the same transcendent/immanent sense of Christian theism. His idea of the divine, more consistent with pantheism (albeit not exactly), was derived from the Continental Enlightenment tradition of ontology traced back to the Portuguese philosopher Baruch Spinoza (1632–1677). If the state is the divine will, then what is the role of religion in the state?

Hegel saw religion in purely subjective terms, the domain of experience and feeling, in a similar way that Immanuel Kant and David Hume saw religion. Religion, according to Hegel, "is a relation to the Absolute, a relation which takes the form of feeling, representative thinking, faith," and is thus subjective. If religion retains this vestige of particularity and subjectivity, then religion has no place in the state. But if religion is "of a genuine kind, it does not run counter to the state." Religion can support the state by shedding its particular and accidental forms and conforming to the universal. When religion complements and upholds the state, contributes to the unity of the state, then "the state should even require all its citizens to belong to a church." There can even be toleration extended to churches dissenting from the state church, provided the members of a dissenting church "fulfill their direct duties to the state passively." The church finally must be governed by the state and cannot exist apart from the state. Still, the state cannot dictate the content of the church's doctrine. Hegel insisted that "the content of a man's faith depends on his private ideas, and the state cannot interfere" and "doctrine as such has its domain in conscience and falls within the right of the subjective freedom of self-consciousness, the sphere of the inner life, which as such is not the domain of the state."[55]

So, the church's relation to the state is marked by complementarity when the church teaches doctrines that comport with the ethical ideal of the state. The state is the senior partner, and the church is the inferior partner, but church and state support one another through establishment. In that establishment, the church supports the unity of the state through its teaching objective ethics, and the state protects the independence of the church by respecting the rights of the inner conscience of the members.

The state exists for itself. The state is the divine mind and the divine will. The laws of the state are the concrete expression of the active will of the state, and obedience to those laws is perfect, objective freedom. Furthermore, Hegel said, "the state is the actually existing, realized moral life. For it is the unity of the universal essential will, with that of the individual; and this is 'morality.'"[56] Hegel rejected the idea that ethics and morality were found in individual moral reflection. Rather, morality should be understood in the way the ancient Athenians understood it—as duty. So since the state is the divine idea, and since the state is essentially the embodiment of morality, perfect freedom is found only in the expression of the law. "Law is the objectivity of spirit; volition in its true form. Only that will which obeys the law is free; for it obeys itself—it is independent and so free," Hegel wrote.[57]

The state, being the universal whole resulting from the unity of particulars, is thus not formed based on, as Alexander Hamilton described in *Federalist* 1, "reflection and choice."[58] The state emerges from the unity of the particular with the universal. It is the concrete reality of the divine idea. Its emergence does not occur by the choices of the particular persons, because the state is the actual manifestation of the spirit. Hegel wrote, "it is not the isolated will of individuals that prevails; individual pretensions are relinquished, and the general will is the essential bond of political union." That unity goes through stages of development in history. The first phase is purely monarchical; in the second phase, particularity begins to be distinguished from the singularity of the monarch through an aristocracy or a democracy; and in the third phase, the universal emerges to bring all particular interests together into the whole.[59]

Hegel equated the universal state with the nation. The state's laws, institutions, citizens, mountains, rivers, and produce Hegel described as belonging to the nation. These are "*their* country, their fatherland, their outward material property." Hegel also saw the history of the nation and the history of the state in equal terms. The nation's history is the "history of *this* state, *their* deeds; what their ancestors have produced belongs to them and lives in their memory." All these claims of the nation are the claims of the state. The claims of the state encompass everything, both spirit and body. Hegel said it this way: "All is their possession, just as they are possessed by it; for it constitutes their existence, their being." Furthermore, the nation is conditioned by its laws; the members of the state find freedom in obedience to those laws; and the laws are the manifestation of the active will of the state, the nation. The nation, the state, represents the citizens as a self-conscious whole, for their own sake. "It is this matured totality which thus constitutes *one* being, the spirit of *one* people," Hegel said. "To it the individual members belong; each unit is the son of his nation, and at the same time, in as far as the state to which he belongs is undergoing development, the son of his age."[60]

Who is the head of the state? Hegel's state—the universal, the ethical ideal that orients its citizens to their highest good, which is the freedom to obey—is a monarchy. The monarchy is based first on the "universality of the constitution and its laws." Hegel meant here that the monarch is the embodiment of the whole nation and its will, expressed in law. Second, the power of the monarch "refers the *particular* to the universal." In other words, the monarch, as a particular person, does not derive his powers nor make his decisions based on an individual caprice, but all his actions have their root in the unity of the state. Third, the monarch possesses "self-determination to which everything else reverts and from which everything else derives the beginning of its actuality." Thus, sovereignty rests with the monarch.[61] The monarch is the single individual in whose person the will of the state is concentrated, and is thus "the ultimate self."[62] The will of the monarch and the will of the state are unified, and it is in this unity that factions, parties, interests, and warfare are kept at bay. Being mere particularities, these threats would have the effect of destroying the unity and the existence of the state, but the monarch, as the majestic head and embodiment of the state, guards the state from dissolution into particularity.[63]

This brief engagement with Hegel only scratches the surface of his theory of the state. In short, Hegel exalted the state to divine status and brought the true Christian faith down to theological degradation and subservience to the state. The state, being defined as ultimate expression of active ethical will through law, defines and orients the nation to what it sees as the highest good: freedom. This freedom is freedom to obey, to fulfill one's duty to the will of the state. The head of the nation-state is the monarch, and the monarch is the ultimate self, just as the state is ultimate. Executive, judicial, and legislative power is in the monarch and carried out by civil magistrates who serve as the extension to the monarchy.

Wolfe's model bears the substance of Hegel's statism. Consider Wolfe's definition of Christian nationalism: "Christian nationalism is a totality of national action, consisting of civil laws and social customs, conducted by a Christian nation as a Christian nation, in order to procure for itself both earthly and heavenly good in Christ."[64] The categories of "totality and national action" are Hegelian, in that they underscore the nature of the nation-state as totalizing and defined by active will. Wolfe used the analogy of a soccer team to explain the nation. Hegel's conception of the unity of the particular with the general fits well with the team analogy also—the members of the team do not lose their identity per se, but they do act as one in a unified interest.

The active will of the nation-state is expressed through "civil law and social customs" in Wolfe's model—the same is true in Hegel's model. The civil laws of Wolfe's Christian nation and the laws of Hegel's nation-state both, in Wolfe's words, "form an interrelated and oftentimes redundant web of obligation that orders everything ultimately to the national good."[65] It is true that Wolfe's national good and Hegel's national good are different—the former is a heavenly life, the latter is concrete freedom. But this is what I mean: Wolfe's model bears the substance of Hegelian statism, even though he refracted it through a Reformed Protestant lens.

Finally, the Christian nation conducts itself as a Christian nation, or as Wolfe later wrote, "The work of the Christian nationalist is convincing his Christian nation to be a nation *for itself*."[66] Hegel's direction is the same—the state is self-conscious of itself, acts for its own sake, and is justified in acting for the good of itself as it defines the good, just as Wolfe's Christian nation does.

Throughout the book, Wolfe conceived of the Christian nation in Hegelian terms. He sought a "reinvigoration of a collective will that asserts and stands up for itself." He understood the term "nation" to "emphasize the unity of the whole."[67] Wolfe conceived of the Christian nation as a perfected nation[68] and defined nationalism as "a nation acting as a nation for its national good,"[69] just as Hegel conceived of the nation as the Whole and had the nation developing into a state of actuality and concrete freedom. Wolfe's "complete nationalism" consists in the "nation *in itself*" having "become a nation *for itself*. Thus, the steps to perfect nationalism begin with a nation moving from implicit to explicit knowledge of itself and then, on the basis of that self-conception, acting for itself by willing its national good."[70] In this striking sentence, Wolfe employed the same categories as Hegel: a nation, equated with a state, having a self-consciousness of itself, defined by active will, bringing about the good as it defines the good. While Wolfe did insist that his model did not immanentize the eschaton "but has ordered itself *to* eternal life,"[71] the logic of his model is inexorable. Hegel lifted the state to divine status, and in so doing, degraded religion by stripping it of transcendence. Wolfe, in making the attainment of eternal life the purview of the state, is on the Hegelian path of doing the same.

Wolfe's conception of the magistrate, and later, the Christian prince, also bears the substance of Hegel's thought. The individual citizen, in Wolfe's model, "cannot always determine appropriate public action for the common good," but "civil leaders, having the whole in view, determine suitable action."[72] The civil laws, Wolfe argued, are both "theonomic and, in a sense, autonomic. The magistrate enacts and enforces laws of his own design, though only as a mediator, a sort of vicar of divine civil rule."[73] Hegel was not as specific in locating the source of authority in a personal God, but the similarities between his and Wolfe's conception of the rule of the magistrate are substantial enough to raise profound concern. Hegel also believed that civil law in the state was just, and that it was the highest good of the people to obey that law. And who made, interpreted, and enforced the law in Hegel's theory? The magistrate, that's who.

Which gets us to Wolfe's Christian prince—"the civil power of the prince comes immediately from God," and "the prince mediates God's divine civil rule," and "he makes public judgments in application of God's natural law, effectively creating law (though derivative of natural law), and he has the power to bring about what he commands."[74] The Christian prince "holds the most excellent office, exceeding even that of the church minister, for it is most like God."[75] In holding judicial, executive, and legislative power in his office, Wolfe's Christian prince bears substantial similarity with Hegel's monarch, who is supreme over the church, the ultimate self, and possesses self-determination to express the will of the state.

One could shrug his shoulders and wonder how any of this matters. What's the problem if Wolfe's model resembles Hegel's? Hegel's theory is totalitarian. The state is ultimatized in Hegel's view. The church is subordinated to the state, and Wolfe admits that the Christian prince is over the minister. The logic that Wolfe uses can only lead in the same direction as Hegel's did for Marx and Heidegger—the totalizing of the state and the degradation of the Christian faith that Wolfe holds dear. That's why it matters!

Wolfe says that his book is not an "action plan."[76] But he does say that we need "some blueprint for Christian civil and moral leadership . . . when our time comes."[77] Like Marx, Wolfe did not see himself as a philosopher but as a prophet. His book was meant to "contribute" to the preparation for the Christian civil and moral leadership that will come under the Christian prince, the one who directs and orients the people to their "highest good."

Wolfe assured the reader that in the Christian nation, while abuse of power is possible, it is unlikely. The magistrate knows the Scriptures, knows the good, and can execute justice reliably. We should all hope that Wolfe's many conflations of "can" with "will," "ought" with "is," and "knowledge" with "right action" will obtain under a civil order ruled by an *Epiphanes*. We should hope that a man of majesty claiming divine right will define the "highest good" aright. I am not at all optimistic that this is possible, because I believe that the Fall of man is a lot more profound than we know. Merely waving off the terrible potentialities for abuse of power as hardly conceivable in a purely conceptual model, as Wolfe does again and again throughout the book, will not do when crafting a manifesto such as this.

Postliberalism, a school of thought into which Wolfe's book fits, is predicated on the idea that the classical liberalism of the American founding has failed. Patrick Deneen's *Why Liberalism Failed* (2019) and Adrian Vermeule's *Common Good Constitutionalism: Recovering the Classical Legal Tradition* (2022) are works by Catholic thinkers who also argue that liberalism has failed. The New Right, a counterrevolutionary, reactionary movement, is made up a growing following of people who are fed up with the failure of liberalism represented by the neoliberal emphasis on the free market on the right and the progressive one-track-mindedness of the left stressing personal identities based on race, sexuality, and gender. Francis Fukuyama has offered a book-length treatment of the collapse of liberalism in his *Liberalism and Its Discontents* (2022).

There is nothing new in counterrevolutionary reactionism in the Western tradition. Richard Hofstadter had his "pseudo-conservatives" in 1955, those he described as "simply the old ultra-conservatism and the old isolationism heightened by the extraordinary pressures of the contemporary world."[78] As I wrote in chapter 1, Viereck argued that two forms of conservatism have prevailed since the French Revolution—the evolutionary conservatism of Burke and the reactionary, counterrevolutionary conservatism of Joseph de Maistre. He coined the term "ottantott" to refer to the reactionary side of conservatism, the side that "seems just as revolutionary against the existing present as the radical Jacobin or Marxist, only in the opposite direction."[79]

Ottantottists have never used the term "conservative" to refer to themselves. Neither did Wolfe.[80] He argued that today's conservatives and progressives are not distinguishable from one another. Even this argument is not all that new since Louis Hartz argued something similar in his *The Liberal Tradition in America* in 1955. Wolfe, however, was wrong to conflate neoliberalism with conservatism. Conservatism in America has always been diverse. For example, historian Patrick Allitt argued that the Civil War was a war between conservatives over what to conserve.[81] Ottantottism has been part of the broad conservative tradition in America since the 1820s. McCarthyite anti-Communism and rightist libertarianism have been important since 1945. American conservatism has never been monolithic.

Aspirational conservatism, predominant in America since the national founding, reveres tradition, constitutionalism, religion, and deliberation in the management of change. Conflating neoliberalism with "conservatism" is simply confused and anachronistic. Neoliberalism refers to the world of the late twentieth and early twenty-first century, whereas evolutionary, aspirational conservatism has its roots in the thought of Edmund Burke.[82]

Both Wolfe and Hegel make much of the nation-state existing for itself, for its own sake. Hegel said the state is the good, per se, because the state births true freedom. Wolfe said the state orients citizens to their good, which is a distinction without a difference from Hegel. If the state exists for its own sake, then it is a good in itself. If it is a good in itself, then the citizens exist for the good of the state. Ironically, there is not much daylight between Wolfe's counterrevolutionary method of statecraft and leftist revolutionary models seen in Marx, Lenin, and so-called democratic socialism of the radical Left today. The Lockean liberal position is the opposite. The state exists for the good of the citizens because the state is a means to an end—the protection of their rights and the extension of their liberties.

Wolfe's model demands that the citizens exist for the state, because he has articulated it in Erastian terms (though he denies his model is Erastian) with a monarch possessing all judicial, legislative, and executive authority. Furthermore, his purely "conceptual" and *a priori* model necessitates that he, like Hegel, know the whole by knowing every conceivable property of the whole, including every relation of all its properties. Wolfe tries to answer every question, every possible objection as he works through his case. But a purely conceptual model cannot possibly attain to that kind of knowledge of the whole.

Wolfe did not go to history for any epistemic justification. Rather than look to history, Wolfe built an ahistorical, *a priori* model. Logical arguments in favor of violent revolution are fine, but when logic collides with realities in space and time, unintended consequences and unforeseen conditions that may not be desirable inevitably come to pass. Look no further than the conceptual plan put forward by Friedrich Engels and Karl Marx in 1848. Ignoring history in favor of pure logical arguments is imprudent, to put it mildly.

Ultimately, why would a reasonable person seek to correct the weaknesses of classical liberalism—many of them real—with authoritarianism at best, and totalitarianism at worst? How does the abuse of freedom justify the jettisoning of freedom? Wolfe has done his readership a worthy service in reinvigorating the Reformed Protestant tradition. But the results of his work are not renewal. His model points to revolution, the overturning of order in the creation of something altogether unprecedented in the American experience.

In 1893, Theodore Roosevelt gave a speech to the Liberal Club of Buffalo, New York, entitled "The Duties of American Citizenship." In that speech, he noted some features that were necessary to active and responsible citizenship. Primary among these was a commitment to invest effort, care, and self-sacrifice because these were necessary in a free society. "You can no more have freedom without striving and suffering for it than you can win success as a banker or lawyer without labor and effort," Roosevelt said.[83] Freedom is not a blessing that a citizen can take for granted. It is hard-won, and also hard-maintained. "Freedom is not a gift that tarries long in the hands of cowards," Roosevelt said.[84] The answer to the challenges that confront citizens today is not to jettison the tradition of ordered liberty that Americans have enjoyed since the national founding. To enjoy the benefits of freedom, citizens have the duty to guard it and hand it down to the next generation, or else it will be lost. The only thing standing between us and despotism is a citizenry that is committed to the conservation of the best of Western and American civilization.

CHAPTER FIVE

Conservatism and History

_____

For 'tis your thoughts that now must deck our kings,
Carry them here and there; jumping o'er times,
Turning the accomplishment of many years
Into an hourglass: for the which supply,
Admit me Chorus to this history;
Who, prologue-like, your humble patience pray,
Gently to hear, kindly to judge, our play.

—William Shakespeare, *The Life of King Henry V*

The past is never dead. It's not even past.

—William Faulkner, *Requiem for a Nun*

Conservatism is the art of listening to the way history grows.

—Peter Viereck, *Conservatism*

_____

On April 2, 1865, Lieutenant General A. P. Hill, in command of the Third Corps of the Army of Northern Virginia, was killed instantly by a shot from Corporal John W. Mauck of the 138th

Pennsylvania Regiment outside Petersburg, Virginia. Hill was performing a reconnaissance on the Confederate right after the Federals had succeeded in breaking through the Southern lines that morning. Mauck's .58 caliber bullet struck Hill in the left hand and then traveled through the heart, spinning the general around in his saddle before he fell sprawled on the ground next to his horse, Champ. He was dead before he hit the ground.

Ambrose Powell Hill had served as a corps commander in the Army of Northern Virginia since the spring of 1863, being promoted by Robert E. Lee to that command just before launching the Gettysburg Campaign that culminated in the great battle fought from July 1 to July 3. At the time of Hill's death, Lee's army was faced with complete collapse. Lee ordered the evacuation of Petersburg the night Hill was killed and surrendered to General U. S. Grant a week later at Appomattox Court House on April 9. The Civil War was all but over.

In his biography of Hill, historian James I. Robertson related the bizarre and unique story of how the general was buried in three separate locations between 1865 and 1891. On the day Hill was killed, members of his staff rushed to secure his body from where it lay and deliver it to his wife, Kitty. She was staying in a house on the outskirts of Petersburg with her two small children and was seven months pregnant. When Colonel William H. Palmer, Hill's chief of staff, came to tell Kitty of her husband's death, she wailed, "The General is dead! You would not be here if he had not been killed!" before he could get the words out.[1] By that afternoon, Kitty and her two daughters, along with Captain Frank Hill (nephew to A. P. Hill), were accompanying the body to Richmond for burial at Hollywood Cemetery. They could not get to the cemetery, however, because people were fleeing Richmond en masse before the expected advance and occupation of the city by the Union army. G. Powell Hill and Henry Hill, cousins of the slain general, were able to work their way into Richmond and secure a coffin from an abandoned furniture store. After the cousins washed the dirt off the general's face and removed his gloves, they found where the bullet had entered the body through the chest and exited out the back. The bullet had also taken the general's left thumb off.

Since they were unable to bury the body in Hollywood, their second plan was to take it to the Fairview Cemetery in Culpeper, Virginia, where Hill's parents and other family were buried. By then, the day was warm and, as G. Powell Hill wrote, "the condition of his remains was such as to give us serious doubts as to the practicability or advisability of attempting to convey them so great a distance across the country" to Culpeper, about a hundred miles from Richmond.[2] The family made the hasty decision to bury the general near G. Powell's home in Chesterfield County in the Winston family cemetery. On April 4, the body was laid to rest there in a temporary, unmarked grave until they could bring it to Culpeper at a more opportune time.[3]

About two years later, a group of veterans proposed the transferal of Hill's body to Hollywood Cemetery outside of Richmond, which was the family's original desire. William H. Palmer (who had brought the news of Hill's death to his wife, Kitty), John R. Cooke, William Mayo, and J. Hampden Chamberlayne led the effort and persuaded the family to allow for the remains' exhumation and interment in Hollywood. Hill's body was exhumed from the Winston cemetery, to the relief of Hill's family. G. Powell wrote, "We felt aggrieved that his grave remained so long unmarked by slab or shaft, or other indication of carrying out such a promise, save the purchase and beautifying of a section in Hollywood, and the removal of the body under the direction of Colonel Palmer and others of his staff and army associates to that beautiful city of the dead."[4] A gravesite was secured at Lot N-35 in Hollywood, and his body was laid to rest there—but yet with no tombstone. All that marked the grave was an inscription in the curb with the words, "Lt.-Gen. A. P. Hill."[5] Neither of Hill's two burials was accompanied by any religious service but was completed in haste and without ceremony.

After Lee died in 1870, "Virginians at their former Confederate capital had begun immortalizing their heroes in bronze," as Robertson described.[6] In 1887, the Pegram Battalion Association began work on formally proposing a Hill statue for Richmond, but Hill's memorial would be distinct. Unlike any other memorial in the city, Hill's would serve as his final resting place. There still was no headstone or marker in Hollywood of any kind, except for the crude inscription on the curb. So, with the support and funding of former Hill staff and, most conspicuously, by Lewis Ginter, the project went forward. Ginter had served as a Confederate major, and by the 1880s had found financial success in real estate development. Ginter was developing land for the construction of suburban neighborhoods, and he wanted the Hill memorial to be the centerpiece of a new neighborhood west of Richmond. The Ginter Real Estate Development Company donated land at the intersection of Laburnum Avenue and Hermitage Road for the memorial site. William L. Sheppard was commissioned to cast the statue of Hill.[7]

The memorial was comprised of a six-foot base with a twenty-four-foot pedestal topped with an eight-foot statue of the general. Under the base was a vault to receive Hill's remains, which had been in the soil of Hollywood Cemetery for over twenty years. On July 1, a group of veterans led by Palmer arrived to exhume Hill from his grave at Hollywood. It took four hours to remove his bones, because the mound did not indicate the exact location of the coffin. His remains were found, and that evening Hill was buried for the third time under the base of the unconstructed memorial without ceremony or religious rites. Heavy granite stones were placed over the grave in preparation for the construction of the pedestal, and a guard of veterans kept vigil over the grave that night.[8]

On May 30, 1892, the memorial to A. P. Hill was dedicated. Fifteen thousand people attended. The dedication was presided over by Henry Heth, Hill's division commander who led the first Confederate infantrymen to the outskirts of Gettysburg, which brought on the titanic battle named for the town. There the memorial stood until December 12, 2022. After the death of George Floyd in 2020, protesters demanded the removal of all statues, markers, and memorials to the Confederacy and those who fought for it. In Richmond, protesters took it upon themselves to pull down the memorial to Jefferson Davis, and city officials in June 2020 ordered the removal of the statues of Lee, Thomas J. "Stonewall" Jackson, cavalry commander J. E. B. Stuart, and others that had stood on Monument Avenue and other sites around Richmond. But removing the Hill statue was more complicated because for almost 130 years it served as his grave. It took two more years of legal wrangling, but finally the statue was removed and given to the Black History Museum and Cultural Center of Virginia. Hill's remains, unearthed for the third time, were brought to Fairview Cemetery in Culpeper for his fourth burial.

What does this strange set of occurrences tell us? Probably a lot of things, but one unmistakable insight we get from the story of A. P. Hill's four burials is that history is basic to our humanity. Over a century after his interment under the pedestal that memorialized him, people continue to care deeply about Hill's legacy, the legacy of the Civil War, and all that followed in its wake. Even while the body was being taken out from the base of the memorial, there was contention among the onlookers between a Confederate sympathizer and an African American man offended by the sight of a Confederate battle flag.[9] Political ideologies do not determine the relevance and significance of history to persons. But conservatives have a special interest in history because they, unlike progressives, are especially oriented toward the past and are disposed to revere tradition.

I have been teaching history since 1992, from the third-grade level to the graduate level. In that time, I have taught students in history classes and seminars in church basements, in single-wide trailers, in private homes, at a maximum-security prison, and on stately university and seminary campuses. I am always struck by the fact that for many students, history consists of little more than an irrelevant litany of dates, names, and obscure places on a map. I try to teach students that historical consciousness is basic to our human nature. Every person has a stake in how the past is interpreted for its meaning, even if we do not understand or appreciate it. The story of Hill's bones is an example of the significance and deep relevance of history to everyone. Consider that human persons are the only living creatures who possess consciousness of past, present, and future. Animals possess no such consciousness. Our family cats, Allen and Jackpot, creatures of habit though they are, have no ability beyond instinct to understand, evaluate, or benefit from knowledge and wisdom gained from their past for the sake of their present. They have no conception of their future to frame hopes, anxieties, or aspirations. Historical consciousness is a salient feature of our bearing the image of God, who is over time, active within time, and has instilled in persons he created a consciousness of their position in time.[10] Wisdom, understanding, the formation of the conscience—these are the benefits of historical consciousness, and they are possible for human persons alone.

Our consideration of the past is part of our pursuit of truth. Because of this, virtue is necessary if we hope to arrive intentionally at coherent and meaningful truth. Virtue is also necessary because it helps us morally evaluate tradition. Not all traditions are worth keeping, and virtue gives us guidance on how to wisely choose which traditions to conserve. Lastly, the pursuit of truth and of virtue offers great rewards to the pursuer. The virtuous pursuit of truth in history both reveals truth and inculcates virtue. We do not gain the whole truth from a God's-eye perspective, in the same way we do not gain virtue to the extent we become morally blameless. But the extent of our gain does not necessarily indicate the quality of that gain. We gain actual truth and virtue in our historical pursuit when that pursuit is virtuous. In sum, the study of history makes one mature. The pursuit of virtue and the pursuit of truth are both aspirational, and they are equally necessary in making sense of the past and responsibly guarding tradition in preparation for handing it down to future generations.

What is history? What is the purpose of history? What are the limits of historical knowledge? These are serious questions that have no simple answers that will satisfy every person. Still, we have reliable guides to help us as we think about how to answer those questions.

Allen Guelzo referred to history as "an answer to the 'second question.'" He meant that the most basic human question—the first question—to satisfy the most elemental curiosity in the mind is, "What is that?" The second question—Guelzo's "historian's question"—is "Where did it come from?" Guelzo argued, "it's the moment that we begin to ask this second question that we've really asked the basic question that underlies all the history that has ever been written."[11] To be sure, since antiquity, persons have relied upon epic poetry, lists, and annals to answer the second question, all of which represent early methods of making sense of the past but none of which are history. History—the Greek root word is ἱστορία (*historia*), meaning inquiry or research—was introduced by Herodotus (ca. 484–between 430 and 420 BC). History has been the primary way we have asked and answered the second question since the fifth century BC. Guelzo's elegant style of framing an understanding of what is essential to history accentuates the reality that the search for historical knowledge is basic to human nature.

Guelzo's own definition of historical writing proceeded in this way: "a humanistic prose narrative of events based upon systematic inquiry into words, deeds, ideas, conflicts, and sufferings which occurred in the past and which have left verifiable evidentiary trails in the present."[12] By humanistic, Guelzo meant that history is concerned with humanity—the events, ideas, and people of the past—rather than with theology, as in God's acts in time, from God's perspective, through providence and miracles. History writing is presented in prose, not in poetry, as in epic literature. History is verifiable through evidence, that is, those artifacts left behind that bear witness to human intellectual, aesthetic, political, religious, economic, military, social, and communal life over time. Consistent with Guelzo, historian John Lukacs described history as "the remembered past."[13] What he meant was this: persons alone among living creatures possess both a conscious and an unconscious awareness of the past. Thinking historically occurs when persons work to construct narratives that make sense of the past in realistic terms. That is, they seek to offer an account of the past that comports with reality, not fiction or allegory. The Greek historians were the first to pursue this project. Lukacs described the Greek historical project as "a striving for truth even more than for justice."[14] They worked to understand and represent real persons and real events in past time.

When Herodotus undertook to write his *History*, he began with these words: "I, Herodotus of Halicarnassus, am here setting forth my history, that time may not draw the color from what man has brought into being, nor those great and wonderful deeds, manifested by both Greeks and barbarians, fail of their report, and, together with all this, the reason why they fought each other."[15] Herodotus wanted to research, using firsthand observation of evidence, the cause-and-effect relationships occurring in the past that brought about the Persian Wars in order to save from oblivion the knowledge of the noteworthy events and actions of those on both sides. The people, places, and events of the past were real, and the account he intended to offer was a realistic account centered on lives and actions of people who had lived, not one of fantasy or a cold collection of lists.

A generation after Herodotus, Thucydides (d. ca. 401 BC) wrote a history of the Peloponnesian War, the war between the Greek *poleis* Athens and Sparta between 431 and 404 BC. Like Herodotus, Thucydides set out to offer a reasonable account, based on observation of various kinds of evidence—anthropological, political, military, biographical, diplomatic, etc.—to account for how the war started and developed to the middle of the twenty-first year of the war, 411 BC, which was the time of his writing. How did this great cataclysm happen, and how did it progress, Thucydides wanted to know. Thucydides intended to write history, not an epic account of the war, nor a mere list of the great figures and their achievements. He consulted "the evidences which an inquiry carried as far back as was practicable," and these evidences led him "to the conclusion that there was nothing on a greater scale, either in war or in other matters."[16] Thucydides was persuaded that the war between Athens and Sparta was the most important and consequential event in history, and he sought to give a realistic account of this great conflict for future readers. "To come to this war," Thucydides wrote, "despite the known disposition of the actors in a struggle to overrate its importance, and when it is over to return to their admiration of earlier events, yet an examination of the facts will show that it was much greater than the wars which preceded it."[17] This was a weighty statement, because the Greeks had fought a series of massive wars with the Persians earlier in the fifth century BC, wars in which their territory was invaded, their cities were burned, and their enemies had the complete subjugation of the people as their objective. If Thucydides was right, and the Peloponnesian War was an even greater event than the Persian Wars, then what the Greeks faced in the late fifth century was an existential crisis that dwarfed even the invasion of their country by a foreign foe decades earlier.

While their methods and aims differed, the ancient historians each fulfilled Guelzo's and Lukacs's primary understandings of that which primarily counted as history—humanistic, evidence-based, prose narratives that were realistic accounts of the events and lives of the past. Plutarch (AD 46–after 119), the first biographer, wrote at the beginning of his consideration of the lives of the great Greeks and Romans, "Let us hope that Fable may, in what shall follow, so submit the purifying processes of Reason as to take the character of exact history."[18] The Roman historian Tacitus (ca. 56–ca. 120), the historian of the early Roman Empire and student of the German tribes beyond the Rhine frontier, said, "My purpose is not to relate at length every motion, but only such as were conspicuous for excellence or notorious for infamy." He had both a civic and a moral purpose in mind for writing history. He said, "This I regard as history's highest function, to let no worthy action be uncommemorated, and to hold out the reprobation of posterity as a terror to evil words and deeds."[19] And Augustine, the most influential Western thinker from the fifth century to the thirteenth, contrasted the writing of history as truth pursuit with fable: "History narrates what has been done, faithfully and with advantage, but the books of the haruspices [diviners who predicted the future using the entrails of animals sacrificed to the gods], and all writings of the same kind, aim at teaching what ought to be done or observed, using the boldness of an adviser, not the fidelity of the narrator."[20] For Augustine, history was a faithful representation of past events by a truth-seeker, not a series of platitudes from a suspect source.

The tradition of the ancients in historical writing continued into the modern period. Thomas Hobbes in *Leviathan* admonished, "In a good history, the judgment must be eminent; because the goodness consisteth in the method, in the truth, and in the choice of actions that are most profitable to be known. Fancy has no place, but only in adorning the style."[21] Lukacs wrote that the modern period witnessed a turn to mature historical consciousness in that history became a project of broad self-reflection and self-awareness. "Toward the end of the seventeenth and during the early eighteenth century, *disposition, character, ego, egoism, conscience, eccentric, melancholy, apathy, agitation, embarrassment, sensible, sentimental, self-conscious* appear in English for the first time in their modern sense." This, for Lukacs, represented a turning point in the history of history writing, in that "our awareness of our historical dimension developed together with our self-awareness."[22] Collective self-knowledge came to be understood by Western moderns as linked to knowledge of history.[23] "The history of mankind," Lukacs argued, "is the history of the evolution of its consciousness."[24]

Richard Weaver, an intellectual historian and professor of English at the University of Chicago in the mid-twentieth century, thought of history in similar terms as Lukacs. He expressed concern that modern Americans were prone to ignore history, and in doing so, lose a key aspect of their humanity. Historical thinking consists in reflection on the past. The past is essential to all the knowledge we possess in the present. Weaver conceived of the present as a thin line, ever advancing with the passage of time.[25] In this moment as I write these lines, the time is 12:32; it is a Friday after midnight; the temperature outdoors is thirty degrees Fahrenheit; and I am listening to Gabriel

Fauré's *Requiem* play in the background. Every second of time that I inhabit, what I know as the "present," is becoming "the past" with the inexorable ticking away of those seconds. Now it is 12:33 a.m., and the line of the present continues to advance.

Contrasted with the present, "the future," Weaver said, is merely a composite of images from the past I display in the theater of my mind. When I imagine what my children will be like in five years, I am taking images of them from my memory and casting those images and their present character traits in terms of what I imagine of them as older versions of themselves. In imagining their futures, I have nothing else to go on but their pasts. Here's how Weaver described past, present, and future: "The present is a line, without width; the future only a screen in our minds on which we project combinations of memory."[26] Present knowledge is ephemeral. Future knowledge is conditional. Our past knowledge, limited though it may be, is real. Since it is real, it has substantive bearing on how we live in the present. Weaver referred to the realistic, substantive remembrance of the past as "piety." As we remember the people of the past as real and living in a world that was also real—as real as we are, and our world is—we take them on their own terms. When we do, we gain wisdom for our lives and our futures. In contrast, Weaver wrote of our proneness to turn away from the past: "The spirit of modern impiety would inter their memory with their bones and hope to create a new world out of good will and ignorance."[27] The impiety of those who would intentionally reject the past begets vain utopianism that would seek to rid society of tradition and order that have served us well in favor of a dreamy new order based on not much more than sentimentality at worst, abstract deductions at best. "Those who would overthrow, or subvert, or revolutionize our society are nearly all of them anti-historical," Weaver wrote.[28] Both revolutionaries of the left and counterrevolutionaries of the right seek to upend tradition in society by fancying utopian, unrealistic whimsy rather than learning from concrete realities observable in past time.

Consider this example from Alexander Hamilton. In January 1788, he turned to the tangibility of history to counter the Anti-Federalist argument that the Constitution would abolish state sovereignty through absolute consolidation. Hamilton denied this. Instead, the states and the federal government would have concurrent jurisdiction. That is, the states would retain their sovereignty in all matters not specified as pertaining to the federal government in the new Constitution. How could Hamilton say this confidently? He did so by considering the Roman republican example, not by any *a priori* philosophical deduction. "To argue upon abstract principles, that this co-ordinate authority cannot exist, would be to set up theory and supposition, against fact and reality," Hamilton said.[29] His point was that theories have little merit compared to concrete experience when it comes to the reliability of a claim. Hamilton knew that by looking to the Romans' achievement of a form of concurrent jurisdiction in their *Comitia Centuriata* and *Comitia Tributa*, he could make the argument that concurrent jurisdiction would work under the Constitution. The Romans found that the interests of the patrician and the plebian classes could both be secured and served, despite the two classes' interests often being at odds.[30] "These two legislatures," Hamilton wrote, "co-existed for ages, and the Roman republic attained to the pinnacle of human greatness."[31] As the Romans were able to achieve harmony between the patricians and plebians, the American states and the federal government could complement each other through partial consolidation of the states under the Constitution. Concrete experience, not abstract philosophizing, carried Hamilton's argument. Hamilton conceived of the Constitution as neither revolutionary nor counterrevolutionary, but a continuation of tradition inherited from experience.

Weaver rightly argued that the purpose of historical thought is the formation of the conscience. "Reflection on what man has done makes sharper in us that faculty by which we distinguish between good and evil," Weaver wrote.[32] He understood the conscience as memory that guides us toward proper actions. Knowledge that comes by memory does not consist in do's and don'ts, "but through an accumulated awareness of the past reminding us that some kinds of actions have produced good and others harm."[33] Thus, for Weaver, history is of profound epistemological and moral importance. "The historian is not only the interpreter of the past; he is also in a sense the guardian of morality."[34] In other words, history is not so objective that one could look at the Holocaust and see it merely as an event alongside other events occurring in twentieth-century Europe. It was that, but much more. It was a moral event with relevance for the whole human race from the 1930s and '40s into the future. As we in the present reflect on that horrendous event, we remember that persons are still morally fallible and that the oft-repeated slogan of "Never Again" is a sentimental pipe dream if we abandon historical reflection that is aimed at truth and conscience formation. Lukacs put it like this: "the purpose of history is understanding even more than accuracy."[35] The necessity of historical accuracy is a given, but history is far more than a quest for accuracy. It is the pursuit of knowledge and understanding, without which life is not worth living.

It is important to acknowledge here that knowledge we have of the past, while real, is limited. Even though the only knowledge we have in time is of the past, and though the only images we conjure of the future are composites of memories, the past is in many ways remote and unreachable to us in the present. Making sense of the past is like drawing a map. There are many types of maps: political, topographical, physical, road, and nautical charts, to name a few. A road map, even when accurate, will not capture every detail of a region. It will leave certain things out to emphasize the position of roads in relation to cities, intersections, places of interest, etc. We would not say that a road map is wrong because it failed to include all the physical features of the topography. Nor would we say that a physical map is wrong because it omitted county boundaries. Similarly, a history of the Hoover presidency will be written from the perspective of a particular author and will cover the details based on the choices that author makes. Those choices do not, in themselves, determine the accuracy of the author's claims. They do reflect the goals, methods, and sources employed by that historian. A history of a period is like a map in that it will include the details the author chose to represent, but it will not include every detail that occurred in the past.

Cold War historian John Lewis Gaddis made this analogy between history and maps. Both history and maps consider a defined surface area. In the case of history, that surface area is comprised of space, time, events, persons, and ideas. For maps, the surface area is made up of natural and man-made features in a particular place. Neither a work of history nor a map can reproduce its subject matter. Reproduction is not the point of either history or cartography. Rather, we are satisfied with the fact that a map attempts to "represent" rather than "replicate."[36] No map tells you everything about a particular geographic region. The same goes for history. No work of history is going to give you everything that actually happened in each span of time. None of this means we are relativists. It means we are realists about what we can call knowledge, and we are sensible about the limitations to our access to truth. The truth is there, it is accessible, and we can know it. But we do not have comprehensive access to the truth of the past in its entirety, because we have a limited amount of source material, and, to put it simply, we do not have God's perspective. What historical truth we have, when secured responsibly, is real, and we can rightly call it knowledge. Gaddis said it like this: "it would be imprudent for historians to decide, from the fact that we have no absolute basis for measuring time and space, that they can't know anything about what happened within them."[37] Of course, we can accurately know and make sense of the past. Our claims to knowledge ought to be tempered by humility. Even the wisest historian is fallible.

The past is gone. Our task is not to get it back. We are not like Doc Brown in *Back to the Future*, building a time machine out of a quirky car to take us to 1955 at 88 miles per hour. Gaddis observed that if we could go back in time, we might be able to understand by experience what it would be like to live in, say, fourteenth-century

England, but we would lack the perspective we have in historical reflection on that period and place. While we could experience the world of Edward III, we would be hemmed in by the moment and would have no ability to intelligibly comprehend that world. Gaddis observed that thinking historically is better than going back in time, if our purpose is to understand the past. The perspective we have in the present gives us a field of vision over the past that allows us to represent a particular life, event, or idea in its context in a more complete way than if we were there. Related to his analogy of history to maps, Gaddis cleverly analogized the past to a broad landscape viewed from a high mountain. When we think historically, we are taking in a vast surface area of times, places, lives, events, and ideas. We see the past from a perspective that no one living in any given moment could have ever had. Gaddis said, "if you think of the past as a landscape, then history is the way we represent it, and it's that act of representation that lifts us above the familiar to let us experience vicariously what we can't experience directly: a wider view."[38]

The effect that such perspective gives us is thrilling. When I wrote my biography of John Foster Dulles, I was struck by the fact that I could know how any given dilemma he faced in his life span (1888–1959) would be resolved, even though he could never have such knowledge in the immediate moments of his experience. For example, Dulles was a wealthy attorney when the stock market crashed in 1929. He was profoundly concerned, just like most people during that time, about his financial security. We now know that his finances would remain secure all through the Great Depression, that he had nothing to worry about, even though such knowledge was high and too wonderful for him to attain in the midst of his circumstances. We also know that Dulles's attitude toward war, peace, nationalism, and diplomacy would undergo great changes from the 1940s to the 1950s, and we also know many of the reasons for those changes. His changing attitudes mystified many of those closest to him, but he seemed to be hardly aware of them. The Dulles of 1944 was starkly different from the Dulles of 1954. From our vantage point in the present, we can see Dulles's entire life span, from the frigid day he was born in his grandparents' house in Washington, DC, to the bright spring day they buried him at Arlington Cemetery. To an extent, we can see the end from the beginning in a dead person's life, and that is one of the profoundly consequential realities of historical thinking. How would you treat the people in your life, or how would you handle your life's joys, dilemmas, and problems if you knew the day and manner of your death? Would you even want to have such knowledge? As his biographer, I had knowledge of Dulles's whole mortal existence. What power historical perspective fetches!

The power of historical perspective can also be pernicious. "I can use the people I encounter in the archives without their consent for my own purposes, for my own pleasures, for my own professional gain," historian Beth Barton Schweiger wrote. "The dead can languish without defense in my books. . . . My purposes may be honest. But what if they are not?"[39] The illusion that historical perspective results in agency over the past leads to idolatry of self over the dead. Historical perspective tempts us to go beyond understanding to embrace delusions of grandeur. We may have an embarrassment of riches of artifacts in an archival collection, but who can discern the motives and thoughts of the human heart? Perspective also tempts us to use our knowledge to justify ourselves or our ideological commitments, to the exclusion of other possible interpretations to which we may object. We often cherry-pick from the historical record the evidence that backs up our preconceived ideologies, while ignoring evidence that undermines them. Hence, we bow before Francis Bacon's Idol of the Tribe,[40] in which we rely on special pleading, or his Idol of the Theatre, in which we indulge in undue allegiance to false schools of thought.[41]

We dare not succumb to the temptation presented by the illusion of omniscience. As soon as we think we have a historical person or event all figured out, we may be surprised to discover we were simply wrong. Dulles is a case in point. As simple a man as he appeared to his contemporaries and even some of his biographers,[42] the reality was much more complicated. He was a man full of paradoxes. Just like you and me, he was complicated.

The knowledge we gain from perspective is a gift, but it comes with a responsibility. While I could take in the span of Dulles's life and times, that perspective came with a simple yet momentous duty. I had to represent him with justice if I wanted to rightly pursue truth about his life and times. The historian's task is to employ justice to the dead before thinking of applying justice through history to the present. Some contemporary historians style themselves "activist historians." If a historian sees his task primarily as social activism, then the tendency to do injustice to the dead is hard to resist. "Activist history" does not foster humility in the pursuit of truth but is tailor-made to mine the useful material from the past and ignore material that doesn't fit so well with a preconceived narrative. Employing justice historically must begin with the past subject matter and then proceed to the present audience. Then justice has a chance of obtaining for the good of the present and with faithfulness to the past.

While Lukacs argued that the purpose of history was understanding, and Weaver wrote that it was for conscience formation, Gaddis said that history grows us into maturity. Each of these three historians' understandings of what history aims for is right. "We understand how much has preceded us and how unimportant we are in relation to it," Gaddis said.[43] Such understanding causes us to "learn our place" and to "feel small"[44] as we stand over the temporal precipice and consider how deep and all-consuming the past is, not only to the dead but one day to ourselves also. The dead say to us, "As you are now, I once was. As I am, you one day will be." How will future generations assess and interpret the meaning of our lives as they employ historical perspective on all the mysteries that face us, that to them are simply part of the historical record? Gaddis said, "Historical consciousness therefore leaves you, as does maturity itself, with a simultaneous sense of your own significance and insignificance."[45]

What a profound statement. Our personal and communal identities are important, but those identities tend to place us at the center of reality. Obsession with personal or group identity, to the extent that such identity serves as the sole frame of reference for truth, is a marker of childishness. Conservatives aim for a realistic assessment of identity that offers wisdom. Historian Robert Tracy McKenzie wrote that history teaches us "the magnitude of our inadequacy" and that our approach to history ought to be like looking up at the night sky. "Our natural response should be one of wonder and awe and a humbling awareness of our own limitations."[46] Instead of being struck with the wonder of history and what wisdom it offers, we can fool ourselves into thinking history is defined by a plotline like the plots in the *Star Wars* movies. History becomes a simple affair of identifying who is evil and who is pure—who is on the "wrong side of history" and who is on the "right side." Or, our knowledge of history may be detailed, but how we deploy that knowledge for present purposes can be puerile, selfish, and dishonest. Do we not find herein the essence of human nature? Persons bear the image of God; they possess profound and invaluable dignity. But persons also are fallible, myopic, sinful, and selfish. Our freedom and knowledge bless us with great privileges, but with the enjoyment of privilege comes immense responsibility. All these considerations as to the meaning and purpose of history relate to human nature. As persons, we possess historical consciousness. We are responsible for both the act and method of employing that consciousness.

Thus, historical thinking requires virtue if historical thinking consists in a pursuit of truth. Specifically, the virtues of prudence, charity, patience, and courage are fitting for historical thinking. Guided by virtue, the study of history is ennobling. Historical thinking both heightens our dignity as persons and chastens us in our predisposition to hubris. A virtue-less pursuit of truth in history is counterfeit and futile. A virtuous pursuit of truth in history is informed by humility before truth itself. We hold in tension the understanding that, in the immediate sense, our access to historical truth is limited, but that in the end, we are subject to the authority of truth. We don't get to just make the past up as we go along according to what suits us.

What do conservatives conserve? Conservatives conserve tradition, and the past is the fount of tradition. How we make sense of the past determines the value we place on tradition. When we employ prudence, we see that some traditions are worthy of conservation but other traditions are not. Aspirational conservatives know that change is not to be eschewed. Change is inevitable, and "stability is not immobility," as Austrian Prince Metternich (1773–1859) said to Tsar Alexander I (1777–1825).[47] Change ought to be managed intentionally, deliberately, procedurally, all while looking to the guiding light of tradition. In this, aspirational conservatives revere tradition but avoid traditionalism, that is, turning tradition per se into an absolute authority. Viereck wrote that "the conservative conserves discriminately, the reactionary indiscriminately."[48] By this he meant that while all conservatives revere tradition, rightist reactionaries accept all tradition uncritically. Rightly understood, tradition, according to Viereck, meant "all the lessons of the past but only the ethically acceptable events." In other words, we conserve the traditions emerging from events that represent the best of human nature and achievement. As to the painful episodes in the past, we repudiate the wrongs done and abandon traditions that preserve those wrongs, but we still maintain the memory of those episodes. Even the frightful events give us truths by which to live. In contrast, the reactionary discerns no ethical nuances in tradition. In nostalgically holding on to the past, the reactionary whitewashes past sins, and thus Viereck said, "he misses all the lessons."[49]

Some traditions are impractical, and some are immoral. Such traditions can and should be abandoned. Progressives may think of all conservatives as despising change and holding to tradition as absolute authority, as in, "we've always done things this way, therefore we must always continue as we have done." Consider how a conservative might challenge this idea by critically assessing certain traditions while revering tradition as a category. Critical reverence of tradition is possible. Tradition, broadly speaking, can be carefully pruned and stewarded, prepared for bequeathal to new generations, or changed to fit new times and circumstances. For example, horses were once ubiquitous, used for all modes of land transportation and communication for millennia. The Botai people in present-day Kazakhstan were the first to domesticate horses in the fourth millennium BC.[50] Horses were used for personal transportation and the transportation of goods. They were used by armies for reconnaissance, hauling weapons and supplies, and as the cavalry arm of the army. They were indispensable for plowing. The invention of the stirrup in the Middle Ages was one of the great advances of technology, enabling the rider to stand in the saddle for stability and dexterity. Until the beginning of the twentieth century, horses were a necessary fixture in the myriad quotidian patterns of everyday life in every condition.

The husbanding of horses is a tradition, but it is now very different than it was in 1900. We have planes, trains, and automobiles to carry us and our stuff hither and thither. Mechanized vehicles plow our fields, transport our goods, and fight our battles. People still raise horses for riding, recreation, exhibition, companionship, and the joy that comes with breeding them. My paternal relatives have been ranchers in Montana for generations, and most of them are still passionate and devoted horse people. The tradition has changed because our way of life has changed. A conservative understands how change facilitated by technology affects tradition. Some traditions are unrecognizable from what they were in the past, but they can take on new forms and meanings for the benefit of individuals and communities.

Other traditions are immoral. Chattel slavery as it existed in the Americas from the sixteenth to the nineteenth centuries is a salient case of an immoral tradition. One of the many features of chattel slavery that made the institution immoral was that it was necessarily predicated upon kidnapping. People were transported against their will from their ancestral lands and their families to distant lands across the ocean and forced to work for another's profit. While chattel slavery was traditional, it has been rightly assessed as immoral and therefore repudiated. In the United States, the repudiation of slavery was bloody, and the legacy of slavery has cast a long shadow over American history that produced another immoral tradition lasting a century after the war: the practice of race segregation predicated on the prejudicial doctrine of "separate but equal." Race prejudice over the generations has come at a bitter cost to our people, and we are still living with its legacy. Witness the controversy surrounding Confederate memorials like A. P. Hill's. Reckoning with sin is necessary to reconciliation and atonement.

Thus, prudence is necessary in thinking historically. We apply prudence as we critically assess the traditions we keep and the traditions we abandon, either because they are impractical, imprudent, or immoral. Even though conservatives revere tradition as a category, they are not traditionalists in that they fight to keep all traditions intact and unchanged. Prudence points to those traditions we ought to conserve for the sake of handing them down to younger generations. What are those? A few examples are the traditions of ordered liberty, federalism, humane letters, localism, voluntary associations, respect for elders, deference to legitimate authorities, freedom of religion, committed marriage between a man and a woman, family life stabilized by the devotion of fathers and mothers in their natural roles, and what Viereck called "the aristocratic spirit." That spirit, Viereck wrote, was marked by "dutiful public service, insistence on quality and standards, the decorum and ethical inner check of *noblesse oblige.*"[51] The aristocratic spirit embraces self-respect and respect for others expressed through wholesome manners; attention to higher purposes that go beyond one's own interest and ambition; a love for all things beautiful; a desire for improvement in society that starts with self-examination; and a circumspection that bears closely in mind the example one sets before a watching world. The employment of prudence in historical thinking searches out the difference between reverence for tradition and traditionalism. Prudence guides us in heeding the successes and failures of the past in terms going beyond mere fastidious concern for accuracy. Understanding, formation of conscience, and growth in maturity all stand at the center of prudence, as the student of history seeks to make sense of the past for the sake of worthy living in the present and the future.

As historical thinkers, we also have a duty to extend charity to the people of the past who are now dead. It may sound strange to say that we owe the dead our love. The kind of love we owe the dead is not mere sentimentality. It is a love that moves the historian to accept the dead for who they were and tell the truth about them. The apostle Paul said that charity "does not rejoice in unrighteousness, but rejoices with the truth."[52] If Burke was right, that society is a contract between the dead, the living, and the yet to be born, then we have as much an obligation to extend charity to the dead as we do to the living—and to the yet to be born. The dead are not merely abstractions or expressionless faces staring back at us from faded black-and-white photographs. The dead were once living, just as we are living in the present. They had struggles, failures, joys, successes, and everything in between. They raised families, enclosed their dead loved ones in clay with grief, looked to the future with hope and anxiety, and wondered what the meaning of their lives might be. They had a nature just like ours. They were persons, with as much dignity and as much fallibility as anyone alive. They sinned in their acts of omission and commission, sometimes doing horrible things to others—just as we do and are prone to do. The study of history is humanistic, that is, it is concerned with real persons living in real times and in real places. The extension of charity to those who cannot speak for themselves any longer, cannot take credit for their triumphs nor answer for their mistakes and sins, is eminently appropriate for those who live in the present and desire to make sense of the past. One day, we will all be as they are: cold ashes in the grave. What will our descendants say of us? Will they judge us by our worst moments, ignoring the admirable elements in our characters? Will they worship us because of our best moments, crassly whitewashing our records and thereby missing the opportunity to gain wisdom from our failures? We would hope that they would neither condemn nor worship us but represent our lives charitably, which entails truth. Charity calls for a balance between valuing a life marked by dignity for what it was and justly and circumspectly critiquing it when fallibility abounded.

The extension of charity entails the restraining of perspectival power. It is neither our place to condemn the dead, nor is it our place to deify them. Condemnation or idolization of the dead usually serves some purpose, but only on behalf of those in the present —a reputation gained, a political opponent defeated, a book contract secured, a promotion won, or a coveted prize acquired. Careers are often built on such inane motivations. Schweiger wrote that the exercise of power in historical thinking is the application of the "desire to possess and master the dead."[53] Virtuous historical thinking involves the simple act of contemplating the dead for what they were, without any thought of using them for narrow, political, or self-centered purposes.

Not so fast! the objector may say. Does not charity entail approval? If we extend charity to the dead, does that not mean we absolve them of their sins? Not in the slightest. The study of history helps us to put away childish things. A childish mentality finds no room for compromise between two opposing positions and absolutizes issues in terms of all one thing or all the other. Childishness ignores complexity and will not abide paradox. In the same way that one can be critically reverent of tradition, a mature person can be both charitable and critical simultaneously. Charity remembers the person's dignity; criticism exposes his fallibility. The responsible historical thinker can walk and chew gum at the same time. He can accept historical complexity and be at peace with a life, event, or idea representing good, bad, and everything in between. Schweiger rightly said that we may extend charity to dead people who disturb us by learning from their mistakes and "learn . . . to look for logs in our own eyes."[54] The sins of the dead reveal our own sins and blind spots if we have eyes to see them. Also, we remember that our own understanding is limited and that we should, in Schweiger's words, "remain open to revision and correction."[55] Childishness puts personal feelings of discomfort at the forefront and seeks to cancel the dead when they push the limits of the moral imaginations of the living. Maturity learns from the dead as they really were—dignified by their humanity and yet fallen in their moral failures.

Ultimately, we must ask ourselves, what kind of persons do *we* aspire to be? Do we aspire to be moral peacocks, preening ourselves and strutting about while quick to condemn others? Historian E. H. Carr wrote, "Study the historian before you study the facts."[56] The character of the historical thinker counts toward the reliability of his conclusions, and that is true not only of others but of ourselves as well. What defines our character as persons? We cannot claim to be persons of charity if we are not willing to extend charity to everyone, living and dead. "Seeing the dead affords practice in seeing the living. The limits of our understanding of those who are gone are matched by our blindness towards the people across the room," Schweiger wrote.[57] What excuse will we offer if we refuse to extend charity to the dead? If we refuse charity to the dead, how will we offer it to the living? The purpose of history is not first to change the world. From the inside out, history changes the historian first. Through the exercise of restraint on the power of historical perspective and realism about human nature that I share with everyone who has ever lived, I can have eyes to see that my problem is not out there but *in here*, that is, in my own tendency to exalt myself at the expense of others. Only after accepting that realization and dedicating myself to a higher destiny may I be able to justly call for change out there.

Along with charity, historical thinking requires the exercise of patience. Patience teaches us to be at peace with complexity. History resists all our attempts to simplify it. It takes time, thought, careful investigation, openness to correction, and recognition of our own limited understanding to undertake responsible, virtuous historical thinking. In the same way we ordinarily must exercise patience with our living neighbors, relatives, and fellow citizens, we have the obligation to exercise patience with the dead. We must first grapple with the foreignness of the world of the past. The world of the past is different than the world of the present, and the deeper the past, the more foreign it appears to us living in the present. We cannot gain understanding of a person who lived in the eighteenth century without understanding the presuppositions of the culture in which he lived, the knowledge he had about the larger world, the understanding he held of reality, his religion, his education, the technology available to him, the perspective he had, the political scene in which he was immersed, or the social realities to which he was subject. Understanding the life and times of a dead person takes an investment of time, respect, mental energy, and concentration. Even after making the investment, we often come away with many more questions than answers.

Patience is a disposition that does not comport well with our insistence on immediate gratification; our convenience-obsessed, technology-riddled culture; or our natural fixations on being *right*. From our earliest experiences, we are accustomed to being resistant to the simple discipline of perseverance. Our food and drink, technology, transportation, entertainment, relationships, and a host of other things are tailored to meet our demands according to the timing of our choosing and the comfort and "safety" as we understand them. Since the COVID-19 lockdowns, practices that required some modicum of effort, such as going to church, attending a public lecture, going to a concert, play, or movie—anything that meant getting out of the house and among other people—no longer require much in the way of submitting ourselves to processes beyond our control. We have been relieved of having to exercise patience by our technology. Artificial intelligence, we are told, will rid humanity of all forms of tedium. Patience and tedium will always be required in the pursuit of historical truth and understanding. Patience is a prerequisite to maturity and wholeness in the person. Wisdom, knowledge, and understanding do not come at the click of a mouse, the threading up of a YouTube video, or looking to AI to do our thinking for us. Historical thinking demands patience if a person desires to have understanding and a formed conscience in the inner self.

We have no choice but to take the past, and the people of the past, on their own terms if we are in search of understanding. We are not able to change past events or outcomes, as much as we would like to go back in time and kill Hitler or stop Kennedy's assassination. We are also powerless to change the people of the past. How difficult it is to change our own intellectual, emotional, spiritual, and physical habits in the present, and how we sometimes long to see our spouses, parents, siblings, friends, neighbors, and fellow citizens be different than they are. As difficult as it is to expect change in the thought and behavior patterns of the living, how much more absurd is it to demand the dead to fit our present moral, intellectual, social, religious, or economic expectations? Yet we often want them to conform to our standards, rather than simply allowing them to be products of their own cultures, backgrounds, attitudes, and behaviors. We tend to anachronistically condemn, for example, eighteenth-century people for failing to look and act like twenty-first-century people. None of this means we cannot think or speak critically of their lives and actions. We need not be moral relativists concerning the past. But the dead really were "products of their times" in the same way that we in the present are "products of our times." The reality of a person being "the product of his time" does not justify sin, but it does help to explain historical realities. Getting down to what it meant for a person to be a product of his time is the nub of the historical issue, and it takes time, thought, realism, and teachability to work to understand why the dead were the way they were as we allow for moral criticisms of their sinful actions.

Finally, courage is necessary to historical thinking. Because the world of the past is so foreign to us in the present, it has the effect of making us feel uncomfortable. Prior to the nineteenth century, the people of the past were accustomed to thinking that slavery was normal, that punishment for crime was meant to humiliate and set an example by gruesomeness, and that religious disagreements could be warrant for exile or torturous execution. Do we defend these realities of the past, conceal them, or minimize them? No! We remember that immorality is a marker of human depravity. We recoil at it because we inherently know the meaning of human dignity.

Monuments and memorials such as the one that served as A. P. Hill's grave once offered the benefit of spurring historical thinking.

It is gone now, and in the case of Hill's statue, we will not have that potential for moral and intellectual benefit any longer. Yet Hill still represents in the present what Americans were in the past, and what they were has relevance for us today, regardless of our acts of willful self-inflicted amnesia. In my years of teaching, I have found that most students have not been trained to accept that they are *supposed* to be uncomfortable with the past. To illustrate: no one would expect a person born and raised in Brownstown, Indiana, to be fully at home in a place like London or Mexico City, must less Tehran or Pyongyang. Visiting a foreign country takes some courage. It is intimidating to be asked questions by a customs official at the airport in a foreign country, to be surrounded by people who look, dress, speak, eat, and live differently than how you are accustomed. Similarly, encountering persons of another time can challenge one's present assumptions and sensibilities. Many people respond to discomfort presented to them by the past with an immediate disposition to rid themselves of the source of the discomfort, as futile a disposition as putting a brown bag over the head and yelling, "You can't see me!" To subject oneself to amnesia takes no courage at all. Rather, it is an act of cowardice to shut one's ears to the past, pretend it did not happen, and remove any and all reminders of it in an effort to assuage negative sentiment or politically incorrect "optics."

In the final analysis, why would people want to choose amnesia for themselves when there are more humanistic alternatives? If historical consciousness is part of what makes us human, is not the act of self-inflicted amnesia inhuman? Courage inspires us as citizens to find ways to acknowledge the features of the past that challenge our sensibilities in the present without resorting either to brute cancellation or blatant intimidation. For example, Washington and Lee University political scientist and historian Lucas Morel spoke to the fraught issues surrounding Lee's presidency of the college after the Civil War. In an interview, Morel (who is African-American) said he regarded Lee as a traitor, expressed openness to changing street names and place-names that memorialize Confederate figures in his town of Lexington, Virginia, but said he resists calls for the removal of Lee's name from the university. Rather, careful consideration and conversation are necessary during such controversies. "History can inform so many of those issues we are embroiled with today."[58] Localities should reasonably deliberate together on the future of place-names and historical monuments. Morel's stated guiding principle on such issues is that if a monument is to come down, it ought to be for the same reasons it went up—reasons the local community articulates and endorses. There are often good reasons to dismantle monuments, but those reasons are for localities to find through honest, lawful, historically aware deliberation.[59]

Guelzo, in reflecting on the controversy over the Robert E. Lee memorial in Charlottesville, Virginia, also called for a reasonable process of deliberation before removing the statue. Like Morel, Guelzo is no Lee apologist. And like Morel's, his was a rare voice—and a conservative one—calling for deliberation about monuments based on historical consciousness rather than politically and emotionally charged iconoclasm. "We need a set of guideposts to get us past name-calling and confrontation, a set of questions that can allow a reasoned discussion," Guelzo wrote.[60] He proposed a few historically informed questions upon which communities could base their deliberations regarding monuments. Then he closed by saying, "There are no obvious or easy answers in most cases. But these questions will allow us to discuss the real historical issues, not the emotional and political ones, and in a sober and directed fashion."[61] Guelzo wrote his piece less than a week after the Unite the Right rally exploded in the streets of a usually quiet and bucolic southern university town. That took courage, no matter what one may think of the specifics of his proposals. In demonstrating courage, the kind shown by Morel and Guelzo, we might be surprised at how the wisdom we learn from the process of hearing each other and being heard could benefit us as a nation.

How can a civilization that chooses to rashly eradicate its collective memories expect to survive and flourish in the future? It is axiomatic that one cannot know where he is going without knowing from whence he came. In American history, there are many shameful episodes. Yet every event, idea, and person that materially and meaningfully contributed to the development of this nation, whether they represent good, evil, or something in between, made America into the country it is in the present. Robertson pointed to the Confederacy as a prime example. Without the rise and fall of the Confederacy, there would be no definition of American citizenship. There would be no conception of an American nationhood that embraced a plurality of peoples under one national purpose. There would be no aspiration of genuine racial unity. America would have lacked the unity necessary to become more than the sum of its parts if it had not had the opportunity to triumph over secession. In other words, Robertson rightly observed that the American union of the twentieth and twenty-first centuries would be impossible without the existence of a Confederate States of America in the nineteenth century, and a Civil War that produced the country we benefit from and call home today.[62]

Historical thinking that begets understanding cannot consist in accepting the dynamics that make us feel good and rejecting those others that make us feel uncomfortable. If we want to pursue truth, we must courageously face whatever discomfort we feel when confronted by a past world that is vastly different than our own and seek to understand it for the sake of benefiting from lessons learned. If we hope to survive and thrive as a nation, we must reckon with our past glories and failures procedurally, reasonably, and virtuously. And if we want our children and grandchildren to enjoy the traditions of liberty and prosperity, we must conserve tradition circumspectly by "listening to the way history grows," as Viereck eloquently said.[63] That also requires the exercise of virtue in the cultivation of historical consciousness. To exercise virtue, we must first be people who pursue virtue.

CHAPTER SIX

Conservatism and Religion

Quid fiet hominibus qui minima contemnunt, majora non credunt?
(What will become of men who mistake small things and do not
believe in greater?)

—Pascal, *Pensées*

There is nothing better for a man than to eat and drink and tell
himself that his labor is good. This also I have seen that it is from
the hand of God. For who can eat and who can have enjoyment
without Him?

—Ecclesiastes 2:24–25

The consciousness of God is vital to human nature. Not everyone
is religious, in terms of subscribing to a specific faith system
or identifying with a particular congregation or sacred community.
Not all conservatives are religious. Some people are unbelievers in
that they might describe themselves as agnostic, secular, or atheist.
There are the famous "nones," those who mark the box "None" on a
questionnaire surveying the religious affiliations of a particular population sample.[1] These social realities aside, human nature is recog-

nizable by a perception and cognizance of the divine unique among all the other living creatures in the world. Conservatives seek to conserve religion and religious institutions because through religion we contemplate the transcendent, pursue truth, and have an objective and just law by which to live. Put simply, all conservatives believe religion and religious institutions have a central place in dignifying human life no matter their personal religious beliefs.

To illustrate, consider how we think about wilderness and wild places. Our attitudes about wilderness help clarify attitudes about God and religion. Why? Wilderness is one of the last remaining realities of the world that presents us with something beyond our capacity to understand and master. Wilderness is marked by mystery, beauty, and even danger. Wilderness captures our imaginations, inspires us to contemplate something older and greater than ourselves, and more profound and expansive than the mundane plane of existence in which we find our being. Wilderness reminds us of our limitations and our mortality when we are faced with great trees or mountains that were here long before us and will endure long after we are dust. A long excursion into the wilderness is at times a thing to be endured because it is physically exhausting and frequently mortally perilous, not to mention comfortless. At the same time, such an excursion is exhilarating and can be life-changing. Even after a challenging, pinching, and laborious experience far from the comforts of home in the wild, an outdoorsman finds himself unable to banish the allure and enchantment of the wilderness from his mind. Wilderness often escapes rational explanation. It can have the paradoxical effect of, in one moment, beckoning us to it with its unutterable beauty and, in the next moment, repelling us with a foreboding, forbidding, and fearful aspect. Speaking of the ancient Greeks, British classicist Gilbert Murray wrote, "Their love for nature was that of a mountaineer and the seaman, who does not talk much about the sea and mountains, but who sickens and pines if he is taken away from them."[2] All who are drawn to wild places know this feeling all too well. The contemplation of the eternal is often like that. Understanding how persons relate to the sublime in the natural world can tell us something about how they relate to the sublime in the supernatural.

Anyone who has spent any time camping, hiking, horseback riding, climbing, hunting, fishing, skiing, boating, or any activity in wild, mysterious, and beautiful places understands the profound draw that the natural world can have on a person. Why is it that a grueling fifteen-mile hike through the rain and cold can have the effect on a person's mind and spirit to go out and do it again as soon as practicable? Why is it that we cannot live without green spaces in our lives, if for nothing more than to be able to see them from a porch, a window, or a car on a road? We are drawn to the created world because we are an organic and spiritual part of the world. Creation is not just out there. We are creatures, we are a part of creation. As a part of creation, it is in our human nature to enjoy it, to apprehend it, and to connect with the One who created the world and who created us.

I wrote earlier that my father and grandfather first introduced me to the outdoors. My father took me hiking and backpacking in the mountains of north Georgia and southwest Montana where the Wilsey family settled in the 1930s. My grandfather, a native Georgian, opened my eyes to the joys of bird hunting—doves, ducks, geese, and quail. My father taught me to respect the land, to love its beauty, and to cherish it for what it was, without seeking to bend it to my own desires. As a boy, I learned wilderness skills like how to tend a clean and tidy camp, prepare meals and sleep comfortably in the wild, build a fire in the rain, read and follow a topographical map, tie knots, take care of gear and supplies, respect native plants and wildlife, and not be afraid of the dark. I also learned patience on long and arduous hikes, courage when conditions changed from placid to tempestuous and familiar to unfamiliar. I was challenged to be cheerful in irksome situations. My grandfather taught me the wonder of mystery in the wild, to respect and love my quarry, the value of waiting to take a shot at the right moment, a code of conduct when hunting with others (like never to command or scold another person's dog), and how to show deference to my elders who accompanied us and often hosted us. With my grandfather, I saw the rhythms of the natural world in the changing of the seasons and the movements of the birds as night gave way to the day, and the day gave way to the night. I also learned to respect a firearm, and that the taking of the life of an animal was a deeply serious matter, that mortality was a thing about which never to be flippant, wasteful, or thoughtless. Being in the mountains and forests of north Georgia and Montana with my father, and in the pine woods of south Georgia, the bayous of Louisiana, and the Eastern Shore of Maryland with my grandfather, opened my eyes to the glories of the wild, the preciousness of life, and the power of awe, respect, quietness, and integrity. Those experiences in my childhood and adolescence permanently formed me, and my desire to pass this heritage down to my children, and if God permits someday, my grandchildren, is profound. The wildness and majesty of the natural world satisfy a person's innate longing for the good, the true, and the beautiful in a similar way as does the honest and humble search for God, who promises that all who seek him on his terms will find him.[3]

Our attitudes toward wilderness are like our attitudes about God. Religious authority and tradition show us how to relate to the eternal, just as recreation, exploration, cultivation, and contemplation are means by which we relate to wilderness. The natural world captures our imaginations. Even if we are not accustomed to wild places, we are intuitively drawn to their beauty and sublimity. Similarly, all persons are naturally captivated by God, even those who would say they have no religion. None of us can escape the consciousness of God—even atheists, those who say they reject the existence of God, frequently consider and articulate attitudes about God. The conservative holds God and the eternal in reverence; thus, religion is necessary to full humanity. A religious consciousness moves us to reckon with God and the world to come. A conservative need not be a devoted religious person, but a conservative will venerate the transcendent and seek to conserve religious tradition.

The bridge between the temporal world we experience in nature and the eternal world we know through faith is moral law. One need not be a philosopher, a theologian, or an ethicist to discern the connections between the world in which we move and have our being and the eternal world. John Foster Dulles is an example of someone whose frame of reference was situated in this world while actively contemplating the next. As one of the most consequential American diplomats of the twentieth century, he applied his observations about how predictable patterns in nature point to religious ideas and precepts. He drew moral and practical lessons from nature and applied them to diplomacy and international law in the crisis-riddled years from the 1930s to the 1950s. Dulles was a consummate outdoorsman. He was a nautical man, not a mountaineer. For years, he plied the waves of the Great Lakes, the St. Lawrence River, and the Gulf of St. Lawrence in his forty-foot yawl, the *Menemsha*. In 1941, he purchased a 700-acre island in Lake Ontario named Duck Island, had a small rustic cabin built on the island, and enjoyed spending weeks at a time in utter isolation on that island with his wife, Janet, until his death in 1959. Dulles was well known by his friends and family for constantly observing moral lessons in the patterns of the lakes, fish, weather, birds, and the seasons. His youngest son, Avery, who became a Catholic cardinal, reflected that his father "would make analogies between things in nature and things in sailing and things which were in the sphere of diplomacy and international finance, or whatever he was working on."[4] Dulles's longtime friend Bob Hart said that one of his favorite sayings on the lake was "everything is fine until you relax." Hart said that by this, Dulles meant that "as long as you're on your toes and watching everything, you get along fine, but the minute you relax, then things happen—the minute you think everything's all right."[5] Perseverance, vigilance, guarding against complacency—these were simple virtues one applies when out sailing on the unpredictable and awesome Lake Ontario, as well as when stewarding the security of the free world in the face of Communist expansionism.

C. S. Lewis, in his classic work *Mere Christianity*, observed a contrast between the way we speak of the law of nature and the way premodern thinkers did. He said that in contemporary times, when we talk of the law of nature, we mean "things like gravitation, or heredity, or the laws of chemistry." Premoderns thought of the law of nature in terms of "the Law of *Human* Nature." Lewis wrote, "the idea was that, just as all bodies are governed by the law of gravitation and organisms by biological laws, so the creature called man also had *his* law—with this great difference, that a body could not choose whether it obeyed the law of gravitation or not, but a man could choose to obey the Law of Human Nature or to disobey it."[6] So while it is useful to look to the natural world for wisdom on the good, the true, and the beautiful, there are limits to what the natural world can teach us. When it comes to the nature of God, truth, and justice, we must reckon with the reality that human nature is fallible, and that persons can abuse their dignity by willfully or ignorantly disobeying the moral law through their misuse of free will, in a way they cannot disobey the second law of thermodynamics.

Still, persons grasp for righteousness. We find common elements of morality in every civilization. While there may be different standards of righteousness across the various civilizations over time, Lewis argued that all civilizations at least have possessed a basic understanding of righteousness. Persons know righteousness and unrighteousness when they see them. "Think of a country where people were admired for running away in battle, or where a man felt proud of double-crossing all the people who had been kindest to him," Lewis wrote. "You might just as well try to imagine a country where two and two made five."[7] Such a country exists only in a fantasy. Righteousness, as an idea, is common to all human communities across time because the desire for righteousness is a part of our bearing the image of God our Creator. Further, Lewis pointed out that not only does every civilization and every individual recognize unrighteousness in others, persons also recognize their own unrighteousness and cannot escape the sense of guilt that attends that recognition. Just as human dignity is concretized in the actual quest for righteousness among communities and individuals, human fallibility is concretized in the individual and corporate recognition of moral failure. Knowledge of the moral law, which comes to us to a limited extent through the natural world, and more fully through religious authority, is common to all. All recognize it due to our human nature, as it is in tension between both dignity and fallibility.[8] As Lewis put it, we have "a real law which we did not invent and which we know we ought to obey."[9]

Where did this moral law originate? Is it merely coincidence that the moral law is displayed in the natural order? Is it nothing more than a fluke that moral law is common to all humanity? God is the source of the moral law, just as he is the source of all that exists. As the source of the universe, God exists over and above the universe and thus does not appear as part of the universe. As Lewis put it, "if there was a controlling power outside the universe, it could not show itself to us as one of the facts inside the universe—no more than the architect of a house could actually be a wall or a staircase or fireplace in that house."[10] While God is hidden in this temporal world of ours, we see and sense his existence in the fact that we know we have a moral law to live by, that God is the source of that law, and that our failure to abide by the moral law makes us answerable to God the Creator. Speaking of Christianity, Lewis wrote, "it is after you have realized that there is a real Moral Law, and a Power behind the law, and that you have broken that law and put yourself wrong with that Power—it is after all this, and not a moment sooner, that Christianity begins to talk."[11] As a religion, Christianity addresses the deepest human need that arises from the core of every person's being—the need to be made right with God, and to know and be known by him. For none of us is immortal. Just as every person who has ever lived and died, you and I also must die. The reality of death places an urgency upon the meeting of this most basic need of ours. Because death is the ultimate reminder of our limitation, fallibility, and moral accountability, we persons look for hope as we contemplate the grave. "Only a being like God," philosopher Thomas V. Morris wrote, "could guarantee a completeness and permanency of meaning for human lives." Morris concluded, "the existence of God is thus no merely theoretical issue. It is an issue of the most ultimate personal importance."[12] The need for God is common to humanity, and the Judeo-Christian religion has pointed humanity to affinity with God for over three thousand years.

In the American experience, Christianity—revealed in the biblical Old and New Testaments—has been the predominant religion of the people. The colonists who settled the British North American colonies beginning in 1607 overwhelmingly subscribed to Christian denominations, and there were some Jewish congregations also in Rhode Island and Georgia. Congregationalists, Presbyterians, Baptists, Anglicans, Quakers, German Reformed, Lutherans, Dutch Reformed, Methodists, Catholics, Moravians, and other Christian groups dominated the American religious landscape by the time the colonies declared their independence. By 1776, there were 3,228 congregations in the thirteen colonies. The Congregationalists were the largest denomination with 668 churches. Jews comprised the smallest group, with five synagogues in America.[13]

By the beginning of the Revolution, Christianity was poised to be one of the major sources influencing the intellectual and spiritual roots of the national founding under the Constitution. Mark David Hall has argued persuasively on this point. Alongside republicanism, liberalism, and the Enlightenment, Christianity was a primary intellectual source for the American founding. Hall posed the question of his book as, "Did America have a Christian founding?" This question is different than the question, "Was America founded as a Christian nation?" While the answer to the latter question may be "it's complicated," Hall's answer to the former question was "a resounding yes."[14] More specifically, Hall argued that Christianity exerted an undeniable and profound influence upon the founders as they established the United States.[15]

Influence is notoriously difficult to justify in historical terms. To make a persuasive case for influence between ideas, persons, and events, the researcher must have evidence. Hall's method was to find and explain evidence demonstrating the influence of Christianity from the founding period, that is, roughly from 1763 to 1800. Hall is not the only scholar to make and defend the argument that Christianity was a primary influence on the founding. Daniel Dreisbach considered the role the Bible played as the ideas generating the American founding developed. He looked at how the Bible was viewed by the public in the late eighteenth century, the ways that various texts of the Bible were used by the founders, and some of the ways biblical teachings were applied in the first decade of the American national career. Like Hall, Dreisbach argued that "for a well-rounded understanding of the ideas that informed the American founding, these biblical influences must be studied alongside republican, Enlightenment, British constitutional, and other intellectual influences."[16]

Hall and Dreisbach looked backward to see how Christianity influenced the founding. Another way to gauge the influence of Christianity on the founding is to consider its effects after the Constitution went into effect in 1789. Two ways in which we might find the influence of Christianity after the American founding are in the development of the African American church traditions and through American culture more generally. First, consider the development of the African American churches. Far from serving in simplistic terms as a "white man's religion," Christianity has historically dominated the religious life of Blacks for well over two centuries. Despite slavery and race discrimination, African American churches were formed, grew exponentially, and resulted in the establishment of domestic and foreign mission organizations, voluntary associations, journals and publication houses, and institutions of higher learning. Specifically, the nineteenth century saw the development and exponential growth of Methodist and Baptist churches. Three Methodist traditions took shape in the 1800s. The African Methodist Episcopal (AME) denomination was formed under Richard Allen (1760–1831) in 1816 in Philadelphia. It started with three congregations and about a thousand parishioners, and by 1900 it had grown to embrace thousands of congregations in twenty-two conferences with two million members.[17] In New York City, the African Methodist Episcopal Zion (AMEZ) denomination came together, electing James Varick as its first bishop in 1821. By 1900, the AMEZ comprised 500,000 members and 3,600 churches across America.[18] The Christian Methodist Episcopal (CME) denomination formed in 1870 after the Civil War, with William H. Miles (1828–1892) and Richard H. Vanderhorst (1813–1872) both serving as its first bishops. The CME churches grew to claim 700,000 members in fifty years.[19]

African American Baptists also flourished in the nineteenth century. The first African American Baptist church was founded at Savannah, Georgia, in 1773 under the ministry of George Liele (1750–1820), and African American Baptists have grown into three major denominations (National Baptist Convention, USA, American Baptist Convention, and Progressive Baptist Convention) and several smaller groups since their beginning.[20] When the National Baptist Convention, USA was formed in 1895, it claimed three million members.[21]

Black colleges proliferated during the nineteenth century thanks to the churches. Some AME-founded institutions of higher learning include Wilberforce University (1856, founded by Daniel Alexander Payne), Paul Quinn College (1872, named for William Paul Quinn, fourth bishop of the AME church), and Morris Brown College (1885, founded by Wesley John Gaines and named for Morris Brown, second bishop of the AME church). Shaw University (1865) was founded in Raleigh, North Carolina, as a Baptist college, as was the venerable Morehouse College (1867) and Spelman College (1881) in Atlanta. Over ninety Black colleges were formed between 1861 and 1900, inspired by the Christian religion.[22]

The expansion of African American Christianity was not always even and harmonious, and it was often complicated by white resistance. Christianity has been used to justify exclusion and oppression, but it has also been called upon as a basis for liberty and rights. Nevertheless, the churches, associations, conferences, and denominations were the most influential institutions in overthrowing Jim Crow segregation in America. Historian Paul Harvey wrote that the civil rights movement emerged from the Black churches in the face of political and religious opposition. Harvey called the civil rights movement a "religious revolution."[23] In the civil rights movement, we have an example of how virtue serves as a guide to the moral assessment of tradition. Traditions of racial hierarchy in America were abandoned because they were immoral, whereas the older traditions of justice under law, respect for human dignity, and religious liberty were protected and extended. The good tradition of American religious liberty ensured the creation of conditions allowing for the growth of churches and religious institutions in every community. Religious liberty was one tradition among many necessary others that substantially contributed to the success of the civil rights movement in burying Jim Crow.

What about the influence of Christianity in the culture of the early republic? When Tocqueville came to the United States in 1831, one of the first features that impressed him most was what a powerful force religion exerted upon American culture. The Second Great Awakening began during the Cane Ridge Revival in Cane Ridge, Kentucky, in August 1801 and continued to have its effects in Jacksonian America decades later. Church attendance had risen from about one-tenth of free American adults in 1789 to between 30 and 40 percent by the middle of the nineteenth century.[24] Reform, as well as conversion, was one of the characteristics distinguishing the First from the Second Awakening. Abolitionism, women's suffrage, temperance, domestic and foreign missions, and the spread of education in the developing regions of the trans-Appalachian and trans-Mississippi West were some of the reforms inspired by the Second Awakening. Tocqueville was especially intrigued by the indirect influence exerted by religion on American culture evidenced in part by these reform movements.

Tocqueville described the positive influence of religion on American mores—what he defined as the Americans' "habits of the heart" and their "whole moral and intellectual state."[25] In the introduction to the first volume of *Democracy in America*, he wrote that liberty was dependent on the mores, and the mores were informed by religion.[26] Toward the end of the first volume, he returned to this theme, stating, "you cannot say that in the United States religion exercises an influence on laws or on the detail of political opinions, but it directs mores."[27]

In tying liberty to mores and mores to religion, Tocqueville argued two things about religion and American society. First, even though there were a great number of distinct Christian sects and groups in America that preached a variety of doctrines, all shared the same principles of morality. Those moral principles reigned everywhere, and were stewarded by the American women in the family and the home. Unlike in France, where citizens escaped domestic misery by engaging in politics and society, in America, citizens drew strength from moral order that prevailed in the home, and thus they carried that private moral order to public life. Second, since there was wide consensus on moral law in America, the mores restrained political passions. Americans did not pursue every political dream because moral laws formed boundaries around what was prudent and just. "These habits of restraint are found in political society," Tocqueville wrote, "and singularly favor the tranquility of the people, as well as the continued existence of the institutions that the people have given themselves."[28] For these reasons, Tocqueville was able to make one of his most famous statements concerning the influence of religion in America—"So religion, which among the Americans never directly takes part in the government of society, must be considered as the first of their political institutions; for if it does not give them the taste for liberty, it singularly facilitates their use of it."[29] Thus, religion exerted influence on American mores beginning with the preaching of the churches. Morality was then nurtured in the home by the wives and mothers, who crafted principles from a commonly held, religiously informed morality into mores. The mores were then translated into society from the order and peace of the home, resulting in political restraint. "Despotism can do without faith, but not liberty," Tocqueville wrote.[30] In a democracy where equality of conditions is the norm, religion is necessary to liberty because it reminds citizens that they are not laws unto themselves. Put simply, Tocqueville found that the consciousness of God and the recognition of human fallibility and limitations contributed to ordered liberty by restraining political passions.

Whereas Tocqueville wrote much about the positive effects of religion on American mores and its necessity to liberty, he also warned his audience about the dangers of its misuse. We must consider Tocqueville's commentary on religion's societal effects, its potentials as well as its dangers. McKenzie reminded us that if we were to stop with Tocqueville's positive assessments of how Americans saw religion, we would be doing a disservice to both Tocqueville and ourselves. "By interrupting him in the middle of his reflections we'll misrepresent him," McKenzie warned.[31]

For example, Tocqueville saw that the secret to religion's positive effects on American society—namely, how religion secures ordered liberty—was the principle of a disestablished church. In fact, Tocqueville used what in contemporary times is a loaded expression. He noted that there was general agreement among the Catholic clergy in America as to how religion and liberty existed in harmony. He said of the members of the Catholic clergy he encountered in America, "all attributed the peaceful dominion that religion exercises in their country principally to the *complete separation of Church and State*."[32]

Far from being a hindrance to the growth and stimulus to religion, church disestablishment quickened religion in American society. Before proceeding, however, we must remember to read Tocqueville's words in historical context. In 1835, when the first volume of *Democracy in America* came out, the phrase "complete separation of church and state" did not have the radically secular entailments it has today. Also, Tocqueville was not describing a *de jure* separation enforced from the top down, but a societal one that grew organically from the local communities. The American clergy Tocqueville interviewed observed a separation of church and state in terms of a separation between worldly and otherworldly concerns. While no national church existed, state establishments persisted until 1833 when Massachusetts became the last state to do away with its state church (the year after Tocqueville departed America and went home to France).

Tocqueville saw how disestablishment focused churches and synagogues on the eternal concerns, while leaving temporal concerns to the government. So, ministers could point their parishioners to God and righteous living without being distracted by the passing political fads and quarrels in Jacksonian America. Tocqueville argued that America proves the thesis that religion does not need the aid of the state but flourishes of its own power. Since religion is innate to human nature, persons will always call upon it to point them to God and the world of the hereafter. "Among all beings," Tocqueville argued, "man alone shows a natural distaste for existence and an immense desire to exist; he scorns life and fears nothingness. These different instincts constantly push his soul toward the contemplation of another world, and it is religion that leads him there."[33]

The problem is that the temptation to ally religion with politics is ever present. In any alliance of religion and politics, politics loses nothing and religion loses everything. That is, religion loses its credibility and influence in society because it becomes too closely associated with fleeting political trends of the day. What political issues seem today to be of apocalyptic importance (as in, "this is the most important election in our lifetimes") in dire need of religious arguments to add weight to pragmatic or prudential considerations tomorrow are forgotten. In the meantime, politics goes on. New issues arise. But religion pays a cost. Once religion has become overly this-worldly, distracted from its focus on God and his redemptive work to the extent that theology is downstream of political interest, it has become just another whim to be tossed aside and rejected when the moment passes. Whereas once religion transcended power politics, now religion is just another tool in political gamesmanship. Religion will still hold sway over religious people, but its authoritative voice will no longer carry in the wider culture. "By allying itself to a political power, religion increases its power over some and loses the hope of reigning over all," Tocqueville said.[34]

Consider these salient statements on how religion loses its great beneficial influence on society when it seals an alliance with politics:

> When religion contracts such an alliance, I am not afraid to say, it acts as a man could: it sacrifices the future with the present in mind, and by obtaining a power that is not its due, it puts its legitimate power at risk.[35]

> Religion cannot share the material strength of those who govern without burdening itself with a portion of the hatreds caused by those who govern.[36]

> When religion wants to rely on the interests of this world, it becomes almost as fragile as all the powers of the earth. Alone, religion can hope for immortality; tied to ephemeral powers, it follows their fortune, and often falls with the passions of the day that sustain those powers.[37]

> By uniting with different political powers, religion can only contract an onerous alliance. It does not need their help to live, and by serving them it can die.[38]

Tocqueville's warnings about the necessity of disestablishment rings true in twenty-first-century America. Christians must guard against putting so much faith in political power that they lose confidence in their first love. It is one thing to advocate for causes that matter for human flourishing, causes like the sanctity of life, the sanctity of marriage, and religious liberty using a biblical frame of reference. But when the faith becomes nothing more than a rallying cry and the Bible nothing more than a talisman to be held aloft for a national candidate in our celebrity-obsessed political culture, then it is neither interesting nor authoritative. While thinkers like Philip Hamburger[39] are right to argue that separation of church and state was never meant to banish religious discourse from the public square, disestablishment has resulted in the widest and most flourishing religious liberty experienced by any nation in modern times.

Disestablishment and religious liberty resulted, early in American history, in competition for converts and congregants among religious communities. The First Great Awakening saw the beginnings of evangelical Christianity, with its itinerant preachers, open-air preaching, and emphasis on the individual's need for a new birth in Christ. The parish system was undermined by the revivals, and religious choice wore down the well-defined grooves of church life defined by cradle-to-grave liturgical routine supported by tax revenue raised by the states and distributed to the clergy. Sociologist Rodney Stark argued that the introduction of choice into American religious life in the eighteenth century served as a spur to growth. "Competition creates energetic churches," Stark wrote, and "the lazy colonial monopolies did not survive in the United States, being replaced by a religious free market."[40]

Two and a half centuries after the founding, the positive effects of disestablishment on religious life endure. Stark compared contemporary religious life in America to European countries with established churches. He found that establishment fosters laziness among the clergy and government intrusion into church concerns, including harassment of churches on the wrong side of political favoritism. More significantly, countries with established churches are more religiously apathetic than in America, which enjoys religious liberty and an open religious marketplace. Magisterial Christian nationalists who favor state establishments should take heed. Citing a 2005–2008 survey of fifteen countries on weekly church attendance, views on the importance of God, and belief in life after death, the United States ranked first with 36 percent attending church weekly, 65 percent claiming that God was important, and 81 percent expressing belief in the afterlife. In contrast, the United Kingdom was in fourth place, with 17 percent church attendance, 27 percent affirming the importance of God, and 58 percent affirming the afterlife. In fifteenth place came Sweden, with its Evangelical Lutheran state establishment—3 percent church attendance, 11 percent affirming the importance of God, and only 46 percent surveyed believing in life after death.[41] Stark concluded in his 2012 book-length study of American religion that, compared to citizens of countries with state churches, Americans enjoyed lower crime, enjoyed better education and home life (due to private religious schools and homeschooling), boasted higher quality of mental and physical health, were more charitable in giving and volunteering, had lower unemployment, were more prone to get married and raise families, had better and more satisfying sex lives (as a result of marriage), and were less credulous regarding the paranormal.[42] All of these benefits Stark credited to the influence of disestablished religion and religious liberty on American society. While his study may now be dated, the lesson he demonstrated—that religion is of enormous and varied benefit to society—is difficult to dispute.

Religion, to be sure, is often abused to wield power over others. Religion also has the effect of dividing people, both in the present and in the past. For those who conflate accidental features of religion with its essence, these facts are evidence that religion ought to have no place in human society. For example, in his book *God Is Not Great: How Religion Poisons Everything*, notable New Atheist Christopher Hitchens set out to convince his readership that religion is necessarily destructive to human flourishing. "*Religion poisons everything,*" Hitchens wrote with emphasis three times in the book.[43] He devoted an entire eponymous chapter to the thesis that "religion kills." He pointed to recent instances where religious people and ideas caused death, destruction, and mayhem: in Belfast, Ireland; Beirut, Lebanon; Bombay (Mumbai), India; Croatia and Serbia; Bethlehem, West Bank, Palestine; finally, Baghdad, Iraq. He went on to argue that September 11 was a classic example of the evil of religion, especially in that Christian celebrity pastors like Jerry Falwell and Pat Robertson publicly stated that the attacks resulting in the deaths of nearly three thousand Americans were the result of God's judgment on Americans' corporate embrace of homosexuality. His chapter is replete with his own personal stories as well as stories ripped from the headlines describing actual events in which religions of all stripes contributed to misery, death, and all kinds of frightfulness. At one point, he wrote, "In all the cases I have mentioned, there were those who protested in the name of religion and who tried to stand athwart the rising tide of fanaticism and the cult of death. I can think of a handful of priests and bishops and rabbis and imams who have put humanity ahead of their own sect or creed. History gives us many other such examples.... But this is a compliment to humanism, not to religion.... In all these cases, anyone concerned with human safety or dignity would have to hope fervently for a mass outbreak of democratic and republican secularism."[44]

Was Hitchens wrong in saying that religion was used destructively in these cases? Was he telling the truth in the chapter in question? We have every reason to accept his narratives of the events he considered as accurate. Then isn't it true that religion kills? Any honest person must acknowledge that religion has been used as a weapon against innocent people, to kill them, enslave them, persecute them, and degrade them. Hitchens's thesis is not original, but it is lurid.

Hitchens was an intelligent man, but he failed to distinguish between that which *periodically attends* religion and that which is *necessary to* religion. Hitchens's unflattering account of religion is further weakened by the fact that he had his mind made up long before he put pen to paper. The case he made is hobbled by special pleading. He proved nothing. He only confirmed his own predetermined conclusions by appealing to evidence that supported those conclusions, while ignoring any evidence that might not suit him. It isn't hard to find examples of frightfulness resulting from religious fanaticism. Still, religion is no more inherently poisonous than is politics, history, technology, music, or any other activity or material that is the product of the human mind or imagination. If we are going to say that religion is by necessity evil and poisonous, that it logically entails murder and destruction, then what should we say about technology, for example? Airplanes firebombed Tokyo; nuked Hiroshima and Nagasaki; spread Agent Orange all over Southeast Asia; killed people on a massive scale in Europe, Asia, and the Middle East; and bring unmitigated misery on millions of (usually) reasonable people who have to resort to them for long-distance travel during holidays. *Airplanes poison everything*. What about politics? Do not political ideas inspire violence through wars of conquest, revolution, and rebellion? Does not politics inherently divide people? Isn't every Thanksgiving dinner around the country ruined year after year by that crazy uncle who constantly stirs up trouble over politics on Facebook? *Politics poisons everything*. We could go on. If religion is inherently divisive and poisonous, then so is politics and technology. Of course, this is absurd. Politics and technology have resulted in death, destruction, and mayhem, as has religion. These have also blessed humanity, and we intuitively regard their demerits to be mitigated by their benefits. For that reason, we should not reckon religion, politics, or technology as necessarily awful just because we can readily find examples of how they have been abused and misused.

It is truer to say that *sin poisons everything*. Human sin is at the root of moral evil, not religion. To understand and combat human sin, we need religion. Christianity, for example, explains human sin and provides a direct Way that defeats both sin and death. While progressives tend to seek correction of injustice by addressing external realities such as economic "inequity" and societal structures, conservatives do so by addressing the source of moral evil, sin, which is internal to the person. Religion plays an indispensable role in that effort.

Tocqueville was right when he said that "religion is only a particular form of hope, and it is as natural to the human heart as hope itself."[45] A religious consciousness is basic to human nature. The Benedictine monk Anselm of Canterbury (1033/1034–1109) reasoned in his work *Proslogion* that it is possible to demonstrate the existence of God through *a priori* existential means. That is, Anselm believed one could argue for the *existence* of a being, in his case God, using *definitions* rather than evidence or prior experience. When Anselm wrote out his argument, he did so in the form of a prayer and reflection on Psalm 14:1, "The fool has said in his heart, 'there is no God.'" Philosopher of religion Stephen T. Davis syllogized Anselm's prayer:

1. Things can exist in only two ways—in the mind and in reality.
2. The GCB [Greatest Conceivable Being, or God] can possibly exist in reality, that is, is not an impossible thing.
3. The GCB exists in the mind.
4. Whatever exists only in the mind and might possibly exist in reality might possibly be greater than it is.
5. The GCB exists only in the mind.
6. The GCB might be greater than it is.
7. The GCB is a being than which a greater is conceivable.
8. It is false that the GCB exists only in the mind.
9. The GCB exists both in the mind and in reality.[46]

Anselm's argument is elegant and enduring. In sum, the argument starts with the given claim that anything that exists has being in reality and in the mind. Existence can have no other iteration except in one or both realms. It follows that God, as the greatest being that can be conceived, is a logically coherent concept (unlike, say, a married bachelor) and thus could be real. The idea of God thus clearly appears to the human mind. If God exists in the mind and possibly in reality, then God would be greater if he existed in reality. In other words, if he only existed in the mind, and not in reality, then he would not be as great as he could be if he were real. In premise five,

Anselm presented the possibility that God is not real, thus employing a *reductio ad absurdum* argument and setting the premise up for negation. Proceeding on, Anselm offered another possibility, this time that God could be a greater being if he existed in reality and not just in the mind. With premise seven, we have our opportunity to negate the contradicting premise five. In other words, if the GCB exists only in the mind, and existing in reality would make it a greater being than merely existing as a figment of the imagination, then it is right to say that the GCB must be real if he is the *greatest* conceivable being. Thus, negating premise five, it is false that the GCB exists only in the mind, because his greatness is diminished if he is not real. The conclusion is that God, the Greatest Conceivable Being, must exist in the mind and in reality.

Anselm wrote his argument in *Proslogion* in the year 1078. For over nine hundred years, Anselm's argument has enjoyed its proponents and endured its opponents. The most famous proponent was probably French mathematician and philosopher René Descartes (1596–1650), and Anselm's most noteworthy opponent would have to be the Prussian Immanuel Kant (1724–1804). More recently, philosophical luminaries such as Karl Barth, Bertrand Russell, Charles Hartshorne, and Alvin Plantinga have engaged the argument either to refute it as fallacious or accept it through explanation and restatement. The point of bringing up Anselm's argument is to concretely illustrate the idea that a consciousness of God is natural to humanity. Whether one accepts Anselm's position, that it is possible to deductively demonstrate the existence of God from the level of *in intellectu* to *in re*, or one dismisses the argument as circular reasoning is irrelevant. The fact that it has taxed some of the greatest minds in human history over the remarkable span of almost a millennium tells us more than that God is merely of passing interest to persons or is just a useful means to an end. If ideas about God and religion were not inherent to human nature, then why has Anselm's argument persisted as a subject of sharp and lively philosophical debate for almost half of the Christian era? At the base minimum, Anselm's argument shows that even the harshest detractor must admit: persons for century after century—even skeptics—have been unable to escape or overcome the thought of God, much less build a lasting civilization without a means of acknowledging and understanding him and his ways.

Religious consciousness is basic to the human condition. Religion is necessary to liberty because it separates libertinism from liberty. God exists, he is the Creator of the universe, and we are his creatures. He made us to seek after him. Augustine was right when he began *Confessions* with the words, "You stir us so that praising you may bring us joy, because you have made us and drawn us to yourself, and our heart is unquiet until it rests in you."[47] Religion is not uniquely divisive, nor is it inherently poisonous. Religion, as the means of drawing near to the divine, is subject to both human dignity and fallibility, just as every other human intellectual, material, and spiritual pursuit.

The Old Testament book of Ecclesiastes offers insight into how a religious consciousness is native to human nature. Moreover, it exhibits an exquisitely conservative view of the nature of God, the human condition, and the basis from which to live the good life with the living God at the center of one's frame of reference. Consider some passages as examples.

> "Vanity of vanities," says the Preacher,
> "Vanity of vanities! All is vanity."
> What advantage does man have in all his work
> Which he does under the sun?
> A generation goes and a generation comes,
> But the earth remains forever.
> Also, the sun rises and the sun sets;
> And hastening to its place it rises there again.
> Blowing toward the south,
> Then turning toward the north,
> The wind continues swirling along;
> And on its circular courses the wind returns.

All the rivers flow into the sea,
Yet the sea is not full.
To the place where the rivers flow,
There they flow again.
All things are wearisome;
Man is not able to tell it.
The eye is not satisfied with seeing,
Nor is the ear filled with hearing.
That which has been is that which will be,
And that which has been done is that which will be done.
So there is nothing new under the sun.
Is there anything of which one might say,
"See this, it is new"?
Already it has existed for ages
Which were before us.
There is no remembrance of earlier things;
And also of the later things which will occur,
There will be for them no remembrance
Among those who will come later still.[48]

The author of Ecclesiastes, identifying himself in 1:1 as "the son of David, king in Jerusalem," is Solomon, the wisest man of the Old Testament. What has Solomon the Preacher told us in these lines? He identified the common belief that "we have it within our power to begin the world over again," as Thomas Paine said in an appendix to *Common Sense* while reflecting on the potentials of American independence.[49] Not only did the Preacher identify this belief, he showed it to be totally false. Later in chapter 1, the Preacher presented his credentials as being one who "set [his] mind to seek and explore by wisdom concerning all that has been done under heaven"[50] and that he had "magnified and increased wisdom more than all who were over Jerusalem before [him]."[51] Thus, he knew something of which he spoke.

The Preacher wrote that all is "vanity." The Hebrew word for vanity is *hebel* and literally means "breath" or "breeze" according to Old Testament scholar David Gibson.[52] Solomon did not mean that everything is worthless, or meaningless. Rather, everything is a mere breath, and like a breath, everything passes away. As soon as you perceive a thing, it is gone. Life, possessions, relationships, careers, reputations, ideas—everything is fleeting, like a breath. Furthermore, everything is "under the sun," thus, everything that we are and all that concerns us is part of this temporal reality, and is subject to limitation, decay, and death. Gibson wrote that this passage underscores the realities that life is short, elusive, and repetitive. As we grasp these realities, we are faced with our own limitations and inevitable death. When we make peace with the reality of death, we find that we may truly learn to live. "The seasons and the natural cycles of the world are content to come and go, but we sweat and toil to make believe that it will not be so with us," Gibson explained.[53] In our hubris, we believe we can set the conditions for our happiness, that past is prologue, that all that matters is the present, and that the future is ours to shape if only our will and heart are strong enough. Ecclesiastes shuts such illusions down as a book of realism. Change is constant, the future is not ours to know or shape, life is unpredictable and fleeting, and we will all die and be forgotten. That is our unavoidable reality. Denying reality will not change it.

Still, the reality of change and death is not cause for despair. To affirm despair would be to adopt a nihilistic approach to life. Consider this passage:

> This is an evil in all that is done under the sun, that there is one fate for all men. Furthermore, the hearts of the sons of men are full of evil and insanity is in their hearts throughout their lives. Afterwards they go to the dead. For whoever is joined with all the living, there is hope; surely a live dog is better than a dead lion. For the living know they will die; but the dead do not know anything,

nor have they any longer a reward, for their memory is forgotten. Indeed their love, their hate and their zeal have already perished, and they will no longer have a share in all that is done under the sun. Go then, eat your bread in happiness and drink your wine with a cheerful heart; for God has already approved your works. Let your clothes be white all the time, and let not oil be lacking on your head. Enjoy life with the woman whom you love all the days of your fleeting life which He has given to you under the sun; for this is your reward in life and in your toil in which you have labored under the sun.[54]

Here we have a contrast between life and death, but in this passage life and death are not equated with blessing and cursing. As ancient Near East scholar C. L. Seow observed, the difference between life and death here is the difference between what is possible and what is impossible.[55] The dead have no choices to make, no forgiveness to ask, no praise to receive, no endeavor to attempt, and no reward to enjoy. They had their chance, and only the living possess any knowledge of anything. The living know that one day they will be as the dead. So, as Seow wrote, "the only appropriate response to the certainty of death is to enjoy life while one is able to do so."[56] Even with such a response, there is the remaining reality that we only have a limited number of days of life allotted to us, so how can we enjoy life in peace, knowing that one day we also will die?

Finally, consider this passage from the end of Ecclesiastes:

The Preacher sought to find delightful words and to write words of truth correctly. The words of wise men are like goads, and masters of these collections are like well-driven nails; they are given by one Shepherd. But beyond this, my son, be warned: the writing of many books is endless, and excessive devotion to books is wearying to the body. The conclusion, when all has been heard, is: fear God and keep His commandments, because this applies to every person. For God will bring every act to judgment, everything which is hidden, whether it is good or evil.[57]

Here, the Shepherd is God himself, and all wisdom has its source in him. To be wise takes long effort and devoted investment of time and resources, so Solomon gives the warning here to study wisdom, knowing the cost. There are no shortcuts to wisdom. When all wisdom has been discovered, understood, taught, and applied, all of life is summed up in one thing: to fear God and obey his commandments. The commandments constitute the wisdom given by the Shepherd. Here, we discover a link between the Old and New Testaments. Christ refers to himself as "the Good Shepherd" in John 10:11, and he admonishes his disciples that those who love him keep his commandments.[58] The beginning of wisdom is the fear of the Lord,[59] so if we want wisdom, we start by revering God and submitting our lives under his authority. We come to know him and his will in revealed Scripture, and we submit ourselves to the authority of Scripture rather than subjecting the Scripture to our own imagined authority. We demonstrate wisdom as we consider our rightful place before our Creator, and that we will be judged after death. As Ecclesiastes commentator Daniel Fredericks wrote, "No definitive statement about divine judgment could ever be made without reference to inspired moral standards."[60] As we contemplate the day of our future judgment, we remember that fear of God requires that we place him at the center of our intellectual, moral, familial, recreational, and civic existence as persons. Fredericks's reminder is apt: "God's very glory and honour, his perfect expectations and perfect love, require that the fullest extent of our sin be realized by all in order to appreciate but a fraction of his grace."[61]

The book of Ecclesiastes is often neglected. Ecclesiastes reminds the living to aspire to that which is greater than themselves. We aspire to a Person and a world that transcends human comprehension, and even if we die in obscurity and are forgotten, our lives will be infinitely dignified by the God who graciously gave himself for us in Christ's atoning sacrifice. Will there be those who will abuse God's name and God's word? Of course. In fearing God and obeying his commandments, we find that while we are in this world, we are called to enjoy it and contribute to its flourishing. We remember that this world and its pleasures are like a vapor, and that a better country awaits us if we put our confidence and trust in the One who rules over all.

CONCLUSION

The Will to Conserve the Harmony of America's Two Spirits

The nations of today cannot make conditions among them not
be equal; but it depends on them whether equality leads them to
servitude or liberty, to enlightenment or barbarism, to prosperity
or misery.

—Alexis de Tocqueville, *Democracy in America*

T he months from May to December 1831 were a whirlwind of
activity for the two young French commissioners traveling
around the northern United States in their official capacity study-
ing American prisons.[1] By December, Gustave de Beaumont and
Alexis de Tocqueville had traveled throughout New England and
New York, had ventured through the Michigan wilderness, and
had explored French Canada. They met American luminaries of the
early republican period. They interviewed Jared Sparks about New
England townships. Tocqueville regarded Sparks as the preeminent
authority on American political institutions. They dined with John
Quincy Adams, the sixth president of the United States, who was
serving as a member of Congress in 1831. Tocqueville conversed
with Adams in French about voluntary associations and Southern

slavery. They encountered the titanic personality of Daniel Webster but were strangely underwhelmed. Webster was a great orator and champion of the Union, but when it came to discussions of prison reform, Tocqueville found him entirely uninterested.[2] Writing to his brother Achille in late September, Beaumont described his and Tocqueville's lives as "a rolling fire of engagements."[3] Tocqueville wrote to his mother that October that "our life consists of prisons, learned societies, and soirées."[4] Life also consisted of mortal danger. Beaumont and Tocqueville could have died during their voyage to Cincinnati in the Ohio River near Wheeling, Virginia (now West Virginia), when their steamship, the *Fourth of July*, struck a rock and nearly sank.[5]

When the pair arrived in Cincinnati on December 1, they had much more on their minds than sinking ships, prisons, and soirées. A few days after arriving in the bustling town, which a mere fifty years earlier was not much more than a wilderness, Tocqueville grew reflective. He wrote to his brother Hippolyte about his fears that revolution may be brewing in England after the passage of the Reform bill (which became the Great Reform Act of 1832). These fears of potential unrest of England reminded him of the troubles in his native France, which seemed to be continually on the brink of revolution. "Are we moving toward freedom?" Tocqueville asked. "Or are we marching toward despotism? God only knows."[6]

France had not known enduring security and liberty rooted in equality and fraternity since the storming of the Bastille in 1789. Tocqueville sorely wanted to know what lessons Americans could teach the French about how to secure liberty in a society dominated by equality of conditions, which tended toward individualism, selfishness, materialism, and tyranny of the majority. Liberty was elusive and fragile, but the Americans seemed to have found a way to fortify and extend it, especially in the towns of New England. Tocqueville expressed surprise that two distinct and oft-warring spirits, "the spirit of religion and the spirit of liberty," were in harmony in America.[7] Tocqueville wrote that these two spirits "have been successfully blended, in a way, and marvelously combined"[8] to the extent that "they reigned together on the same soil."[9] Throughout both volumes of *Democracy in America*, Tocqueville shed light on what harmonized the spirit of religion and the spirit of liberty. The mediating influence of public spirit, that is, the voluntary balancing of public and private interests, was essential to the harmony Tocqueville saw between religion and liberty in the townships of the northern American states. Public spirit and religion were distinct but complementary forces in America shaping the mores and mitigating the effects of tyranny by giving citizens a deep loyalty to their communities that could only be fostered by a sense of civic ownership manifested in thoroughgoing voluntarism. Public spirit can thus be understood as local patriotism.

In two volumes of *Democracy in America*, Tocqueville foresaw and warned his audience of several risks attending the rise and irresistible spread of equality of conditions in human societies. For our purposes, we will consider three specific warnings Tocqueville offered, and his argument that religion was necessary to prevent tyranny and preserve liberty in a democratic arrangement.

First, Tocqueville was concerned about the risk of majoritarian tyranny in a democracy. Democracies are predicated upon the fundamental principle that power arises from the bottom up, not from the top down. The sovereign power of a democratic nation is held, not by the head of state, the legislative assembly, or the court system, but by the people themselves. The fact that sovereignty rests with the people means that the people have the liberty to make whatever laws they want, provided those laws represent the attitudes and preferences of the majority. Tocqueville was struck by the fact that one need not refer to the abstract principle of popular sovereignty to grasp its significance. One need only to look to the concrete example America set. "If there is a single country in the world where the true value of the dogma of the sovereignty of the people can hope to be appreciated . . . that country is assuredly America," Tocqueville wrote.[10] In democratic America, rule by majority was the standard because sovereignty rested with the people, but how easy it could be for majorities to use their power to tyrannize minorities. Tocqueville observed, "once the majority has formed on a question, there is, so to speak, no obstacle that can, I will not say stop, but even slow its course and leave time for the majority to hear the cries of those whom it crushes as it goes."[11] In other words, once an issue has been decided by the majority, the minority position is ground to powder. A salient example of this reality in contemporary times is the issue of same-sex marriage. This issue was debated in communities all over America for many years, and people on both sides of the issue spoke their peace freely. But when *Obergefell v. Hodges* was handed down in 2015, all debate ceased. If you continued to hold to traditional marriage between one man and one woman, your minority view no longer had any credibility in public discourse.

A second risk to liberty that Tocqueville observed was that of democratic peoples' innate preference for equality over liberty. Americans viewed equality as an ideal for which to strive in democracies, but Tocqueville stressed that equality of conditions tended toward tyranny more so than it tended toward liberty. The lack of a hereditary aristocracy meant that citizens in an equal society could pursue well-being and pleasure in the same ways, but Tocqueville observed that political power could still be reserved to a select few. A despot could be the equal of his fellow citizens, except in that he possessed consolidated political power and his fellow citizens did not. Furthermore, equality yielded short-term gains measured in material possessions and pleasures, but liberty was attained through sacrifices over long periods of time. Taste for equality was more suited to human nature than that for liberty because its benefits inspired short-term gains motivated by passion, whereas the benefits that citizens enjoyed from liberty were hard won and might not be realized for generations. Tocqueville observed that democratic people impatiently "want equality in liberty, and if they cannot obtain that, they still want equality in slavery. They will suffer poverty, enslavement, barbarism, but they will not suffer aristocracy."[12]

A third danger to democratic societies was a form of despotism that Tocqueville feared was uniquely pernicious when equality of conditions prevailed. This kind of despotism, Tocqueville believed, "will resemble nothing that has preceded it in the world; our contemporaries cannot find the image of it in their memories."[13] Tocqueville could not find the right word for such despotism, so he described its characteristics and effects. This despotism started with equality in which everyone indulged in the "small and vulgar pleasures with which they fill their souls."[14] People possessed their material wealth and their creature comforts, those things that filled their time and captured their attention. Such people cut themselves off from civic life and surrounded themselves with their immediate family and friends. In so doing, they become isolated from their neighbors and other members of their communities, resulting in losing their ability to empathize with others with different backgrounds and beliefs. People such as this lived for themselves, and they had no mind for the well-being of their fellow citizens because they paid them no attention. When people's immediate needs and wants could be satisfied with material pleasures, and when citizens no longer conducted themselves out of concern for the common good, then "there arises an immense and tutelary power that alone takes charge of assuring their enjoyment and of looking after their fate."[15] Such a despotic power would rule over citizens like children, taking care to provide for their whims as long as they ceased from thinking for themselves, from acting on their free will, and from taking responsibility for their own well-being. Citizens become content with entrusting themselves to governmental guardianship. Political power would become supreme in the hands of such a benevolent tyrant, one that relieved citizens of "the trouble to think and the difficulty of living."[16] Equality of conditions, Tocqueville wrote, prepared people for such a fate. This is what he meant when he argued that democratic people would more readily give up liberty than equality. Equality's promise was cheap. Liberty's benefits just cost too much. The America of today seems to have become what Tocqueville feared. Dominated by a secular majority obsessed with "equity," mesmerized by technological marvels and creature comforts, and governed by an overpowering nanny state, the America of the twenty-first century has taken the path of Tocqueville's democratic despotism.

How to preserve liberty when equality of conditions sets the stage for a distinctive kind of despotism tailored for democracy? Tocqueville argued that religion was necessary for the lessening of the threat of despotism and the preservation of liberty. Christianity was the dominant religion in 1831 America, and Christianity was also best suited for liberty in a democracy. Comparing Christianity to Islam, Tocqueville remarked that the Qur'an was a political document as much as a religious one. But the religion of Jesus was focused primarily on the person's relation to God and to others.[17] Historian Norman Graebner noted that "it was this quality in Christianity . . . that permitted it to exist in a cultivated, democratic civilization."[18]

Tocqueville's famous "point of departure" for *Democracy in America* was the Pilgrim and Puritan founding of New England, and the singular form of Christianity these colonial founders brought with them to American shores.[19] He described this brand of Christianity as "democratic and republican" and "in accord" with politics from the moment of colonial inception to the moment of Tocqueville's writing.[20] While there was no federally established religion in America, Tocqueville argued that religion was indispensable to American political and social life. Tocqueville's assertion that religion was "the first of their political institutions"[21] meant that it was essential to liberty. Ordered liberty was not possible without a consensus on morality, and morality was informed by religion. Because of this, Tocqueville could say, "if [religion] does not give them the taste for liberty, it singularly facilitates their use of it."[22] Americans so closely regarded religion's necessity to liberty that they often conflated the two. Furthermore, Tocqueville was astonished to find that disestablished religion's power was so great that Americans saw the need to preserve religion as a bulwark for republican institutions in the settled eastern states for the sake of the emerging American civilization in the western states and territories where those institutions were fragile. Americans thus perceived a duty to protect the rights and freedoms of others to protect their own, and protecting freedom meant protecting religion.[23]

Religion served as democracy's greatest advantage, according to Tocqueville. While equality was good for society, it encouraged humanity's base instincts of selfishness, isolation, and materialism. Every religion, especially Christianity, pointed people beyond their immediate fortunes and cast their attention on things that transcended mere creature comforts, like the immortality of the soul. Religion also imposed responsibilities along with privileges, so that people looked to the flourishing of others as well as themselves. Democratic societies, dictated by equality of conditions, encouraged individuals to be obsessed with self, but religion mitigated those selfish, materialistic tendencies by balancing rights with duties. "So religious peoples are naturally strong precisely in the places where democratic peoples are weak," Tocqueville wrote. "This makes very clear how important it is for men to keep their religion while becoming equal."[24]

Tocqueville also thought religion was necessary to human liberty because he saw religion springing from human nature. Since religion was innate to human nature, and religion concerned itself with the eternal, religious belief was prior to government's mere temporal claim on human obedience. Every human action was rooted in the human conception of God, of their place in human society, and of their duties to their fellows.[25] Corresponding to this, while persons pursued their own interests, religion guided the pursuit of those interests, especially in America. One of the great ironies Tocqueville saw among Americans was that they were not particularly virtuous, but they were willing to do virtuous things in order to gain something of benefit to themselves.[26] Americans, Tocqueville wrote, "show with satisfaction how enlightened love of themselves leads them constantly to help each other and disposes them willingly to sacrifice for the good of the State a portion of their time and their wealth."[27] For Tocqueville, human action was informed by religion along with the pursuit of *l'interêt bien entendu*, or self-interest well understood—"you find it no less in the mouths of the poor than in that of the rich."²⁸ Both religion and self-interest were basic to human nature.

While religion had its source in human nature, in America it had further strength in the constitutional division between the sacred and the secular, or as we have already seen, what Tocqueville referred to as "the complete separation of church and state."²⁹ Tocqueville saw that everyone in America, clergy included, agreed on the necessity of this separation in order that religion might maintain its social force. In France, religious and political concerns were so closely joined as to make it difficult to know where one began and the other ended. The effect was that religion devolved into just another political faction with a short life span. In America, religion transcended political squabbling. Clergymen focused their attention on "the consolation of all miseries" and the "contemplation of another world."³⁰ The effect of this dynamic was that believers and unbelievers alike recognized the power of religion and its role in preserving freedom. Because religion was natural to human nature, any kind of artificial support lent to it by the state would render it impotent.

Importantly then, for Tocqueville, religion was simultaneously a product and creator of free institutions and behaviors in America. Specifically, religion was reflected in Americans' public spirit—that patriotism in which public and private interest were merged through active citizenship on the local level.³¹ Religion also created a diverse array of voluntary associations like hospitals, schools, colleges, and reform societies. Tocqueville could find no voluntary associations in England or France. Associations were uniquely American because they were voluntary, not imposed by the government or by the aristocracy. They arose out of Americans' awareness of the necessity of self-reliance rather than reliance on distant authorities to solve practical problems. Americans formed associations "for purposes of public security, commerce and industry, morality and religion."³² Additionally, the doctrine of self-interest well understood meant that every American understood how and when to make small sacrifices for the good of the whole. Voluntary associations and self-interest rightly understood made for an ordered and self-controlled society.[33] Order was a virtue learned first in the home where religion fundamentally informed the mores, the basic intellectual and moral character of the people, and the mores the laws.[34]

As both a product and inspiration of free institutions and behaviors, religion was indispensable to liberty in democratic America. But religion by itself could not preserve liberty if isolated from public spirit. Without public spirit, religion could be used against liberty. Conversely, liberty could be used against religion especially if religion was enlisted in the aid of a particular political faction.[35] Religion could also be used by greedy entrepreneurs for financial gain, in James Schleifer's words, as "simply another business within a wider commercial society."[36] Moreover, Tocqueville feared that Catholic Christians were prone to deny religious liberty to non-Catholics. Tocqueville worried that if Catholics ever became the majority in America, they would persecute Protestants.[37] And if Christians overlooked the present in favor of the afterlife, religion would become too individualistic, too otherworldly, and too moralistic for any public benefit.[38] Public spirit, however, directed both religion and liberty to their best ends. Because public spirit was focused on a voluntary balancing of private and public goods, of rights with responsibilities, of individual privileges and duties to others, it directed religion away from despotic, individualistic, or base tendencies and toward the ideals of right fellowship with God and with others. Public spirit also directed liberty away from license and toward self-restraint. Harvey Mansfield summarized Tocqueville's meaning: "a people, like an individual person, makes itself more powerful with self-restraint, not less."[39]

Specifically, Tocqueville observed public spirit facilitating harmony between the spirits of religion and liberty through Puritan covenantalism, which produced what Barbara Allen called a "federal matrix";[40] through voluntary associations; through self-interest well understood; by separating church and state; and by establishing conditions for both sincere religious belief and a common acknowledgment among citizens that religion be publicly useful.

First, let us consider the role of Puritan covenantalism. Tocqueville was so struck by the influence of Puritan thought on American culture that he believed that the Puritan stress on self-government was normative throughout America. He wrote, "it seems to me that I see the whole destiny of America contained in the first Puritan who landed on its shores, like the whole human race in the first man."[41] Tocqueville thought that self-government was the most important Puritan contribution to American culture, and the Puritans saw self-government as a covenantal arrangement among citizens with God. Practically, Puritan political theology knitted together a network of covenants into what Allen called a "matrix of church, civil, and personal covenants," and later, a "federal matrix comprised of citizens and their governmental and voluntary associations."[42] Allen traced the origins of this federal matrix to the political theology expressed by Johannes Althusius (1557–1638) and William Ames (1576–1633), noting their stress on covenantal society as consisting of a network of associations—an "association of associations."[43] Such a society depended on give and take between individuals and the community, a mutual commitment that resulted in the common good through consent of the governed, self-restraint, and balancing the interests of private citizens with the interests of the whole.[44] When Tocqueville visited America in 1831–1832, he found that "early exponents of federalism such as Althusius and Ames expressed the germ of later associational forms."[45] The Puritan covenantalism established in the early seventeenth century had yielded the habit of self-government in the New England townships, a habit reinforced by the naturally occurring associating together of citizens to solve everyday problems and meet common needs.

Tocqueville found that much had changed by the nineteenth century, but the habit of self-government had matured, not deteriorated, by the time of his visit. Allen observed that Tocqueville was impressed with how the townships "laid the foundation for American federalism" by establishing balance between private and public interest through "equity volition, and the principle of federal or civil liberty."[46] Sanford Kessler noted that American scholars such as Andrew C. McLaughlin, Edmund S. Morgan, Daniel J. Elazar, Donald S. Lutz, and Robert N. Bellah supported Tocqueville's overall contention that Puritan covenantalism laid the basis for American federalism, limited government, and society informed by moral/religious underpinnings essential to ordered liberty.[47]

Puritan covenantalism formed the intellectual and practical basis for self-government, and by extension, voluntary associations. The townships' independence, which impressed Tocqueville, meant that citizens possessed power to direct their own destiny without reliance on distant or higher jurisdictions like county, state, or federal government. Citizens of different backgrounds came together and worked for a common goal, which meant that they avoided isolation, built common ground, and exercised power to effect solutions and change in pursuit of political or civil goals. Dana Villa expressed the power of associations as Tocqueville observed them: "they create ... an experience and expectation of citizenship *directly opposed* to that fostered by a centralized, administrative state."[48] Associations accomplished what neither individual effort nor state action could accomplish alone— the balancing of rights against duties, and of public and private interests as individuals saw their own flourishing as being dependent on the flourishing of the whole. They represented what Villa called "the definitive triumph of society—not only over a self-centered individualism, but over the state and *le monde politique* as well."[49]

Allen noted another important factor relevant to the role of associations in promoting harmony between religion and liberty. By associating together for political and civic goals, citizens were introduced and reintroduced to American founding ideals through practical experience. Allen said, "Opportunities for making constitutional and collective choices not only renewed an individual's attachment to founding ideas but also tested those ideas, permitting reflection and change as well as renewal."[50] The moral value of sacrificing individual desires for the good of the community, of putting aside differences for the sake of solving a common problem, and the good inherent in taking responsibility for one's own destiny through the exercise of power responsibly—these were learned by citizens by associating together. These values were consistent with Christian morality, and they helped form the mores on which society was based—what Allen described as "a public philosophy developed through common action and the beliefs these experiences inspired."[51]

Tocqueville found that citizens formed associations to advance a balanced set of individual and corporate interests. They exercised a right—that of association—to fulfill the duty of advancing the common good. They did not associate together primarily because they were virtuous. They found they had something to gain individually when the good of the community was served. This is, in short, Tocqueville's doctrine of self-interest well understood. Catherine Zuckert contrasted Tocqueville's understanding of self-interest with that of French political thinkers Montesquieu and Rousseau. Montesquieu thought republics had to be made up of virtuous citizens, trained by the state, who sacrificed their individual interests for the sake of virtue. Rousseau thought that Christianity distracted citizens from their temporal duties and made them obsessed with the afterlife, resulting in the neglect of state interests. Rousseau called for a new state-approved civil religion that would render the church the servant of the state. Unlike Montesquieu, Tocqueville argued that virtue is important but not primary in preserving liberty; and unlike Montesquieu and Rousseau, Tocqueville believed that religion sprang from human nature and could not be enforced by the state without dire consequences for religion and freedom.[52] Religion, whether civil or revealed, could not be the source of balancing private and public interest in America. "Calculations of self-interest prove to be the immediate and primary cause of individual self-restraint in America," according to Zuckert.[53] Religion's role in striking that balance mitigates materialism and selfishness, rather than through "moral suasion."[54] Religion also provided a set of moral standards

Americans commonly accepted, and this consensus informed an agreed standard for that in which the common good consisted.[55] Self-interest well understood was thus chastened by religion, and it encouraged flourishing of one and all in a community. Religion exerted an indirect, natural influence on self-interest, rather than an artificial influence through an established church.

Allowing religion to grow and take hold of society as a product of human nature rather than the active sponsorship of the state was essential to the harmony between religion and politics in America, as Tocqueville observed it. When states provide artificial support for religion, both the state and religion suffer—the religious wars of the seventeenth century demonstrated this dynamic plainly. Aristide Tessitore wrote that "America reveals in an unprecedented way that the natural horizon for religion is not politics but the family" and that the source of religion was in human nature itself.[56] Harvey Mansfield noted Tocqueville's assertion that religion naturally limits liberty, and not in a deleterious way. Religion prevents liberty from devolving into license by defining it in terms of justice; that is, liberty concerns itself with the good of the individual and the good of the community.[57] Mansfield noted that "the task of politics . . . is to cooperate with religion and to guide our lives so that our virtue is rewarded and our freedom preserved."[58] If church and state do not remain separated, Tocqueville foresaw the dissolution of religion and an open door to tyranny.

The separation of church from state was necessary for the preservation of liberty for Tocqueville. What effect did that separation have on citizens' actual faith in the dogmas of religion? Did it matter if citizens sincerely believed in those dogmas, or would it suffice merely to accept religion as a force for public good? Ralph C. Hancock argued that Tocqueville did not allow for such a bifurcation. He did argue that Tocqueville "clearly subordinates the question of the truth of Christianity to that of its political utility"[59] but that he did so from the perspective of a religious neutral, so to speak, looking in from the outside. From such a perspective, Tocqueville accepted both the necessity of sincere religious belief *and* a serious acknowledgment of religion's public utility in a democracy formed by a particular set of mores.

Sincere belief introduced spiritual and intellectual convictions that undergirded citizens' duties to God and to others. As Oliver Hidalgo wrote, "without religious convictions, the citizens are . . . not able to recognize that there are more important things than leading a life of pleasure."[60] The society's mores, informed as they were by religion, had to be passed down from one generation to the next. For that to happen, the older generation must have been inwardly persuaded of the truth of what they were teaching their children. It is true that Tocqueville acknowledged the existence of many competing sects within Christianity, but Christian morals were everywhere accepted. Pierre Manent wrote that, when it comes to religion's power to regulate society through mores, "it is necessary to see further than [religion's] utility."[61] Still, for religion to have public utility, citizens have to actually believe that its teachings are true. Manent, reading Tocqueville, concluded that "for religion to have its proper force, it is necessary for men to be devoted to it for itself and not for social utility or by love of the political institutions to which it can be fused. . . . The religion of the Americans loses its utility proportional to the attachment to it for reasons of utility."[62] For Tocqueville, both sincerity of belief in religious dogma and the public usefulness of that religion went together if a society of individuals was to put public spirit into practice to harmonize religion with liberty.

When Tocqueville observed the New England townships, he was struck by their independence and their power. They were independent from county and state government action, and able to act without reference to other jurisdictions. While no one citizen possessed much power, when citizens associated together in the pursuit of a common goal, they found that their collected power was sufficient to meet any problem. Tocqueville said, "The inhabitant of New England is attached to his township not so much because he was born there as because he sees in that township a free and strong corporation that he is a part of and that is worth his trouble to seek to direct."[63] This was the essence of public spirit—the township's ability to balance individual rights with duties toward others, and private interests with the interests of the whole. Public spiritedness served as the impetus behind citizens' forming political and civil associations. It also served to reveal the benefits of self-interest well understood, benefits for both the individual and the community.

Tocqueville argued that religion was necessary to liberty in a society dominated by equality of conditions, like American and French societies were. Religion would have an indirect influence on American society because it expanded organically rather than through state sponsorship. Americans felt this influence in the production of mores, the mitigation of selfishness, the teaching of duties, and the care of the soul through fellowship with God and with others. Tocqueville understood that public spirit and religion were distinct, but they had similar features. Neither religion nor public spirit needed artificial support from the state to flourish. Both public spirit and religion required sincerity on the part of citizens for their public force to be felt. Both public spirit and religion were integral to human nature, and their edifying influence on society to preserve liberty was organic, growing from the bottom up, not from top to bottom.

In France, Tocqueville saw that the spirit of religion and the spirit of liberty were at odds with one another. Americans, however, had harmonized them. Tocqueville saw that through the symbiotic interaction between public spirit and religion in citizens' exercise of rights and fulfilling of duties, Americans maintained liberty. We have wisdom to gain from Tocqueville's observations of how public spirit mediated between religion and liberty in the early nineteenth century. We should resist the urge to look back on 1831 America with overweening nostalgia, but we also should resist the tendency to ignore our history and expel religion to the outermost corners of society, rendering it null and void. Religious people today should heed Tocqueville's warnings about mixing religion with political agendas, rendering it as nothing more than another political faction. While much has changed since the nineteenth century, much of what Tocqueville offered us in his masterful *Democracy in America* serves to give admonition and encouragement about the prospects for maintaining liberty in a democratic age.

The aspirational conservative disposition seeks to preserve and extend the best of the American tradition because that tradition is an inheritance passed down to us from our ancestors who strove and sacrificed to secure it for us. The tradition of religious liberty is part of the American tradition. America is not perfect, and Americans have not applied religious liberty flawlessly and consistently according to the ideals of the founding documents. Similarly, conservatives are not always faithful to their own traditions, nor do they perfectly balance public and private interests, or social obligations with their attending privileges. There are no "true" conservatives in this sense, just as there is no such thing as "true" Americans. We are all on the path toward improvement, striving for the attainment of ideals, but recognizing that we have miles to go before we arrive at the ideal.

Take the example of the American founders. There were fifty-five delegates to the Philadelphia convention that drafted the Constitution in the summer of 1787. Twenty-five of those delegates were slave-owners. Thomas Jefferson, who was in France during that summer, penned the immortal words of the Declaration of Independence, "we hold these truths to be self-evident that all men are created equal, that they are endowed by their Creator with certain unalienable rights, that among these are life, liberty, and the pursuit of happiness." Jefferson owned hundreds of slaves over the course of his lifetime at his Virginia plantations of Monticello and Poplar Forest. It is fashionable today to call the founders "hypocrites" because many of them owned slaves all the while endorsing Jefferson's ideals in the Declaration. Such people who resort to one-dimensional judgments of the founders are unable to hold two historical realities in tension with one another. They also seem not to have the capacity to grasp the concept of aspiration. To aspire to an ideal, one first understands that he has not arrived, but has a path to follow. He is willing to take that path and stay on that path no matter how difficult the way may be, because the upward path he is on is the path of improvement, and thus it offers its own reward. Americans have historically exhibited perseverance on the path to improvement, albeit by fits and starts.

Abraham Lincoln gave a speech in Chicago during his 1858 Senate campaign against Stephen Douglas, in which he modeled how to hold in tension the reality that the founders maintained the institution of slavery while setting the nation on the aspirational path of abolishing it. Lincoln argued that the founders kept the institution of slavery in the United States at the national founding, not because they thought it was morally good but because it was necessary to achieve the federal union of the states. The Constitution that created the federal union made the states greater than the sum of their parts, better than they would have ever been if they had pursued their own national careers as independent states or if they had formed separate and smaller unions. "We had slavery among us, we could not get our Constitution unless we permitted them to remain in slavery, we could not secure the good we did secure if we grasped for more, and having by necessity submitted to that much, it does not destroy the principle that is the charter of our liberties," Lincoln said.[64] In other words, the necessity of keeping slavery for the sake of creating the federal union does not render the Constitution false to its dedication to liberty.

Lincoln explained his meaning by appealing to the biblical passage in which Jesus taught his disciples, "you are to be perfect, as your heavenly Father is perfect."[65] As Jesus doubtless knew that the disciples would always be unable to attain to divine perfection in this life, he also knew that to lay the aspiration before them was central to their fulfilling their calling as his disciples. Lincoln said, "So I say in relation to the principle that all men are created equal, let it be as nearly reached as we can. . . . Let us then turn this government back into the channel in which the framers of the Constitution originally placed it."[66] Christ's moral teachings were aspirational, in the same way that the founding documents like the Declaration and the Constitution were aspirational.

Lincoln denied that the Constitution was a proslavery document. Rather, it was developed on the basis of the principle of liberty for all. If the Constitution were a proslavery document, then the Constitution would have affirmed that slavery was a positive moral good. But this was not so. "'Necessity,'" Lincoln said, "was the only argument they ever admitted in favor of slavery.... They found the institution existing among us, which they could not help; and they cast blame upon the British King for having permitted its introduction."[67] Lincoln said that the founders were ashamed of slavery, like one is ashamed of a cancerous growth, in that they never used the term "slavery" in the Constitution, but instead used euphemistic language like "person held to service or labor." True, the founders left the cancer alone in 1787, and like the victim of the cancer one dares "not cut out at once, lest he bleed to death." Nevertheless, the victim trusts to a future day when "the cutting may begin at the end of a given time."[68] The first Congresses under the Constitution acted toward slavery in ways that demonstrated, in Lincoln's words, "hostility to PRINCIPLE, and toleration ONLY BY NECESSITY."[69] Central to Lincoln's arguments against proslavery Democrats was that the founders intended Jefferson's equality clause to be meant for everyone and the Constitution to set the nation on the path toward the extinction of slavery.

This is a small example of how America is historically an aspirational nation. America was founded on principles of human dignity, individual liberty, free exercise of religion, and equality under the law. Have Americans been perfect in living up to these moral standards? Of course not. Americans have been conscious of their flaws and have given much to follow the path of improvement. America was not founded to preserve slavery. Quite the opposite: it was founded on a principle that made slavery untenable, as well as any form of legal or economic oppression. That is one of the reasons why millions of people from all over the world have sacrificed all they possessed to get here for over two centuries.

Similarly, American conservatives of the Burkean tradition are aspirational because they have taken on the aspirational quality of their country. Being a conservative commits a person to the flourishing of individuals, communities, and the nation guided by tradition, just law, and an ethic of love informed by the Bible. Conservatives are often vilified by the Left as being inhuman. Nonsense. Faithful conservatives aspire to the good, true, and beautiful. Conservative aspirations are not mere dreams of a perfect society. They are realistic, aimed at a real society inhabited by real persons with both dignity and fallibility, guided by concrete experience learned from the past, not utopian visions.

The tradition of harmony between religion and liberty has prevailed in America since the national founding. Have there been past exceptions? Undoubtedly. Has religious liberty been unstained in America? Certainly not. Despite American failures to consistently live up to the ideals of the founding, what Lincoln said of the founders' attitudes toward slavery applies to the principle of harmony between religion and liberty. That harmony has been the standard since the beginning of our national life. Aspirational conservatives are among the only ones in America today who have the will to conserve that harmony. Among self-described Democrats, the political party of the Left, only 23 percent consider themselves to be patriots, while 59 percent of Republicans, the party representing conservatives, do. Twenty-three percent of Democrats value religion, while 53 percent of Republicans say the same.[70] It is not exaggeration to say that conservatives have a greater will to conserve the traditions of patriotism and religious liberty than do progressives. It is also not an exaggeration to argue that conservatives are more interested in conserving religious liberty than the Ottantotts who support magisterial Christian nationalism and the establishment of state churches.

If we are going to be conservatives, and if we are going to conserve the American tradition of harmonizing religion and liberty through public spirit, then we must know what a conservative is and what conservatives value. In other words, we must know what conservatives are before we can know what conservatives do. The aspirational conservative is prepolitical. The one possessing a conservative disposition aims for a higher moral destiny for persons and societies, guided by the light of permanent things, tradition, and just order. He also understands human fallibility and the real world. He reckons with the human condition marked as it is by limitation, imperfection, and change. The moral profit and ordered liberty of the human person is the primary consideration of the conservative disposition. For those goods to obtain in the real world of scarcity, sin, and death, we must heed the proven experience of generations past that reveals to us how we understand concepts like rights, freedoms, and ethics. We turn our backs on the past and on tradition at our peril.

Conservatives value a well-ordered imagination, because an imagination that realistically takes stock of the intersection between the eternal and the temporal prepares the person to accept the world as it is, but with hope. Conservatives order their love for their nation as an extension of their family and understand that the nation is neither innocent of great wrongdoing, nor is it the earthly manifestation of the infernal region. Conservatives know that liberty apart from order is a lie. Liberty without moral order is slavery to vice, but too much order stifles liberty. Balance between liberty and order is difficult but attainable, as earlier generations have learned over time. Conservatives look to the past and read history to grow out of childishness and into maturity. As the apostle Paul wrote, "when I was a child, I used to speak like a child, think like a child, reason like a child; when I became a man, I did away with childish things." Conservatives know that history puts us on the path to maturity. Finally, conservatives value religion, because religion expands our view from our mundane concerns and our selfishness to our common fate that awaits us, as well as the world to which we go. If we do not fear God, how can we expect to find peace and contentment here on earth?

Those things that harmonize liberty and religion on earth are the things that conservatives cherish. We love and seek to cultivate public spirit, because public spirit is a form of patriotism, or a well-ordered love of country. We want to continue voluntarily associating for civil and religious causes, because in doing so we cooperate with our neighbors, make new friends and associates, and find strength in the numbers of like-minded citizens. We see self-interest through the lens of the interests of the whole, thereby obtaining goods for ourselves and for others at the same time. We support the separation of church and state, not because we want to empower the state against the church or redefine religious liberty as a tame and lifeless "freedom of worship," but for the sake of free religious exercise resulting in the securing of liberty for all. And we want to create a culture that values religion and religious people, because a nation that values faith also values morality, truth, and just order. Those traditional features of American life that foster the health of religion and augment the scope and quality of religion are not utopian aspirations. They are concrete, because we have examples of their beneficial manifestations in the experiences of those who have preceded us. As we have enjoyed the inheritance we have obtained from earlier generations, it is our duty to the younger generations to hand them down unsullied.

We live in uncertain times. No matter. Every generation has lived in such times. No person has ever been able to see his end from his beginning. Every person who has ever lived had struggles, failures, hopes, and triumphs. It is so with all of us. Unlike the dead, our story is not finished yet, and we have the hope that tomorrow is another day. We have a God who is in control of our circumstances. We have a faith built on the truthfulness of God's character. We have a truly great country—not a perfect one, but a great one nonetheless because it serves as the stage for the fulfillment of foundational human potential goods. America has historically recognized the prepolitical right of all persons to worship, obey, and speak publicly for the God they serve. Let us not be ashamed of the inheritance we enjoy from our forebears, nor let us be ashamed to be known as true patriots. In patriotism there is courage, gratitude, vigilance, and charity. In authentic patriotism, there is hope.

Every Christmas, the *Wall Street Journal* publishes an editorial first written and published in 1949 by Vermont Royster. Royster eloquently called to mind the world of Rome, the world in which Jesus was born and Paul was converted from a persecutor to a preacher of Jesus's gospel. That world, like ours, sought salvation in power—power to redistribute wealth and power to enforce conformity. What Augustine called the City of Man has and will continue to exalt itself and oppose any and all that stand in its way. The human tendency to grasp for power and worship self-appointed gods for the sake of selfish ambition remains dominant, even in the freest and most democratic of societies. Only those who are realistic about the paradox of human dignity and human fallibility, who venerate tradition without worshiping it, and who understand that liberty is only manifested through just order are in the position to hold the powers of tyranny at bay. In the face of darkness, malice, ignorance, selfishness, guile, and hypocrisy, let us find courage in Royster's closing words as we guard and steward our American heritage of religious liberty for the sake of our children and grandchildren: "And so Paul, the apostle of the Son of Man, spoke to his brethren, the Galatians, the words he would have us remember afterward in each of the years of his Lord: Stand fast therefore in the liberty wherewith Christ has made us free and be not entangled again with the yoke of bondage."[71]

Acknowledgments

This book has been in the making for many years. One of the first persons to believe in the project was my friend David Bratt, who advocated for it as an editor at Eerdmans. James Ernest, who took the project on in 2021 as editor, has been an invaluable source of wisdom in my research and writing. I am proud to call him a friend.

I owe a profound debt of gratitude to the Center for Religion, Culture, and Democracy (CRCD), an initiative of the First Liberty Institute. The CRCD has provided faithful support for me as a research fellow in the writing of this book. I am particularly grateful to my longtime friend Trey Dimsdale, the Executive Director of the CRCD, and to Jordan Ballor, the CRCD's Research Director. The CRCD provided me with funds for a research assistant, and I could not have asked for a more helpful, conscientious, and efficient person than Mary Beth Latham to serve in that role. The Russell Kirk Center for Cultural Renewal at Piety Hill in Mecosta, Michigan, also provided support by hosting me during a portion of the summer of 2023 as a Wilbur Fellow. My sincere thanks go to Mrs. Annette Kirk, Jeff and Cecilia Nelson, and Wesley Reynolds, who graciously hosted me at the Kirk Center as I resided there and researched, wrote, and lectured on the conservatism of Russell Kirk. Dan Churchwell at the Acton Institute for the Study of Religion and Liberty invited me to give lectures on conservatism at Acton's annual conference for three years, and Gary L. Gregg, Director of the McConnell Center at the

University of Louisville, graciously supported my work by inviting me to serve as a nonresident fellow at the Center as coleading faculty with him on a yearlong study of Alexis de Tocqueville's *Democracy in America* during the academic year 2023–2024. Finally, my institution, The Southern Baptist Theological Seminary, granted me a sabbatical in the spring semester of 2023. The sabbatical was indispensable to my research and writing.

Faithful friends read chapter drafts and excerpts and offered helpful feedback: Daniel G. Hummel, Bradford Wilson, Matthew Franck, Michael A. G. Haykin, Boleslaw "Bolek" Z. Kabala, Glenn Moots, my father, David L. Wilsey, my wife, Mandy Wilsey, and my daughter Caroline C. Wilsey. Thanks to friends who were instrumental in helping me shape ideas through deep conversations, especially R. Albert Mohler Jr., Lisa Bradford, George Nash, Mark David Hall, Stephen O. Presley, Chris Armstrong, James M. Patterson, Josh Bowman, Andrew T. Walker, Darrell Falconburg, and Claire Aguda.

During my research, I wrote several articles on related topics, some of which I adapted for use in the chapters herein with the generous permission of each publisher. Here is the bibliographic information of the pieces I adapted for the book. See the specific citations that appear in the places where the adaptations occur.

"At Its Best, American Patriotism Is Blessed with Two-Dimensional Vision." *Christianity Today*, July 1, 2021. https://www.christianity today.com/ct/2021/july-web-only/reclaiming-patriotism-steven -smith-america-nationalism.html.

"The Christian Prince against the Dad Bod: An Assessment of the Case for Christian Nationalism." *London Lyceum*, April 28, 2023. https://thelondonlyceum.com/book-review-the-case-for -christian-nationalism-stephen-wolfe/.

"God and Government: Tocqueville and Revolution." Acton University Online video lecture. Acton Institute for the Study of Religion and Liberty. February 2020.

"The Many Faces of Christian Nationalism." *Law and Liberty*, September 26, 2021. https://lawliberty.org/features/the-many-faces-of-christian-nationalism/.

"Public Spirit as Mediating Influence between Tocqueville's 'Spirit of Religion' and 'Spirit of Freedom.'" In *The Palgrave Handbook of Religion and State: Theoretical Perspectives*, vol. 1, edited by Shannon Holzer. Cham, Switzerland: Palgrave Macmillan, 2023.

Many thanks to John Pinheiro of the Acton Institute, Rachel Lu of *Law and Liberty*, Matt Reynolds of *Christianity Today*, Jordan Steffaniak of the *London Lyceum*, and Shannon Holzer, editor of *The Palgrave Handbook of Religion and State*, for accepting these pieces over the past several months.

Kenwood Baptist Church has been a very great source of encouragement, especially my fellow elders and my pastor and colleague at Southern Seminary, James M. Hamilton Jr. My inimitably wonderful daughters, Caroline and Sally, have given me their unconditional love and loyalty throughout my research and writing. This book is for them, and I hope and pray it serves as an apt invitation from their father to the conservative aspiration. Finally, my wife, Mandy, is the greatest encourager of all. She, more than any other single person, deserves my gratitude not only for her supporting me through the ups and downs of this project, but also for abiding with me despite all my hang-ups and foibles. She is, in every way, an excellent wife. I am amazed at God for giving me the grace to have found her (Prov. 31:10).

Notes

INTRODUCTION

1. Alexis de Tocqueville, *Democracy in America*, ed. Eduardo Nolla, trans. James T. Schleifer, 2 vols. (Indianapolis: Liberty Fund, 2010), 1:69.

2. See Donald S. Lutz, *The Origins of American Constitutionalism* (Baton Rouge: Louisiana State University Press, 1988), for an impressive quantified study of the impact of Protestantism on the ideas of the American founding. See also Barry Alan Shain, *The Myth of American Individualism: The Protestant Origins of American Political Thought* (Princeton: Princeton University Press, 1994), and Bernard Bailyn, *The Ideological Origins of the American Revolution* (Cambridge, MA: Belknap Press of Harvard University Press, 2017), for secondary source material on Protestantism and the founding. See Daniel L. Dreisbach and Mark David Hall, eds., *Faith and the Founders of the American Republic* (Oxford: Oxford University Press, 2014), for a collection of essays by prominent historians on religion and the founding. And finally, see Daniel L. Dreisbach and Mark David Hall, *The Sacred Rights of Conscience* (Indianapolis: Liberty Fund, 2009), for a collection of primary-source documents pertinent to liberty and religion from the ancient period through the early nineteenth century.

3. Aaron Zitner, "America Pulls Back from Values That Once Defined It, WSJ-NORC Poll Finds," *Wall Street Journal*, March 27, 2023, https://tinyurl.com/465e4cs7.

4. Andrew J. Bloeser et al., "Are Stealth Democrats Really Committed to Democracy? Process Preferences Revisited," *Perspectives on Politics*, 2022, 1–15. For a breakdown of results with commentary, see Tarah Williams, Andrew Bloeser, and Brian Howard, "Large Numbers of Americans Want a Strong, Rough, Anti-democratic Leader," *Nextgov*, February 7, 2023, https://tinyurl.com/2atemcfp.

5. Theodore Roosevelt, "True Americanism," in *The Works of Theodore Roosevelt, National Edition*, vol. 13 (New York: Scribner's, 1926), 13–26.

6. Nikole Hannah-Jones, ed., *The 1619 Project: A New Origin Story* (New York: One World, 2021), xxxii. See also Leslie M. Harris, "I Helped Fact-Check the 1619 Project. The Times Ignored Me," *Politico*, March 6, 2020, https://tiny url.com/2me2jhrn, and Adam Serwer, "The Fight over the 1619 Project Is Not about the Facts," *Atlantic*, December 23, 2019, https://tinyurl.com/3y2fkbb8.

7. Patrick J. Deneen, *Why Liberalism Failed* (New Haven: Yale University Press, 2018), 3.

8. Thomas Crean and Alan Fimister, *Integralism: A Manual for Political Philosophy* (Seelscheid, Germany: Editiones Scholasticae, 2020), 101.

9. Crean and Fimister, *Integralism*, 171, 179.

10. Stephen Wolfe, *The Case for Christian Nationalism* (Moscow, ID: Canon, 2022), 381.

11. Wolfe, *Christian Nationalism*, 31, 286.

12. Wolfe, *Christian Nationalism*, 352.

13. Robert J. Morrell, *Up from History: The Life of Booker T. Washington* (Cambridge, MA: Belknap Press of Harvard University Press, 2009), 12.

14. Rosa Parks with Jim Haskins, *My Story* (New York: Puffin, 1992), 2.

15. Sylvia Jukes Morris, *Price of Fame: The Honorable Clare Boothe Luce* (New York: Random House, 2014), 397–98.

16. *The Historical Collections of the Danvers Historical Society*, vol. 8 (Danvers, MA: Danvers Historical Society, 1920), 70.

17. Walter Blair, "The Popularity of Nineteenth-Century American Humorists," *American Literature* 3, no. 2 (May 1931): 190.

18. DaCosta, Morton, dir., *Auntie Mame* (Warner Bros., 1958; Blu-ray DVD: Warner Bros., 2017), featuring Rosalind Russell, Forrest Tucker, Coral Browne, Roger Smith, and Peggy Cass.

19. Dennis M. Powell, "Wake Up, America: Laughter Is Healing," *Hill*, March 4, 2021, https://tinyurl.com/572ncumx.

20. C. S. Lewis, "On the Reading of Old Books," in *God in the Dock* (Grand Rapids: Eerdmans, 1970), 200.

21. Eric Foner, quoted in Michael J. Connolly, "Daniel Boorstin against the Barbarians," *Imaginative Conservative*, October 16, 2023, https://tinyurl.com/dx6b43sc.

22. Daniel J. Boorstin, *The Genius of American Politics* (Chicago: University of Chicago Press, 1953), 1.

23. Boorstin, *Genius*, 8.

24. Boorstin, *Genius*, 9.

25. Boorstin, *Genius*, 9.

26. Boorstin, *Genius*, 10.

27. Gordon S. Wood, *Revolutionary Characters: What Made the Founders Different* (New York: Penguin Books, 2006), 3.

28. Gordon S. Wood, *The Idea of America: Reflections on the Birth of the United States* (New York: Penguin Books, 2011), 3.

29. Boorstin, *Genius*, 18.

30. Allen C. Guelzo, "Preaching a Conspiracy Theory," *City Journal*, December 8, 2019, https://tinyurl.com/4wr7pbaw.

31. Boorstin, *Genius*, 11.

32. Boorstin, *Genius*, 16.

33. Lemuel Haynes, "Liberty Further Extended: Or, Free thoughts on the illegality of Slave-keeping; Wherein those arguments that Are useed in its vindication Are plainly confuted. Together with an humble Address to such as are Concearned in the practice," quoted in Ruth Bogin, "'Liberty Further Extended': A 1776 Antislavery Manuscript by Lemuel Haynes," *William and Mary Quarterly* 40, no. 1 (January 1983): 94.

34. Haynes, "Liberty Further Extended," 94.

35. Boorstin, *Genius*, 33.

36. With the kind permission of the Acton Institute for the Study of Religion and Liberty, I have adapted a portion of the next few paragraphs from a series of presentations I made for the Acton Institute in 2020 entitled "God and Government: Tocqueville and Revolution," which was produced as a video course for Acton University Online.

37. Daniel Walker Howe, *What Hath God Wrought: The Transformation of America, 1815–1848* (New York: Oxford University Press, 2007), 31–32.

38. Howe, *What Hath God Wrought*, 32.

39. Richard Swedberg, *Tocqueville's Political Economy* (Princeton: Princeton University Press, 2009), 9.

40. Swedberg, *Tocqueville's Political Economy*, 19.

41. Tocqueville, *Democracy in America*, 1:27.

42. Alexis de Tocqueville, *The Ancien Regime and the French Revolution*, ed. John Elster, trans. Arthur Goldhammer (New York: Cambridge University Press, 2011), 1:17.

43. George Wilson Pierson, *Tocqueville in America* (Baltimore: Johns Hopkins University Press, 1996), 14–15.

44. Pierson, *Tocqueville in America*, 15.

45. Tocqueville, *Ancien Regime*, 1:16–17.

46. Tocqueville, *Democracy in America*, 1:25.

47. Tocqueville, *Democracy in America*, 1:466–67, 499–500.

48. Tocqueville, *Democracy in America*, 1:28.

49. Tocqueville, *Ancien Regime*, foreword, 6.

CHAPTER ONE

1. Jonathan Healey, *The Blazing World: A New History of Revolutionary England, 1603–1689* (New York: Knopf, 2023), 26; W. E. Lunt, *History of England* (New York: Harper & Row, 1957), 388.

2. Matthew Continetti, *The Right: The Hundred Year War for American Conservatism* (New York: Basic Books, 2022), 8–9.

3. Peter Viereck, *Conservatism Revisited: The Revolt against Ideology* (reprint, New Brunswick, NJ: Transaction, 2005), 70.

4. C. S. Lewis, *The Last Battle*, Chronicles of Narnia (New York: HarperCollins, 2004), 762.

5. Continetti, *The Right*, 13.

6. John Stuart Mill, *Considerations on Representative Government*, with an introduction by F. A. Hayek (Chicago: Regnery, 1962), 147. Mill did not actually describe conservatives in this way. He made reference to the British Conservative Party in a footnote to chapter 7 of *Representative Government*. He was charging Benjamin Disraeli for being a member of the party and yet failing to understand conservative principles. "Well would it be for England if Conservatives voted for everything conservative, and Liberals for everything liberal. . . . The Conservatives, as being by the law of their existence the stupidest party, have much the greatest sins of this description to answer for." Mill was attacking Disraeli and the party for being overly partisan, while betraying their own principles for short-term gain over their political rivals. He was not merely engaging in a petty *ad hominem* attack, nor was he suggesting that all conservatives were stupid.

7. Russell Kirk, "Russell Kirk and the Vision for Piety Hill," video recording, 1993, Vimeo video, 8:42, https://vimeo.com/119700546.

8. Kirk, "Vision."

9. Russell Kirk, "A Cautionary Note on the Ghostly Tale," in *Ancestral Shadows: An Anthology of Ghostly Tales*, ed. Vigen Guroian (Grand Rapids: Eerdmans, 2004), 405.

10. Patrick Allitt, *The Conservatives: Ideas and Personalities throughout American History* (New Haven: Yale University Press, 2009), 168.

11. William H. Honan, "Russell Kirk Is Dead at 75: Seminal Conservative Author," *New York Times*, April 30, 1994, https://tinyurl.com/5zcnbvh.

12. "Russell Kirk: Voice for Conservatism," *Los Angeles Times*, April 30, 1994, https://tinyurl.com/bdebs9z3 (emphasis added).

13. Russell Kirk, *The Conservative Mind: From Burke to Eliot*, 7th rev. ed (Washington: Regnery, 2001), 8.

14. Kirk, *The Conservative Mind*, 8–9.

15. Russell Kirk, "Prescription, Authority, and Ordered Freedom," in *What Is Conservatism?*, ed. Frank S. Meyer, 2nd ed. (Wilmington, DE: ISI, 2017), 29.

16. Irving Babbitt, *Democracy and Leadership*, with an introduction by Russell Kirk (1924; reprint, Indianapolis: Liberty Fund, 1979), 27.

17. Rom. 7:19. All references to the Bible are in the New American Standard Bible (1995), unless otherwise specified.

18. Babbitt, *Democracy and Leadership*, 28.

19. Karl Marx, "The Eighteenth Brumaire of Louis Napoleon," Works of Marx and Engels, 1852, Marxists Internet Archive, https://tinyurl.com/mrxw6z2j.

20. Kirk, "Prescription, Authority, and Ordered Freedom," 30.

21. Kirk, *The Conservative Mind*, 9.

22. Kirk, *The Conservative Mind*, 10.

23. Kirk, *The Conservative Mind*, 10.

24. Russell Kirk, *The Roots of American Order*, with an introduction by Forrest MacDonald, 4th ed. (Wilmington, DE: ISI, 2003), 5.

25. Claes Ryn wrote a brilliant introduction to the 2005 reprint of Viereck's 1949 *Conservatism Revisited*; Robert Lacey has an excellent chapter on Viereck in his *Pragmatic Conservatism: Edmund Burke and His Intellectual Heirs* (New York: Palgrave Macmillan, 2018); Daniel McCarthy wrote a reconsideration of Viereck for the *American Conservative* in 2007 ("Viereck Revisited," *American Conservative*, June 18, 2007, https://tinyurl.com/3c3a5ch7); and Lisa Bradford of Pacific University is working on a history of the Viereck family.

26. Peter Viereck, *Metapolitics: From Wagner and the German Romantics to Hitler*, expanded ed. (New Brunswick, NJ: Transaction, 2004; original 1941), 4–5.

27. Lacey, *Pragmatic Conservatism*, 166.

28. McCarthy, "Viereck Revisited."

29. Claes G. Ryn, "Conservative Revival and Controversy," introduction to Viereck, *Conservatism Revisited*, 3.

30. Peter Viereck, "Conservatism under the Elms," *New York Times*, November 4, 1951, https://tinyurl.com/fahh5h63.

31. Ryn, "Conservative Revival and Controversy," 6.

32. Ryn, "Conservative Revival and Controversy," 6.

33. Viereck, *Conservatism Revisited*, 70.

34. Marian Strobel, email message to author, January 27, 2023.

35. John Locke, *Second Essay concerning the True Original Extent and End of Civil Government*, Great Books of the Western World, vol. 35 (Chicago: Encyclopedia Britannica, 1952), 2:4.

36. Francis Canavan, foreword to Edmund Burke, *Reflections on the Revolution in France*, vol. 2 of *Select Works of Edmund Burke*, ed. Francis Canavan (Indianapolis: Liberty Fund, 1999), x.

37. Burke, *Reflections*, 192–93.

38. Burke, *Reflections*, 193.

39. Burke, *Reflections*, 193 (emphasis added).

40. Peter Viereck, *Conservatism: From John Adams to Churchill* (Princeton: Nostrand, 1956), 11.

41. Viereck, *Conservatism*, 12.

42. Viereck, *Conservatism*, 12.

43. Jean-Jacques Rousseau, *The Social Contract and Other Later Political Writings*, ed. Victor Gourevitch (Cambridge: Cambridge University Press, 1997), 41.

44. Viereck, *Conservatism*, 13.

45. Viereck, *Conservatism Revisited*, 155.

46. Viereck, *Conservatism Revisited*, 53, 155.

47. Patrick Henry, "Give Me Liberty, or Give Me Death," March 23, 1775, Yale Law School, Lillian Goldman Law Library, the Avalon Project, https://tinyurl.com/2fcn2777.

48. Russell Kirk, "The Framers: Not Philosophes, but Gentlemen," in *The Essential Russell Kirk: Selected Essays*, ed. George A. Panichas (Wilmington, DE: ISI, 2007), 452.

49. Angela K. Lewis, *Conservatism in the Black Community: To the Right and Misunderstood* (New York: Routledge, 2013), 142.

50. Angela K. Lewis, *Conservatism in the Black Community*, 3.

51. Angela K. Lewis, *Conservatism in the Black Community*, 5.

52. Angela K. Lewis, *Conservatism in the Black Community*, 55–61.

53. Angela K. Lewis, *Conservatism in the Black Community*, 29–30.

54. Lee H. Walker, *Rediscovering Black Conservatism* (Chicago: Heartland Institute, 2009), 3.

55. Walker, *Rediscovering Black Conservatism*, 10.

56. Walker, *Rediscovering Black Conservatism*, 10.

57. Peter Eisenstadt, introduction to *Black Conservatism: Essays in Intellectual and Political History*, ed. Peter Eisenstadt, 2nd ed. (New York: Routledge, 2012), x.

58. Eisenstadt, introduction to *Black Conservatism*, xi.

59. Eisenstadt, introduction to *Black Conservatism*, xi.

60. Eisenstadt, introduction to *Black Conservatism*, xii.

61. Walker, *Rediscovering Black Conservatism*, 11.

62. Eisenstadt, introduction to *Black Conservatism*, xiii.

63. Eisenstadt, introduction to *Black Conservatism*, xiii.

64. Irving Babbitt, *Rousseau and Romanticism* (New York: Houghton Mifflin, 1919), xiii.

CHAPTER TWO

1. Dante Alighieri, "Epistle X to Can Grande," in *A Translation of the Latin Works of Dante Alighieri*, trans. A. G. Ferrers Howell and Philip H. Wicksteed (London: Dent, 1904), 350.

2. Dante Alighieri, *The Divine Comedy: Inferno, Purgatorio, Paradiso*, trans. Allen Mandelbaum, with an introduction by Eugenio Montale (New York: Knopf, 1995), *Inferno*, canto 1, lines 73–74.

3. Dante Alighieri, *Inferno*, canto 1, lines 115–117.

4. Dante Alighieri, *Inferno*, canto 1, lines 118, 120.

5. Dante Alighieri, *Inferno*, canto 1, lines 124–125.

6. Luke 10:18.

7. Dante Alighieri, *Purgatorio*, canto 7, lines 73–75.

8. Dante Alighieri, *Purgatorio*, canto 7, lines 90–96.

9. See Neil J. Young, *We Gather Together: The Religious Right and the Problem of Interfaith Politics* (New York: Oxford University Press, 2016).

10. Andrew R. Flores, "National Trends in Public Opinion on LGBT Rights in the United States," UCLA School of Law, Williams Institute, November 2014, https://tinyurl.com/mwh3ytkc.

11. Stephen Collinson, "The US Now Faces Simultaneous Showdowns with China and Russia," CNN, February 14, 2023, https://tinyurl.com/7yvmzmck.

12. Eleanor Mueller and Victoria Guida, "Washington Blinks as Debt Costs Begin to Bite," *Politico*, November 20, 2023, https://tinyurl.com/39e26s9f.

13. Carrie Gates, "'On the Brink of a New Civil War': New National Survey Highlights Fragility of American Democracy, Stark Partisan Divides," *Notre Dame News*, November 3, 2022, https://tinyurl.com/2ynu8pnz.

14. Paul C. Light, "The True Size of Government Is Nearing a Record High," Brookings, October 7, 2020, https://tinyurl.com/4suxrs28.

15. J. Sellers Hill and Nia L. Orakwue, "Harvard Student Groups Face Intense Backlash for Statement Calling Israel 'Entirely Responsible' for Hamas

Attack," *Harvard Crimson*, October 10, 2023, https://tinyurl.com/266r27wx; Drew Harwell and Victoria Bisset, "How Osama bin Laden's 'Letter to America' Reached Millions Online," *Washington Post*, November 16, 2023, https://tinyurl.com/2xzje86z.

16. Claes Ryn, *The Failure of American Conservatism and the Road Not Taken* (New York: Republic, 2023), 7.

17. Kevin J. Hayes, *George Washington: A Life in Books* (New York: Oxford University Press, 2017), 5.

18. Ryn, *Failure of American Conservatism*, 24.

19. Ryn, *Failure of American Conservatism*, 29.

20. Zena Hitz, *Lost in Thought: The Hidden Pleasures of an Intellectual Life* (Princeton: Princeton University Press, 2020), 53.

21. Peter Viereck, *Unadjusted Man in the Age of Overadjustment: Where History and Literature Intersect* (New York: Transaction, 2004), 2.

22. In his introduction to the 2004 revised edition, Viereck made clear that he meant male and female when using the term "man." He wrote, "I use the 'man' of 'overadjusted man' in the sense of mankind, female or male, and whatever the ethnic clan. Too bad English lacks a short word like the German 'Mensch,' meaning both genders. My concern, needless to say (or not needless?), is with our shared humanity." Viereck, *Unadjusted Man in the Age of Overadjustment*, ix. When I use the pronoun "he" to generically refer to a person, I mean it to include both male and female, and thus I am following the same method as Viereck.

23. L. Russ Bush, *A Handbook for Christian Philosophy* (Grand Rapids: Zondervan, 1991), 23.

24. Viereck, *Unadjusted Man in the Age of Overadjustment*, x.

25. Viereck, *Unadjusted Man in the Age of Overadjustment*, 6.

26. Hitz, *Lost in Thought*, 58.

27. See Alfred Lansing, *Endurance: Shackleton's Incredible Voyage* (New York: Basic Books, 2014).

28. Kevin J. Vanhoozer, *Pictures at a Theological Exhibition: Scenes of the Church's Worship, Witness, and Wisdom* (Downers Grove, IL: IVP Academic, 2016), 105.

29. Robert M. Hutchins, *The Great Conversation: The Substance of a Liberal Education*, Great Books of the Western World, vol. 1 (Chicago: Encyclopedia Britannica, 1952), 1, 9.

30. Augustine, *The Confessions*, trans. Maria Boulding, Works of Saint Augustine: A Translation for the 21st Century, vol. 1, part 1 (1997; reprint, New York: New City, 2012), 8.7.17.

31. Augustine, *Confessions* 8.5.10.

32. Augustine, *Confessions* 6.3.4.

33. Augustine, *Confessions* 8.12.29.

34. Augustine, *Confessions* 8.12.29.

35. Kirk, *The Conservative Mind*, 8.

36. Augustine, "On Faith and the Creed," in *Nicene and Post-Nicene Fathers*, vol. 3, *Augustin on the Holy Trinity, Doctrinal Treatises, Moral Treatises*, ed. Philip Schaff (Peabody, MA: Hendrickson, 1999), 2.2.

37. Gen. 2:7.

38. Augustine, "Faith and the Creed," 2.2.

39. Augustine, "Faith and the Creed," 2.2.

40. Augustine, "Faith and the Creed," 2.2.

41. Augustine, *Confessions* 7.11.17.

42. Augustine, *Confessions* 7.13.19.

43. Augustine, *City of God*, trans. Marcus Dods (London: Folio, 2012), 12.6.

44. Augustine, *City of God* 12.8.

45. Augustine, *City of God* 12.8.

46. Augustine, *Confessions* 7.15.21.

47. Augustine, *Confessions* 10.34.53.

48. Augustine, *Confessions* 10.6.8, 9. The pre-Socratic figure Anaximenes was of the Milesian School, flourishing prior to 494 BC. He taught that air is the basic substance of reality. "Just as our soul, being air, holds us together, so do breath and air encompass the whole world." Bertrand Russell, *The History of Western Philosophy* (1945; reprint, New York: Touchstone, 1973), 28.

49. See John William Draper, *History of the Conflict between Religion and Science* (New York: Appleton, 1874), and Andrew Dickson White, *The Warfare of Science* (London: King & Co., 1876) for two nineteenth-century examples of conflict thesis historiography.

50. There are excellent reasons to reject the conflict thesis as too simplistic. Historian of science Colin Russell identified six weaknesses in particular: First, the conflict thesis "hinders the recognition of other relationships between science and religion," namely, that science and religion have often been "independent, mutually encouraging, or even symbiotic." Second, it "ignores the many documented examples of science and religion operating in close alliance." Third, it "enshrines a flawed view of history in which 'progress' or . . . 'victory' has been portrayed as inevitable." Fourth, it "obscures the rich diversity of ideas in both science and religion" since the categories of *science* and *religion* change over time. Fifth, it "engenders a distorted view of disputes resulting from causes other than those of religion versus science." And sixth, it "exalts minor squabbles . . . to the

status of major conflicts." Colin A. Russell, "The Conflict of Science and Religion," in *Science and Religion: A Historical Introduction*, ed. Gary B. Ferngren (Baltimore: Johns Hopkins University Press, 2002), 7–9.

51. Rom. 1:19–20.

52. Augustine, "Sermon 43: On What Is Written in Isaiah; Unless You Believe, You Shall Not Understand," in *Sermons on the Old Testament, 20–50*, trans. Edmund Hill, Works of Saint Augustine: A New Translation for the 21st Century, vol. 2, part 3 (Brooklyn, NY: New City, 1990), 43.1.

53. Augustine, "Sermon 43," 43.3.

54. Augustine, "Sermon 43," 43.9.

55. Benedict XVI, "General Audience of 30 January 2008: Saint Augustine of Hippo," Libreria Editrice Vaticana, https://tinyurl.com/yryxward.

56. Augustine, *Soliloquies*, in *Nicene and Post-Nicene Fathers*, vol. 7, *Augustin: Homilies on the Gospel of John, Homilies on the First Epistle of John, Soliloquies*, ed. Philip Schaff (Peabody, MA: Hendrickson, 1999), 1.13.

57. Augustine, "On Grace and Free Will," in *Nicene and Post-Nicene Fathers*, vol. 5, *Augustin: Anti-Pelagian Writings*, ed. Philip Schaff (Peabody, MA: Hendrickson, 1999), chap. 4, p. 445.

58. Augustine, "Grace and Free Will," chap. 31, p. 456.

59. J. Peter Burkholder, Donald Jay Grout, and Claude V. Palisca, *History of Western Music* (1960; reprint, London: Folio, 2006), 360.

60. Kirk, "Cautionary Note," 402.

61. Kirk, "Cautionary Note," 403.

62. Kirk, "Cautionary Note," 406.

63. Henry David Thoreau, *Walden*, with an introduction by Bill McKibben (Boston: Beacon, 2004), 87.

64. Viereck, *Unadjusted Man*, ix.

CHAPTER THREE

1. See Lester J. Cappon, ed., *The Adams-Jefferson Letters: The Complete Correspondence between Thomas Jefferson and Abigail and John Adams* (1959; reprint, Chapel Hill: University of North Carolina Press, 1987).

2. Daniel Webster, *Adams and Jefferson: Discourse in Commemoration of the Lives and Services of John Adams and Thomas Jefferson, Delivered in Faneuil Hall, Boston, on the 2d of August, 1826*, English Classic Series, vol. 51, ed. Albert F. Blaisdell (New York: Clark & Maynard, 1885), 8.

3. Webster, *Adams and Jefferson*, 9.

4. Webster, *Adams and Jefferson*, 10.

5. Webster, *Adams and Jefferson*, 10.

6. Paul C. Nagel, *This Sacred Trust: American Nationality, 1798–1898* (New York: Oxford University Press, 1971), xii.

7. I have adapted this section on the various manifestations of nationality in America from Puritan millennialism to the Christian America thesis from an essay I wrote in September 2021, with the kind permission of the editors of *Law and Liberty*. See John D. Wilsey, "The Many Faces of Christian Nationalism," *Law and Liberty*, September 26, 2021, https://tinyurl.com/ycya4mwc.

8. See John D. Wilsey, *One Nation under God: An Evangelical Critique of Christian America* (Eugene, OR: Pickwick, 2011); John D. Wilsey, *American Exceptionalism and Civil Religion* (Downers Grove, IL: IVP Academic, 2015); John D. Wilsey, *God's Cold Warrior: The Life and Faith of John Foster Dulles*, Library of Religious Biography (Grand Rapids: Eerdmans, 2021).

9. See, for example, Andrew L. Seidel, *The Founding Myth: Why Christian Nationalism Is Un-American* (New York: Sterling, 2019); Andrew L. Whitehead and Samuel L. Perry, *Taking America Back for God: Christian Nationalism in the United States* (New York: Oxford University Press, 2020); Kristin Kobes DuMez, *Jesus and John Wayne: How White Evangelicals Corrupted a Faith and Fractured a Nation* (New York: Liveright, 2020); Philip L. Gorski and Samuel L. Perry, *The Flag and the Cross: White Christian Nationalism and the Threat to American Democracy* (New York: Oxford University Press, 2022); Pamela Cooper-White, *The Psychology of Christian Nationalism: Why People Are Drawn in and How to Talk across the Divide* (Minneapolis: Fortress, 2022); Andrew L. Whitehead, *American Idolatry: How Christian Nationalism Betrays the Gospel and Threatens the Church* (Grand Rapids: Brazos, 2023), to name just a few.

10. Whitehead and Perry, *Taking America*, 119.

11. Whitehead and Perry, *Taking America*, 148–49.

12. Nagel, *This Sacred Trust*, xii.

13. Nagel, *This Sacred Trust*, xii.

14. Nagel, *This Sacred Trust*, xii.

15. Anthony D. Smith, *Chosen Peoples: Sacred Sources of National Identities* (New York: Oxford University Press, 2003), 18.

16. Steven B. Smith, *Reclaiming Patriotism in an Age of Extremes* (New Haven: Yale University Press, 2021), 157.

17. Steven B. Smith, *Reclaiming Patriotism*, 157.

18. Tocqueville, *Democracy in America*, 1:385.

19. Tocqueville, *Democracy in America*, 1:385.

20. See Theodore Roosevelt, "International Duty and Hyphenated Amer-

icanism," in *The Works of Theodore Roosevelt, National Edition*, vol. 18 (New York: Scribner's, 1926), 278–94.

21. See Howe, *What Hath God Wrought*, and Charles Sellers, *The Market Revolution: Jacksonian America, 1815–1846* (New York: Oxford University Press, 1991).

22. George McKenna, *The Puritan Origins of American Patriotism* (New Haven: Yale University Press, 2007), 6.

23. Of course, the New England Puritans of the seventeenth century did not see themselves as Americans. I use this term to refer broadly to those who came to North America during the colonial period, either voluntarily or against their will, and who ultimately won independence from Great Britain in 1783 to create the United States.

24. Tocqueville, *Democracy in America*, 1:385, 388.

25. Tocqueville, *Democracy in America*, 1:385.

26. Tocqueville, *Democracy in America*, 1:386.

27. Tocqueville, *Democracy in America*, 1:386.

28. John Winthrop, "A Modell of Christian Charity," in *God's New Israel: Religious Interpretations of American Destiny*, ed. Conrad Cherry, rev. ed. (1971; reprint, Chapel Hill: University of North Carolina Press, 1998), 39.

29. See Samuel Danforth and Paul Royster (transcriber and editor), "A Brief Recognition of New-Englands Errand into the Wilderness: An Online Electronic Text Edition," 1670, University of Nebraska–Lincoln Digital Commons, Paper 35, https://tinyurl.com/y82sc6wa.

30. Cotton Mather, *Magnalia Christi Americana, or The Ecclesiastical History of New England*, University of Southern Maine, Osher Map Library Rare Books, 9, https://tinyurl.com/bdefu6mt.

31. Ernest Lee Tuveson, *Redeemer Nation: The Idea of America's Millennial Role* (Chicago: University of Chicago Press, 1968), 19.

32. Mark Noll, *America's God: From Jonathan Edwards to Abraham Lincoln* (New York: Oxford University Press, 2002), 78.

33. Lutz, *Origins of American Constitutionalism*, 141.

34. Pauline Maier, *From Resistance to Revolution: Colonial Radicals and the Development of American Opposition to Britain, 1765–1776* (New York: Norton, 1991), xx.

35. See Noll, *America's God*, 73–92.

36. Jonathan Mayhew, "A Discourse concerning Unlimited Submission," in *The Puritans: A Sourcebook of Their Writings*, ed. Perry Miller and Thomas H. Johnson (1963; reprint, Mineola, NY: Dover, 2001), 1:280.

37. Samuel Sherwood, "The Church's Flight into the Wilderness," in *Polit-*

ical Sermons of the American Founding Era, 1730–1805, ed. Ellis Sandoz (Indianapolis: Liberty Fund, 1991), 520–22.

38. Nicholas Street, "The American States Acting over the Part of the Children of Israel in the Wilderness and Thereby Impeding Their Entrance into Canaan's Rest," in *God's New Israel: Religious Interpretations of American Destiny* (1971; reprint, Chapel Hill: University of North Carolina Press, 1998), 67–81.

39. John L. O'Sullivan. "Annexation," *United States Magazine and Democratic Review* 17, no. 85 (July–August 1845): 5, https://tinyurl.com/3katvv6u.

40. See Anders Stephanson, *Manifest Destiny: American Expansion and the Empire of Right* (New York: Hill & Wang, 1995), 28–111.

41. Anthony D. Smith, *Chosen Peoples*, 13.

42. John L. O'Sullivan, "Introduction," *United States Magazine and Democratic Review* 1, no. 1 (October 1837): 14, https://tinyurl.com/4j95cp6n.

43. John L. O'Sullivan, "The Great Nation of Futurity," *United States Magazine and Democratic Review* 6, no. 23 (November 1839): 430, https://tinyurl.com/ynm6bnxw.

44. Abraham Lincoln, "Annual Message to Congress, December 1, 1862," in *Selected Speeches and Writings*, ed. Don E. Fehrenbacher (New York: Library of America, 2009), 364.

45. Abraham Lincoln, "Second Inaugural Address," in *The Annals of America, 1858–1865: The Crisis of the Union*, vol. 9 (Chicago: Encyclopedia Britannica, 1968), 556.

46. Ward Hill Lamon, *Recollections of Abraham Lincoln, 1847–1865*, ed. Dorothy Lamon Teillard (1895; reprint, Cambridge, MA: University, 1911), 91.

47. Abraham Lincoln, "The Gettysburg Address," in *The Annals of America, 1858–1865*, 462.

48. Lincoln, "The Gettysburg Address," 463.

49. "Historian Allen Guelzo Speaks on the 150th Anniversary of the Battle of Gettysburg," World Socialist Web Site, YouTube, July 4, 2013, https://tinyurl.com/msu25f53.

50. "Historian Allen Guelzo Speaks on the 150th Anniversary of the Battle of Gettysburg."

51. Milan Babík, *Statecraft and Salvation: Wilsonian Liberal Internationalism as Secularized Eschatology* (Waco, TX: Baylor University Press, 2013), 198.

52. John Foster Dulles, "Patriotism" (speech given at Indiana University, Bloomington, June 12, 1955, John Foster Dulles Papers, box 337, Public Policy Papers, Department of Rare Books and Special Collections, Seeley G. Mudd Manuscript Library, Princeton University).

53. Richard M. Gamble, *The War for Righteousness: Progressive Christianity,*

the Great War, and the Rise of the Messianic Nation (Wilmington, DE: ISI, 2003), 5.

54. Peter Marshall and David Manuel, *The Light and the Glory* (Grand Rapids: Baker Books, 1977), 23.

55. Marshall and Manuel, *Light and the Glory*, 23.

56. Lincoln, "Second Inaugural Address," 556.

57. Augustine, *City of God* 15.22.

58. John Lukacs, *The End of the Twentieth Century and the End of the Modern Age* (New York: Ticknor & Fields, 1993), 19.

59. The section opening with the story of Henry Johnson is adapted from an article I wrote with the kind permission of the editors of *Christianity Today*. See John D. Wilsey, "At Its Best, American Patriotism Is Blessed with Two-Dimensional Vision," *Christianity Today*, July 1, 2021, https://tinyurl.com/2n2sw2jk.

60. "Sergeant Henry Johnson, Medal of Honor, World War I," U.S. Army, https://tinyurl.com/3ydx5ahp.

61. "Sergeant Henry Johnson, Medal of Honor, World War I."

62. Steven B. Smith, *Reclaiming Patriotism*, 164.

63. Steven B. Smith, *Reclaiming Patriotism*, 5.

64. Steven B. Smith, *Reclaiming Patriotism*, 31.

65. Steven B. Smith, *Reclaiming Patriotism*, 157.

66. Steven B. Smith, *Reclaiming Patriotism*, 158.

67. Steven B. Smith, *Reclaiming Patriotism*, 165.

68. Steven B. Smith, *Reclaiming Patriotism*, 201.

CHAPTER FOUR

1. Sidney Lumet, dir., *Fail Safe* (Columbia Pictures, 1964), DVD (Sony Pictures, 2000), featuring Henry Fonda, Dan O'Herlihy, Walter Matthau, Frank Overton, and Larry Hagman.

2. There is a plethora of worthy resources to explore on the relation between human nature and human liberty, and ramifications for political and social order. See, for example, Robert P. George, *Making Men Moral: Civil Liberties and Public Morality* (1993; reprint, New York: Oxford University Press, 2002); O. Carter Snead, *What It Means to Be Human: The Case for the Body in Public Bioethics* (Cambridge, MA: Harvard University Press, 2020); John F. Kilner, *Duty and Destiny: Humanity in the Image of God* (Grand Rapids: Eerdmans, 2015); Jacques Maritain, *The Rights of Man and Natural Law*, trans. Doris C. Anson (New York: Scribner's, 1943); John Finnis, *Natural Law and Natural Rights*, 2nd ed. (New York: Oxford University Press, 2011); Jonathan

Sacks, *Morality: Restoring the Common Good in Divided Times* (New York: Basic Books, 2020).

3. Aristotle, *Nicomachean Ethics*, trans. W. D. Ross, Great Books of the Western World, vol. 9 (Chicago: Encyclopedia Britannica, 1952), 1.13.

4. Rom. 7:21–23.

5. William Shakespeare, *Hamlet, Prince of Denmark*, ed. William George Clarke and William Aldis Wright, Great Books of the Western World, vol. 27 (Chicago: Encyclopedia Britannica, 1952), act 4, scene 4, line 38.

6. Shakespeare, *Hamlet*, act 4, scene 4, lines 46–47.

7. Shakespeare, *Hamlet*, act 4, scene 4, lines 42–43.

8. Shakespeare, *Hamlet*, act 4, scene 4, line 66.

9. Thomas Aquinas, *Summa Theologica*, trans. Fathers of the English Dominican Province, rev. Daniel J. Sullivan, Great Books of the Western World, vol. 19 (Chicago: Encyclopedia Britannica, 1952), I, q. 83, art. 1.

10. Aquinas, *Summa Theologica* I, q. 83, art. 1.

11. Aristotle, *Nicomachean Ethics* 5.6.

12. Aristotle, *Nicomachean Ethics* 5.6.

13. Aristotle, *Nicomachean Ethics* 5.6.

14. Aristotle, *Politics*, trans. Benjamin Jowett, Great Books of the Western World, vol. 9 (Chicago: Encyclopedia Britannica, 1952), 3.6.

15. Aristotle, *Politics* 3.6.

16. Locke, *Second Essay*, 4:21.

17. Locke, *Second Essay*, 6:57.

18. Locke, *Second Essay*, 6:57.

19. Charles de Secondat, Baron de Montesquieu, *The Spirit of Laws*, trans. Thomas Nugent, rev. J. V. Prichard, Great Books of the Western World, vol. 38 (Chicago: Encyclopedia Britannica, 1952), 11.3.

20. Montesquieu, *Spirit of Laws*, 11.4.69c.

21. Alexander Hamilton, *Federalist* 1, in *The Federalist*, ed. J. R. Pole (Indianapolis: Hackett, 2005), 3.

22. James Madison, *Federalist* 37, in Pole, *The Federalist*, 193–94.

23. Madison, *Federalist* 37, in Pole, *The Federalist*, 194.

24. James Madison, *Federalist* 57, in Pole, *The Federalist*, 311.

25. James Madison, *Federalist* 51, in Pole, *The Federalist*, 283.

26. Locke, *Second Essay*, 9:124.

27. James Madison, *Federalist* 39, in Pole, *The Federalist*, 207.

28. Madison, *Federalist* 39, in Pole, *The Federalist*, 207–8.

29. Madison, *Federalist* 39, in Pole, *The Federalist*, 211.

30. James Madison, *Federalist* 52, in Pole, *The Federalist*, 286.

31. Madison, *Federalist* 57, in Pole, *The Federalist*, 310.

32. I have adapted this section on Wolfe's Christian nationalism from an essay I wrote in April 2023 with the kind permission of the editors of the *London Lyceum*. See John D. Wilsey, "The Christian Prince against the Dad Bod: An Assessment of the Case for Christian Nationalism," *London Lyceum*, April 28, 2023, https://tinyurl.com/2s4f4m23.

33. Wolfe, *Christian Nationalism*, 470.

34. Wolfe, *Christian Nationalism*, 31.

35. Wolfe, *Christian Nationalism*, 381.

36. Wolfe, *Christian Nationalism*, 326.

37. Wolfe, *Christian Nationalism*, 26.

38. Wolfe, *Christian Nationalism*, 26.

39. Wolfe, *Christian Nationalism*, 88.

40. Wolfe, *Christian Nationalism*, 118.

41. Wolfe, *Christian Nationalism*, 164, 183.

42. Wolfe, *Christian Nationalism*, 208.

43. Wolfe, *Christian Nationalism*, 209.

44. Wolfe, *Christian Nationalism*, 323.

45. Mark David Hall has made this critique repeatedly and persuasively in several places. See, for example, Mark David Hall, "Towards a More Reasonable Account of Christian Nationalism," *Providence*, December 20, 2023, https://tinyurl.com/yc43buny.

46. Wolfe, *Christian Nationalism*, 9.

47. Wolfe, *Christian Nationalism*, 248.

48. C. Bradley Thompson, *America's Revolutionary Mind: A Moral History of the American Revolution and the Declaration That Defined It* (New York: Encounter, 2019), 210.

49. Georg Wilhelm Friedrich Hegel, *The Philosophy of Right*, trans. T. M. Knox, Great Books of the Western World, vol. 46 (Chicago: Encyclopedia Britannica, 1952), 3.3.257.

50. Hegel, *The Philosophy of Right*, 2.3.129.

51. Hegel, *The Philosophy of Right*, 3.3.258.

52. Bertrand Russell, *The History of Western Philosophy* (New York: Simon & Schuster, 1945), 737.

53. Hegel, *The Philosophy of Right*, 3.3.260.

54. Hegel, *The Philosophy of Right*, 3.3.270.

55. Hegel, *The Philosophy of Right*, 3.3.270.

56. Georg Wilhelm Friedrich Hegel, *The Philosophy of History*, trans. J. Sibree, Great Books of the Western World, vol. 46 (Chicago: Encyclopedia Britannica, 1952), introduction, 170.

57. Hegel, *The Philosophy of History*, introduction, 171.

58. Hamilton, *Federalist* 1, 1.

59. Hegel, *The Philosophy of History*, introduction, 174.

60. Hegel, *The Philosophy of History*, introduction, 177.

61. Hegel, *The Philosophy of Right*, 3.3.275.

62. Hegel, *The Philosophy of Right*, 3.3.280.

63. Hegel, *The Philosophy of Right*, 3.3.281.

64. Wolfe, *Christian Nationalism*, 9.

65. Wolfe, *Christian Nationalism*, 13.

66. Wolfe, *Christian Nationalism*, 38.

67. Wolfe, *Christian Nationalism*, 135.

68. Wolfe, *Christian Nationalism*, 26.

69. Wolfe, *Christian Nationalism*, 164.

70. Wolfe, *Christian Nationalism*, 166.

71. Wolfe, *Christian Nationalism*, 180.

72. Wolfe, *Christian Nationalism*, 30.

73. Wolfe, *Christian Nationalism*, 269.

74. Wolfe, *Christian Nationalism*, 31.

75. Wolfe, *Christian Nationalism*, 286.

76. Wolfe, *Christian Nationalism*, 433.

77. Wolfe, *Christian Nationalism*, 322.

78. Richard Hofstadter, "The Pseudo-Conservative Revolt," *American Scholar* 24, no. 1 (Winter 1954–1955): 14.

79. Viereck, *Conservatism*, 11–12.

80. Wolfe, *Christian Nationalism*, 38, 437.

81. Allitt, *The Conservatives*, 67.

82. Wolfe rightly but ironically cites Burke favorably in defining society as embracing the dead, the living, and the yet to be born. See Wolfe, *Christian Nationalism*, 137.

83. Theodore Roosevelt, "The Duties of American Citizenship," in *Works of Theodore Roosevelt*, vol. 13, 282.

84. Roosevelt, "Duties of American Citizenship," 282.

CHAPTER FIVE

1. James I. Robertson, *General A. P. Hill: The Story of a Confederate Warrior* (New York: Vintage, 1987), 319.

2. G. Powell Hill, "First Burial of General Hill's Remains," *Southern Historical Society Papers* 31 (1891): 183–86, https://tinyurl.com/39y2v268.

3. Robertson, *A. P. Hill*, 321.

4. Hill, "First Burial," 186.

5. Robertson, *A. P. Hill*, 322.

6. Robertson, *A. P. Hill*, 322.

7. Robertson, *A. P. Hill*, 323.

8. Robertson, *A. P. Hill*, 324.

9. Joi Fultz, "Confederate General A. P. Hill's Remains Removed from Richmond Monument," CBS 6 News Richmond, December 13, 2022, https://tinyurl.com/z37rz7fu.

10. Isa. 44:6–7; John 8:58.

11. Allen Guelzo, *Making History: How Great Historians Interpret the Past* (Chantilly, VA: Teaching Co., 2008), 12.

12. Guelzo, *Making History*, 12.

13. John Lukacs, *Historical Consciousness: The Remembered Past* (1968; reprint, New Brunswick, NJ: Transaction, 2009), 9.

14. Lukacs, *Historical Consciousness*, 11.

15. Herodotus, *The History*, trans. David Grene (Chicago: University of Chicago Press, 1987), 33.

16. Thucydides, *The History of the Peloponnesian War*, trans. Richard Crawley, Great Books of the Western World, vol. 6 (Chicago: Encyclopedia Britannica, 1952), 1.1.1.

17. Thucydides, *Peloponnesian War* 1.1.21.

18. Plutarch, *The Lives of the Noble Grecians and Romans: Theseus*, trans. John Dryden, Great Books of the Western World, vol. 14 (Chicago: Encyclopedia Britannica, 1952), 1.1.21.

19. P. Cornelius Tacitus, *The Annals*, trans. Alfred John Church and William Jackson Brodribb, Great Books of the Western World, vol. 15 (Chicago: Encyclopedia Britannica, 1952), 2.65.

20. Augustine, *On Christian Doctrine*, trans. J. F. Shaw, Great Books of the Western World, vol. 18 (Chicago: Encyclopedia Britannica, 1952), 2.28.44.

21. Thomas Hobbes, *Leviathan, Or, Matter, Form, and Power of a Commonwealth Ecclesiastical and Civil*, Great Books of the Western World, vol. 23 (Chicago: Encyclopedia Britannica, 1952), 1.8.

22. Lukacs, *Historical Consciousness*, 14.

23. Lukacs, *Historical Consciousness*, 31.

24. John Lukacs, *The Hitler of History* (New York: Knopf, 1998), 251.

25. Richard M. Weaver, *Ideas Have Consequences* (1948; reprint, Chicago: University of Chicago Press, 1984), 176.

26. Weaver, *Ideas Have Consequences*, 176.

27. Weaver, *Ideas Have Consequences*, 177.

28. Richard M. Weaver, "The Role of Education in Shaping Our Society," in *In Defense of Tradition: Collected Shorter Writings of Richard M. Weaver, 1929–1963*, ed. Ted J. Smith III (Indianapolis: Liberty Fund, 2000), 217.

29. Alexander Hamilton, *Federalist* 34, in Pole, *The Federalist*, 176.

30. Hamilton, *Federalist* 34, in Pole, *The Federalist*, 177.

31. Hamilton, *Federalist* 34, in Pole, *The Federalist*, 177.

32. Richard M. Weaver, "Lord Acton: The Historian as Thinker," in Smith, *In Defense of Tradition*, 631.

33. Weaver, "Lord Acton," 631.

34. Weaver, "Lord Acton," 631.

35. John Lukacs, *History and the Human Condition: A Historian's Pursuit of Knowledge* (Wilmington, DE: ISI, 2013), 6.

36. John Lewis Gaddis, *The Landscape of History: How Historians Map the Past* (New York: Oxford University Press, 2002), 32.

37. Gaddis, *The Landscape of History*, 34.

38. Gaddis, *The Landscape of History*, 5.

39. Beth Barton Schweiger, "Seeing Things: Knowledge and Love in History," in *Confessing History: Explorations in Christian Faith and the Historian's Vocation*, ed. John Fea, Jay Green, and Eric Miller (Notre Dame: University of Notre Dame Press, 2010), 62.

40. Francis Bacon, *Novum Organum*, Great Books of the Western World, vol. 30 (Chicago: Encyclopedia Britannica, 1952), 1.41, 50, 52.

41. Bacon, *Novum Organum*, 1.44.

42. See Stephen Kinzer, *The Brothers: John Foster Dulles, Allen Dulles, and Their Secret World War* (New York: Holt, 2013), for a particularly egregious example of a biographer who was sure he had Dulles all figured out.

43. Gaddis, *The Landscape of History*, 6.

44. Gaddis, *The Landscape of History*, 6, 7.

45. Gaddis, *The Landscape of History*, 8.

46. Robert Tracy McKenzie, *The First Thanksgiving: What the Real Story Tells Us about Loving God and Learning from History* (Downers Grove, IL: IVP Academic, 2013), 18.

47. Klemens von Metternich, *Memoirs*, III, 430, quoted in Viereck, *Conservatism Revisited*, 74.

48. Viereck, *Conservatism Revisited*, 70.

49. Viereck, *Conservatism Revisited*, 70.

50. Michael Price, "These Asian Hunter-Gatherers May Have Been the First to Domesticate Horses," *Science*, May 9, 2018, https://tinyurl.com/ythf964f.

51. Viereck, *Conservatism Revisited*, 74.

52. 1 Cor. 13:6.

53. Schweiger, "Seeing Things," 65.

54. Schweiger, "Seeing Things," 70.

55. Schweiger, "Seeing Things," 70.

56. Edward Hallett Carr, *What Is History?* (1961; reprint, New York: Knopf, 1964), 26.

57. Schweiger, "Seeing Things," 77.

58. Rachel Lucas, "A Progressive City with Confederate Roots: Lexington's Unique Path to Racial Equality," WSLS 10 News, August 7, 2020, https://tinyurl.com/yjhfwy8c.

59. Morel interview, in Lucas, "A Progressive City with Confederate Roots."

60. Allen Guelzo, "Should We Banish Robert E. Lee and His Confederate Friends? Let's Talk," *USA Today*, August 16, 2017, https://tinyurl.com/mvstvwsk.

61. Guelzo, "Should We Banish Robert E. Lee and His Confederate Friends?"

62. James I. Robertson, "The Civil War: Debate over Confederate Monuments," C-Span, July 28, 2018, https://tinyurl.com/yckssbpa.

63. Viereck, *Conservatism Revisited*, 153.

CHAPTER SIX

1. Jason DeRose, "Religious 'Nones' Are Now the Largest Single Group in the U.S.," NPR, January 24, 2024, https://tinyurl.com/ynp5thby.

2. Gilbert Murray, introduction to *Greek and English Tragedy: A Contrast*, quoted in Marjorie Hope Nicolson, *Mountain Gloom and Mountain Glory: The Development of the Aesthetics of the Infinite* (1959; reprint, Seattle: University of Washington Press, 1997), 39.

3. Isa. 55:6–7; Jer. 29:12; 33:2–3; Matt. 7:7–8; Rev. 22:17.

4. Avery Dulles, oral interview, July 30, 1966, Woodstock College, MD, 14, conducted by Philip A. Crowl, John Foster Dulles Oral History Collection, Seeley G. Mudd Manuscript Library, Princeton University.

5. Robert F. Hart, oral interview, July 6, 1965, Chaumont, NY, 29, conducted by Philip A. Crowl, John Foster Dulles Oral History Collection, Seeley G. Mudd Manuscript Library, Princeton University.

6. C. S. Lewis, *Mere Christianity* (1943; reprint, New York: Touchstone, 1980), 18.

7. Lewis, *Mere Christianity*, 19.

8. Lewis, *Mere Christianity*, 21.

9. Lewis, *Mere Christianity*, 31.

10. Lewis, *Mere Christianity*, 33.

11. Lewis, *Mere Christianity*, 39.

12. Thomas V. Morris, *Making Sense of It All: Pascal and the Meaning of Life* (Grand Rapids: Eerdmans, 1992), 62.

13. Rodney Stark, *The Victory of Reason: How Christianity Led to Freedom, Capitalism, and Western Success* (New York: Random House, 2005), 208.

14. Mark David Hall, *Did America Have a Christian Founding?* (Nashville: Nelson, 2019), xviii.

15. Hall, *Christian Founding*, xxii.

16. Daniel L. Dreisbach, *Reading the Bible with the Founding Fathers* (New York: Oxford University Press, 2017), 17.

17. Anne H. Pinn and Anthony B. Pinn, *Fortress Introduction of Black Church History* (Minneapolis: Fortress, 2002), 37.

18. Pinn and Pinn, *Black Church History*, 47.

19. Pinn and Pinn, *Black Church History*, 56.

20. Pinn and Pinn, *Black Church History*, 63–101.

21. "The Black Church in America: A Story," African American Registry, https://tinyurl.com/364knnzr.

22. "5 Things to Know: HBCU Edition," National Museum of African American History and Culture, https://tinyurl.com/bdenb3wr.

23. Paul Harvey, *Through the Storm, through the Night: A History of African American Christianity* (Lanham, MD: Rowman & Littlefield, 2011), 5.

24. Robert Tracy McKenzie, *We the Fallen People: The Founders and the Future of American Democracy* (Downers Grove, IL: IVP Academic, 2021), 235.

25. Tocqueville, *Democracy in America*, 1:466.

26. Tocqueville, *Democracy in America*, 1:25.

27. Tocqueville, *Democracy in America*, 1:473.

28. Tocqueville, *Democracy in America*, 1:475.

29. Tocqueville, *Democracy in America*, 1:475.

30. Tocqueville, *Democracy in America*, 1:478.

31. McKenzie, *We the Fallen People*, 238.

32. Tocqueville, *Democracy in America*, 1:480 (emphasis added).

33. Tocqueville, *Democracy in America*, 1:482.

34. Tocqueville, *Democracy in America*, 1:483.

35. Tocqueville, *Democracy in America*, 1:483.

36. Tocqueville, *Democracy in America*, 1:483.

37. Tocqueville, *Democracy in America*, 1:483–84.

38. Tocqueville, *Democracy in America*, 1:484.

39. "The First Amendment has often been understood to limit religious freedom in ways never imagined by the late eighteenth-century dissenters who demanded constitutional guarantees of religious liberty. For example, the dissenters who campaigned for constitutional barriers to any government establishment of religion had no desire more generally to prevent contact between religion and government." Philip Hamburger, *Separation of Church and State* (Cambridge, MA: Harvard University Press, 2002), 13.

40. Rodney Stark, *America's Blessings: How Religion Benefits Everyone, Including Atheists* (West Conshohocken, PA: Templeton, 2012), 11.

41. Stark, *America's Blessings*, 30.

42. Stark, *America's Blessings*, 4–5.

43. Christopher Hitchens, *God Is Not Great: How Religion Poisons Everything* (New York: Twelve, 2007), 23, 37, 41.

44. Hitchens, *God Is Not Great*, 46–47.

45. Tocqueville, *Democracy in America*, 1:482.

46. Stephen T. Davis, *God, Reason, and Theistic Proofs* (Grand Rapids: Eerdmans, 1997), 22–26.

47. Augustine, *Confessions* 1.1.

48. Eccles. 1:2–11.

49. Thomas Paine, *Common Sense*, in *"Common Sense," "The Rights of Man," and Other Essential Writings of Thomas Paine* (New York: Meridian, 1984), 66.

50. Eccles. 1:13.

51. Eccles. 1:16.

52. David Gibson, *Living Life Backward: How Ecclesiastes Teaches Us to Live in Light of the End* (Wheaton, IL: Crossway, 2017), 19.

53. Gibson, *Living Life Backward*, 30.

54. Eccles. 9:3–9.

55. C. L. Seow, *Ecclesiastes: A New Translation with Introduction and Commentary*, Anchor Bible, vol. 18c (New York: Doubleday, 1997), 305.

56. Seow, *Ecclesiastes*, 305.

57. Eccles. 12:10–14.

58. John 14:15.

59. Prov. 9:10.

60. Daniel C. Fredericks, *Ecclesiastes*, in *Ecclesiastes and the Song of Songs*, Apollos Old Testament Commentary, vol. 16 (Downers Grove, IL: IVP, 2010), 250.

61. Fredericks, *Ecclesiastes*, 251.

CONCLUSION

1. I have adapted this section on how Tocqueville saw the Americans harmonize religion and liberty from an essay I wrote in the summer of 2020, with the kind permission of Springer Nature Switzerland AG. See John D. Wilsey, "Public Spirit as Mediating Influence between Tocqueville's 'Spirit of Religion' and 'Spirit of Freedom,'" in *The Palgrave Handbook of Religion and State: Theoretical Perspectives*, vol. 1, ed. Shannon Holzer (Cham, Switzerland: Palgrave Macmillan, 2023), 417–31.

2. Pierson, *Tocqueville in America*, 393–94, 406–7, 417–18.

3. Alexis de Tocqueville, *Letters from America* (New Haven: Yale University Press, 2010), 191.

4. Tocqueville, *Letters from America*, 220.

5. Tocqueville, *Letters from America*, 238.

6. Tocqueville, *Letters from America*, 239.

7. Tocqueville, *Democracy in America*, 1:69, 479.

8. Tocqueville, *Democracy in America*, 1:69.

9. Tocqueville, *Democracy in America*, 1:479.

10. Tocqueville, *Democracy in America*, 1:92.

11. Tocqueville, *Democracy in America*, 1:407.

12. Tocqueville, *Democracy in America*, 1:878.

13. Tocqueville, *Democracy in America*, 2:1248.

14. Tocqueville, *Democracy in America*, 2:1249.

15. Tocqueville, *Democracy in America*, 2:1250.

16. Tocqueville, *Democracy in America*, 2:1251.

17. Tocqueville, *Democracy in America*, 2:746–47.

18. Norman A. Graebner, "Christianity and Democracy: Tocqueville's Views of Religion in America," *Journal of Religion* 56, no. 3 (July 1976): 264.

19. Tocqueville, *Democracy in America*, 1:45–73.

20. Tocqueville, *Democracy in America*, 1:467.

21. Tocqueville, *Democracy in America*, 1:475.

22. Tocqueville, *Democracy in America*, 1:475.

23. Tocqueville, *Democracy in America*, 1:478.

24. Tocqueville, *Democracy in America*, 2:746.

25. Tocqueville, *Democracy in America*, 2:741.

26. Wilfred McClay, *The Masterless: Self and Society in Modern America* (Chapel Hill: University of North Carolina Press, 1994), 44.

27. Tocqueville, *Democracy in America*, 2:921.

28. Tocqueville, *Democracy in America*, 2:920.

29. Tocqueville, *Democracy in America*, 1:480.

30. Tocqueville, *Democracy in America*, 1:482–83.

31. Tocqueville, *Democracy in America*, 1:385.

32. Tocqueville, *Democracy in America*, 1:303.

33. Tocqueville, *Democracy in America*, 2:921–22.

34. Tocqueville, *Democracy in America*, 1:494–504.

35. Tocqueville, *Democracy in America*, 1:26.

36. James T. Schleifer, "Tocqueville, Religion, and Democracy in America: Some Essential Questions," *American Political Thought* 3, no. 2 (Fall 2014): 263.

37. Schleifer, "Tocqueville, Religion, and Democracy," 263.

38. Schleifer, "Tocqueville, Religion, and Democracy," 263.

39. Harvey C. Mansfield, "Tocqueville on Religion and Liberty," *American Political Thought* 5, no. 2 (Spring 2016): 256.

40. Barbara Allen, *Tocqueville, Covenant, and the Democratic Revolution: Harmonizing Earth with Heaven* (Lanham, MD: Rowman & Littlefield, 2005), 131.

41. Tocqueville, *Democracy in America*, 1.2.9.455.

42. Allen, *Tocqueville, Covenant, and the Democratic Revolution*, 13, 131.

43. Allen, *Tocqueville, Covenant, and the Democratic Revolution*, 13.

44. Allen, *Tocqueville, Covenant, and the Democratic Revolution*, 14–17.

45. Allen, *Tocqueville, Covenant, and the Democratic Revolution*, 135.

46. Allen, *Tocqueville, Covenant, and the Democratic Revolution*, 137.

47. Sanford Kessler, "Tocqueville's Puritans: Christianity and the American Founding," *Journal of Politics* 54, no. 3 (August 1992): 779.

48. Dana Villa, "Tocqueville and Civil Society," in *The Cambridge Companion to Tocqueville*, ed. Cheryl B. Welch (Cambridge: Cambridge University Press, 2006), 228.

49. Villa, "Tocqueville and Civil Society," 229.

50. Allen, *Tocqueville, Covenant, and the Democratic Revolution*, 131.

51. Allen, *Tocqueville, Covenant, and the Democratic Revolution*, 131.

52. Catherine Zuckert, "Not by Preaching: Tocqueville on the Role of Religion in American Democracy," *Review of Politics* 43, no. 2 (April 1981): 262–63.

53. Zuckert, "Not by Preaching," 266.

54. Zuckert, "Not by Preaching," 266.

55. Allen, *Tocqueville, Covenant, and the Democratic Revolution*, 124.

56. Aristide Tessitore, "Alexis de Tocqueville on the Natural State of Religion in the Age of Democracy," *Journal of Politics* 64, no. 4 (November 2002): 1144.

57. Mansfield, "Tocqueville on Religion and Liberty," 256.

58. Mansfield, "Tocqueville on Religion and Liberty," 273.

59. Ralph C. Hancock, "The Uses and Hazards of Christianity in Tocque-

ville's Attempt to Save Democratic Souls," in *Interpreting Tocqueville's "Democracy in America,"* ed. Ken Masugi (Lanham, MD: Rowman & Littlefield, 1991), 349.

60. Oliver Hidalgo, "America as a Delusive Model—Tocqueville on Religion," *Amerikastudien/American Studies* 52, no. 4 (2007): 563.

61. Pierre Manent, *Tocqueville and the Nature of Democracy* (Lanham, MD: Rowman & Littlefield, 1996), 87.

62. Manent, *Tocqueville and the Nature of Democracy*, 91.

63. Tocqueville, *Democracy in America*, 1:111.

64. Abraham Lincoln, "Speech at Chicago, Illinois, July 10, 1858," in *Abraham Lincoln: Selected Speeches and Writings*, ed. Don E. Fehrenbacher (New York: Library of America, 2009), 147.

65. Matt. 5:48.

66. Lincoln, "Speech at Chicago," 147.

67. Abraham Lincoln, "Speech on the Kansas-Nebraska Act at Peoria, Illinois, October 16, 1854," in Fehrenbacher, *Abraham Lincoln*, 96.

68. Lincoln, "Speech on the Kansas-Nebraska Act," 97.

69. Lincoln, "Speech on the Kansas-Nebraska Act," 97.

70. Zitner, "America Pulls Back from Values That Once Defined It, WSJ-NORC Poll Finds."

71. Vermont Royster, "*In Hoc Anno Domini*," *Wall Street Journal*, December 22, 2023, https://tinyurl.com/ycywaw3b.

Bibliography

Alighieri, Dante. *The Divine Comedy: Inferno, Purgatorio, Paradiso.* Translated by Allen Mandelbaum, with an introduction by Eugenio Montale. New York: Knopf, 1995.

———. "Epistle X to Can Grande." In *A Translation of the Latin Works of Dante Alighieri,* translated by A. G. Ferrers Howell and Philip H. Wicksteed. London: Dent, 1904.

Allen, Barbara. *Tocqueville, Covenant, and the Democratic Revolution: Harmonizing Earth with Heaven.* Lanham, MD: Rowman & Littlefield, 2005.

Allitt, Patrick. *The Conservatives: Ideas and Personalities throughout American History.* New Haven: Yale University Press, 2009.

Aquinas, Thomas. *Summa Theologica.* Translated by Fathers of the English Dominican Province. Revised by Daniel J. Sullivan. Great Books of the Western World, vol. 19. Chicago: Encyclopedia Britannica, 1952.

Aristotle. *Nicomachean Ethics.* Translated by W. D. Ross. Great Books of the Western World, vol. 9. Chicago: Encyclopedia Britannica, 1952.

———. *Politics.* Translated by Benjamin Jowett. Great Books of the Western World, vol. 9. Chicago: Encyclopedia Britannica, 1952.

Augustine. *City of God.* Translated by Marcus Dods. London: Folio, 2012.

———. *The Confessions.* Translated by Maria Boulding. Works of Saint Augustine: A Translation for the 21st Century, vol. 1, part 1. 1997. Reprint, New York: New City, 2012.

———. *On Christian Doctrine.* Translated by J. F. Shaw. Great Books of the Western World, vol. 18. Chicago: Encyclopedia Britannica, 1952.

———. "On Faith and the Creed." In *Nicene and Post-Nicene Fathers,* vol. 3, *Augustin on the Holy Trinity, Doctrinal Treatises, Moral Treatises,* edited by Philip Schaff. Peabody, MA: Hendrickson, 1999.

———. "On Grace and Free Will." In *Nicene and Post-Nicene Fathers,* vol. 5,

Augustin: Anti-Pelagian Writings, edited by Philip Schaff. Peabody, MA: Hendrickson, 1999.

———. "Sermon 43: On What Is Written in Isaiah; Unless You Believe, You Shall Not Understand." In *Sermons on the Old Testament, 20–50*, translated by Edmund Hill. Works of Saint Augustine: A New Translation for the 21st Century, vol. 2, part 3. Brooklyn, NY: New City, 1990.

———. *Soliloquies*. In *Nicene and Post-Nicene Fathers*, vol. 7, *Augustin: Homilies on the Gospel of John, Homilies on the First Epistle of John, Soliloquies*, edited by Philip Schaff. Peabody, MA: Hendrickson, 1999.

Babbitt, Irving. *Democracy and Leadership*. With an introduction by Russell Kirk. 1924. Reprint, Indianapolis: Liberty Fund, 1979.

———. *Rousseau and Romanticism*. New York: Houghton Mifflin, 1919.

Babík, Milan. *Statecraft and Salvation: Wilsonian Liberal Internationalism as Secularized Eschatology*. Waco, TX: Baylor University Press, 2013.

Bacon, Francis. *Novum Organum*. Great Books of the Western World, vol. 30. Chicago: Encyclopedia Britannica, 1952.

Bailyn, Bernard. *The Ideological Origins of the American Revolution*. Cambridge, MA: Belknap Press of Harvard University Press, 2017.

Benedict XVI. "General Audience of 30 January 2008: Saint Augustine of Hippo." Libreria Editrice Vaticana. https://tinyurl.com/yryxward.

"The Black Church in America: A Story." African American Registry. https://tinyurl.com/364knnzr.

Blair, Walter. "The Popularity of Nineteenth-Century American Humorists." *American Literature* 3, no. 2 (May 1931): 175–93.

Bloeser, Andrew J., Tarah Williams, Candaisy Crawford, and Brian Harward. "Are Stealth Democrats Really Committed to Democracy? Process Preferences Revisited." *Perspectives on Politics*, 2022, 116–30.

Boorstin, Daniel J. *The Genius of American Politics*. Chicago: University of Chicago Press, 1953.

Burke, Edmund. *Reflections on the Revolution in France*. In *Select Works of Edmund Burke*, vol. 2, edited by Francis Canavan. Indianapolis: Liberty Fund, 1999.

Burkholder, J. Peter. Donald Jay Grout, and Claude V. Palisca, *History of Western Music*. 1960. Reprint, London: Folio, 2006.

Bush, L. Russ. *A Handbook for Christian Philosophy*. Grand Rapids: Zondervan, 1991.

Canavan, Francis. Foreword to Edmund Burke, *Reflections on the Revolution in France*, vol. 2 of *Select Works of Edmund Burke*, edited by Francis Canavan. Indianapolis: Liberty Fund, 1999.

Bibliography

Cappon, Lester J., ed. *The Adams-Jefferson Letters: The Complete Correspondence between Thomas Jefferson and Abigail and John Adams.* 1959. Reprint, Chapel Hill: University of North Carolina Press, 1987.

Carr, Edward Hallett. *What Is History?* 1961. Reprint, New York: Knopf, 1964.

Collinson, Stephen. "The US Now Faces Simultaneous Showdowns with China and Russia." CNN, February 14, 2023. https://tinyurl.com/7yvmzmck.

Connolly, Michael J. "Daniel Boorstin against the Barbarians." *Imaginative Conservative,* October 16, 2023. https://tinyurl.com/dx6b43sc.

Continetti, Matthew. *The Right: The Hundred Year War for American Conservatism.* New York: Basic Books, 2022.

Cooper-White, Pamela. *The Psychology of Christian Nationalism: Why People Are Drawn in and How to Talk across the Divide.* Minneapolis: Fortress, 2022.

Crean, Thomas, and Alan Fimister. *Integralism: A Manual for Political Philosophy.* Seelscheid, Germany: Editiones Scholasticae, 2020.

DaCosta, Morton, director. *Auntie Mame.* Warner Bros., 1958. Blu-ray DVD. Warner Bros., 2017. Featuring Rosalind Russell, Forrest Tucker, Coral Browne, Roger Smith, and Peggy Cass.

Danforth, Samuel, and Paul Royster (transcriber and editor). "A Brief Recognition of New-Englands Errand into the Wilderness: An Online Electronic Text Edition." 1670. University of Nebraska–Lincoln Digital Commons. Paper 35. https://tinyurl.com/y82sc6wa.

Davis, Stephen T. *God, Reason, and Theistic Proofs.* Grand Rapids: Eerdmans, 1997.

Deneen, Patrick J. *Why Liberalism Failed.* New Haven: Yale University Press, 2018.

DeRose, Jason. "Religious 'Nones' Are Now the Largest Single Group in the U. S." NPR, January 24, 2024. https://tinyurl.com/ynp5thby.

Draper, John William. *History of the Conflict between Religion and Science.* New York: Appleton, 1874.

Dreisbach, Daniel L. *Reading the Bible with the Founding Fathers.* New York: Oxford University Press, 2017.

Dreisbach, Daniel L., and Mark David Hall, eds. *Faith and the Founders of the American Republic.* Oxford: Oxford University Press, 2014.

———. *The Sacred Rights of Conscience.* Indianapolis: Liberty Fund, 2009.

Dulles, Avery. Oral interview, July 30, 1966, Woodstock College, MD, 14. Conducted by Philip A. Crowl. John Foster Dulles Oral History Collection. Seeley G. Mudd Manuscript Library, Princeton University.

Dulles, John Foster. "Patriotism." Speech given at Indiana University, Bloomington, June 12, 1955. John Foster Dulles Papers, box 337. Public Policy

Papers, Department of Rare Books and Special Collections. Seeley G. Mudd Manuscript Library, Princeton University.

DuMez, Kristin Kobes. *Jesus and John Wayne: How White Evangelicals Corrupted a Faith and Fractured a Nation*. New York: Liveright, 2020.

Eisenstadt, Peter, ed. *Black Conservatism: Essays in Intellectual and Political History*. 2nd ed. New York: Routledge, 2012.

Faulkner, William. *Requiem for a Nun*. Reprint, New York: Random House, 1966.

Finnis, John. *Natural Law and Natural Rights*. 2nd ed. New York: Oxford University Press, 2011.

"5 Things to Know: HBCU Edition." National Museum of African American History and Culture. https://tinyurl.com/bdenb3wr.

Flores, Andrew R. "National Trends in Public Opinion on LGBT Rights in the United States." UCLA School of Law, Williams Institute, November 2014. https://tinyurl.com/mwh3ytkc.

Fredericks, Daniel C. *Ecclesiastes*. In *Ecclesiastes and the Song of Songs*. Apollos Old Testament Commentary, vol. 16. Downers Grove, IL: IVP, 2010.

Fultz, Joi. "Confederate General A. P. Hill's Remains Removed from Richmond Monument." CBS 6 News Richmond, December 13, 2022. https://tinyurl.com/z37rz7fu.

Gaddis, John Lewis. *The Landscape of History: How Historians Map the Past*. New York: Oxford University Press, 2002.

Gamble, Richard M. *The War for Righteousness: Progressive Christianity, the Great War, and the Rise of the Messianic Nation*. Wilmington, DE: ISI, 2003.

Gates, Carrie. "'On the Brink of a New Civil War': New National Survey Highlights Fragility of American Democracy, Stark Partisan Divides." *Notre Dame News*, November 3, 2022. https://tinyurl.com/2ynu8pnz.

George, Robert P. *Making Men Moral: Civil Liberties and Public Morality*. 1993. Reprint, New York: Oxford University Press, 2002.

Gibson, David. *Living Life Backward: How Ecclesiastes Teaches Us to Live in Light of the End*. Wheaton, IL: Crossway, 2017.

Gorski, Philip L., and Samuel L. Perry. *The Flag and the Cross: White Christian Nationalism and the Threat to American Democracy*. New York: Oxford University Press, 2022.

Graebner, Norman A. "Christianity and Democracy: Tocqueville's Views of Religion in America." *Journal of Religion* 56, no. 3 (July 1976): 263–73.

Guelzo, Allen C. *Making History: How Great Historians Interpret the Past*. Chantilly, VA: Teaching Co., 2008.

———. "Preaching a Conspiracy Theory." *City Journal*, December 8, 2019. https://tinyurl.com/4wr7pbaw.

———. "Should We Banish Robert E. Lee and His Confederate Friends? Let's Talk." *USA Today*, August 16, 2017. https://tinyurl.com/mvstvwsk.

Hall, Mark David. *Did America Have a Christian Founding?* Nashville: Nelson, 2019.

———. "Towards a More Reasonable Account of Christian Nationalism." *Providence*, December 20, 2023. https://tinyurl.com/yc43buny.

Hamburger, Philip. *Separation of Church and State*. Cambridge, MA: Harvard University Press, 2002.

Hamilton, Alexander. *Federalist 1*. In *The Federalist*, edited by J. R. Pole. Indianapolis: Hackett, 2005.

———. *Federalist 34*. In *The Federalist*, edited by J. R. Pole. Indianapolis: Hackett, 2005.

Hancock, Ralph C. "The Uses and Hazards of Christianity in Tocqueville's Attempt to Save Democratic Souls." In *Interpreting Tocqueville's "Democracy in America,"* edited by Ken Masugi. Lanham, MD: Rowman & Littlefield, 1991.

Hannah-Jones, Nikole, ed. *The 1619 Project: A New Origin Story*. New York: One World, 2021.

Harris, Leslie M. "I Helped Fact-Check the 1619 Project. The Times Ignored Me." *Politico*, March 6, 2020. https://tinyurl.com/2me2jhrn.

Hart, Robert F. Oral interview, July 6, 1965, Chaumont, NY, 29. Conducted by Philip A. Crowl. John Foster Dulles Oral History Collection, Seeley G. Mudd Manuscript Library, Princeton University.

Harvey, Paul. *Through the Storm, through the Night: A History of African American Christianity*. Lanham, MD: Rowman & Littlefield, 2011.

Harwell, Drew, and Victoria Bisset. "How Osama bin Laden's 'Letter to America' Reached Millions Online." *Washington Post*, November 16, 2023. https://tinyurl.com/2xzje86z.

Hayes, Kevin J. *George Washington: A Life in Books*. New York: Oxford University Press, 2017.

Haynes, Lemuel. "Liberty Further Extended: Or, Free thoughts on the illegality of Slave-keeping; Wherein those arguments that Are useed in its vindication Are plainly confuted. Together with an humble Address to such as are Concearned in the practice." Quoted in Ruth Bogin, "'Liberty Further Extended': A 1776 Antislavery Manuscript by Lemuel Haynes." *William and Mary Quarterly* 40, no. 1 (January 1983): 85–105.

Healey, Jonathan. *The Blazing World: A New History of Revolutionary England, 1603–1689*. New York: Knopf, 2023.

Hegel, Georg Wilhelm Friedrich. *The Philosophy of History*. Translated by J. Sibree. Great Books of the Western World, vol. 46. Chicago: Encyclopedia Britannica, 1952.

——. *The Philosophy of Right*. Translated by T. M. Knox. Great Books of the Western World, vol. 46. Chicago: Encyclopedia Britannica, 1952.

Henry, Patrick. "Give Me Liberty, or Give Me Death." March 23, 1775. Yale Law School, Lillian Goldman Law Library, the Avalon Project. https://tinyurl.com/2fcn2777.

Herodotus, *The History*. Translated by David Grene. Chicago: University of Chicago Press, 1987.

Hidalgo, Oliver. "America as a Delusive Model—Tocqueville on Religion." *Amerikastudien/American Studies* 52, no. 4 (2007): 561–78.

Hill, G. Powell. "First Burial of General Hill's Remains." *Southern Historical Society Papers* 31 (1891): 183–86. https://tinyurl.com/39y2v268.

Hill, J. Sellers, and Nia L. Orakwue. "Harvard Student Groups Face Intense Backlash for Statement Calling Israel 'Entirely Responsible' for Hamas Attack." *Harvard Crimson*, October 10, 2023. https://tinyurl.com/266r27wx.

"Historian Allen Guelzo Speaks on the 150th Anniversary of the Battle of Gettysburg." World Socialist Web Site. YouTube, July 4, 2013. https://tinyurl.com/msu25f53.

The Historical Collections of the Danvers Historical Society. Vol. 8. Danvers, MA: Danvers Historical Society, 1920.

Hitchens, Christopher. *God Is Not Great: How Religion Poisons Everything*. New York: Twelve, 2007.

Hitz, Zena. *Lost in Thought: The Hidden Pleasures of an Intellectual Life*. Princeton: Princeton University Press, 2020.

Hobbes, Thomas. *Leviathan, Or, Matter, Form, and Power of a Commonwealth Ecclesiastical and Civil*. Great Books of the Western World, vol. 23. Chicago: Encyclopedia Britannica, 1952.

Hofstadter, Richard. "The Pseudo-Conservative Revolt." *American Scholar* 24, no. 1 (Winter 1954–1955): 9–27.

Honan, William H. "Russell Kirk Is Dead at 75: Seminal Conservative Author." *New York Times*, April 30, 1994. https://tinyurl.com/5zcnbvh.

Howe, Daniel Walker. *What Hath God Wrought: The Transformation of America, 1815–1848*. New York: Oxford University Press, 2007.

Hutchins, Robert M. *The Great Conversation: The Substance of a Liberal Education*. Great Books of the Western World, vol. 1. Chicago: Encyclopedia Britannica, 1952.

Kessler, Sanford. "Tocqueville's Puritans: Christianity and the American Founding." *Journal of Politics* 54, no. 3 (August 1992): 776–92.

Kilner, John F. *Duty and Destiny: Humanity in the Image of God.* Grand Rapids: Eerdmans, 2015.

Kinzer, Stephen. *The Brothers: John Foster Dulles, Allen Dulles, and Their Secret World War.* New York: Holt, 2013.

Kirk, Russell. "A Cautionary Note on the Ghostly Tale." In *Ancestral Shadows: An Anthology of Ghostly Tales,* edited by Vigen Guroian. Grand Rapids: Eerdmans, 2004.

———. *The Conservative Mind: From Burke to Eliot.* 7th rev. ed. Washington: Regnery, 2001.

———. "The Framers: Not Philosophes, but Gentlemen." In *The Essential Russell Kirk: Selected Essays,* edited by George A. Panichas. Wilmington, DE: ISI, 2007.

———. "Prescription, Authority, and Ordered Freedom." In *What Is Conservatism?,* edited by Frank S. Meyer, 2nd ed. Wilmington, DE: ISI, 2017.

———. *The Roots of American Order.* With an introduction by Forrest MacDonald. 4th ed. Wilmington, DE: ISI, 2003.

———. "Russell Kirk and the Vision for Piety Hill." Video recording. 1993. Vimeo video. 8:42. https://vimeo.com/119700546.

Lacey, Robert J. *Pragmatic Conservatism: Edmund Burke and His Intellectual Heirs.* New York: Palgrave Macmillan, 2018.

Lamon, Ward Hill. *Recollections of Abraham Lincoln, 1847–1865.* Edited by Dorothy Lamon Teillard. 1895. Reprint, Cambridge, MA: University, 1911.

Lansing, Alfred. *Endurance: Shackleton's Incredible Voyage.* New York: Basic Books, 2014.

Lewis, Angela K. *Conservatism in the Black Community: To the Right and Misunderstood.* New York: Routledge, 2013.

Lewis, C. S. *Mere Christianity.* 1943. Reprint, New York: Touchstone, 1980.

———. "On the Reading of Old Books." In *God in the Dock.* Grand Rapids: Eerdmans, 1970.

———. *The Silver Chair.* Reprint, London: Folio Society, 2012.

———. *The Last Battle.* Chronicles of Narnia. New York: HarperCollins, 2004.

Light, Paul C. "The True Size of Government Is Nearing a Record High." Brookings, October 7, 2020. https://tinyurl.com/4suxrs28.

Lincoln, Abraham. "Annual Message to Congress, December 1, 1862." In *Selected Speeches and Writings,* edited by Don E. Fehrenbacher. New York: Library of America, 2009.

———. "The Gettysburg Address." In *The Annals of America, 1858–1865: The Crisis of the Union*. Vol. 9. Chicago: Encyclopedia Britannica, 1968.

———. "Second Inaugural Address." In *The Annals of America, 1858–1865: The Crisis of the Union*. Vol. 9. Chicago: Encyclopedia Britannica, 1968.

———. "Speech at Chicago, Illinois, July 10, 1858." In *Abraham Lincoln: Selected Speeches and Writings*, edited by Don E. Fehrenbacher. New York: Library of America, 2009.

———. "Speech on the Kansas-Nebraska Act at Peoria, Illinois, October 16, 1854." In *Abraham Lincoln: Selected Speeches and Writings*, edited by Don E. Fehrenbacher. New York: Library of America, 2009.

Locke, John. *Second Essay concerning the True Original Extent and End of Civil Government*. Great Books of the Western World, vol. 35. Chicago: Encyclopedia Britannica, 1952.

———. *"Two Treatises of Government" and "A Letter concerning Toleration."* Edited by Ian Shapiro. New Haven: Yale University Press, 2003.

Lucas, Rachel. "A Progressive City with Confederate Roots: Lexington's Unique Path to Racial Equality." WSLS 10 News, August 7, 2020. https://tinyurl.com/yjhfwy8c.

Lukacs, John. *The End of the Twentieth Century and the End of the Modern Age*. New York: Ticknor & Fields, 1993.

———. *Historical Consciousness: The Remembered Past*. 1968. Reprint, New Brunswick, NJ: Transaction, 2009.

———. *History and the Human Condition: A Historian's Pursuit of Knowledge*. Wilmington, DE: ISI, 2013.

———. *The Hitler of History*. New York: Knopf, 1998.

Lumet, Sidney, director. *Fail Safe*. Columbia Pictures, 1964, DVD Sony Pictures, 2000. Featuring Henry Fonda, Dan O'Herlihy, Walter Matthau, Frank Overton, and Larry Hagman.

Lunt, W. E. *History of England*. New York: Harper & Row, 1957.

Lutz, Donald S. *The Origins of American Constitutionalism*. Baton Rouge: Louisiana State University Press, 1988.

Madison, James. *Federalist 37*. In *The Federalist*, edited by J. R. Pole. Indianapolis: Hackett, 2005.

———. *Federalist 39*. In *The Federalist*, edited by J. R. Pole. Indianapolis: Hackett, 2005.

———. *Federalist 51*. In *The Federalist*, edited by J. R. Pole. Indianapolis: Hackett, 2005.

———. *Federalist 52*. In *The Federalist*, edited by J. R. Pole. Indianapolis: Hackett, 2005.

Bibliography

———. *Federalist* 57. In *The Federalist*, edited by J. R. Pole. Indianapolis: Hackett, 2005.

Maier, Pauline. *From Resistance to Revolution: Colonial Radicals and the Development of American Opposition to Britain, 1765–1776.* New York: Norton, 1991.

Manent, Pierre. *Tocqueville and the Nature of Democracy.* Lanham, MD: Rowman & Littlefield, 1996.

Mansfield, Harvey C. "Tocqueville on Religion and Liberty." *American Political Thought* 5, no. 2 (Spring 2016): 250–76.

Maritain, Jacques. *The Rights of Man and Natural Law.* Translated by Doris C. Anson. New York: Scribner's, 1943.

Marshall, Peter, and David Manuel. *The Light and the Glory.* Grand Rapids: Baker Books, 1977.

Marx, Karl. "The Eighteenth Brumaire of Louis Napoleon." Works of Marx and Engels, 1852. Marxists Internet Archive. https://tinyurl.com/mrxw6z2j.

Mather, Cotton, and Thomas Parkhurst. "Magnalia Christi Americana" (1702). *Osher Map Library Rare Books*, 9. https://tinyurl.com/bdefu6mt.

Mayhew, Jonathan. "A Discourse concerning Unlimited Submission." In *The Puritans: A Sourcebook of Their Writings*, edited by Perry Miller and Thomas H. Johnson. 1963. Reprint, Mineola, NY: Dover, 2001.

McCarthy, Daniel. "Viereck Revisited." *American Conservative*, June 18, 2007. https://tinyurl.com/3c3a5ch7.

McClay, Wilfred. *The Masterless: Self and Society in Modern America.* Chapel Hill: University of North Carolina Press, 1994.

McKenna, George. *The Puritan Origins of American Patriotism.* New Haven: Yale University Press, 2007.

McKenzie, Robert Tracy. *The First Thanksgiving: What the Real Story Tells Us about Loving God and Learning from History.* Downers Grove, IL: IVP Academic, 2013.

———. *We the Fallen People: The Founders and the Future of American Democracy.* Downers Grove, IL: IVP Academic, 2021.

Mill, John Stuart. *Considerations on Representative Government.* With an introduction by F. A. Hayek. Chicago: Regnery, 1962.

Montesquieu, Charles de Secondat, Baron de. *The Spirit of Laws.* Translated by Thomas Nugent. Revised by J. V. Prichard. Great Books of the Western World, vol. 38. Chicago: Encyclopedia Britannica, 1952.

Morrell, Robert J. *Up from History: The Life of Booker T. Washington.* Cambridge, MA: Belknap Press of Harvard University Press, 2009.

Morris, Sylvia Jukes. *Price of Fame: The Honorable Clare Boothe Luce*. New York: Random House, 2014.

Morris, Thomas V. *Making Sense of It All: Pascal and the Meaning of Life*. Grand Rapids: Eerdmans, 1992.

Mueller, Eleanor, and Victoria Guida. "Washington Blinks as Debt Costs Begin to Bite." *Politico*, November 20, 2023. https://tinyurl.com/39e26s9f.

Murray, Gilbert. Introduction to *Greek and English Tragedy: A Contrast*. Quoted in Marjorie Hope Nicolson, *Mountain Gloom and Mountain Glory: The Development of the Aesthetics of the Infinite*. 1959. Reprint, Seattle: University of Washington Press, 1997.

Nagel, Paul C. *This Sacred Trust: American Nationality, 1798–1898*. New York: Oxford University Press, 1971.

Noll, Mark. *America's God: From Jonathan Edwards to Abraham Lincoln*. New York: Oxford University Press, 2002.

O'Sullivan, John L. "Annexation." *United States Magazine and Democratic Review* 17, no. 85 (July–August 1845): 5–10. https://tinyurl.com/3katvv6u.

———. "The Great Nation of Futurity." *United States Magazine and Democratic Review* 6, no. 23 (November 1839): 426–30. https://tinyurl.com/ynm6bnxw.

———. "Introduction." *United States Magazine and Democratic Review* 1, no. 1 (October 1837). https://tinyurl.com/4j95cp6n.

Paine, Thomas. *Common Sense*. In *"Common Sense," "The Rights of Man," and Other Essential Writings of Thomas Paine*. New York: Meridian, 1984.

Pascal. *Pensées*. Translated by W. F. Trotter. Great Books of the Western World, vol. 33. Chicago: Encyclopedia Britannica, 1952.

Pierson, George Wilson. *Tocqueville in America*. Baltimore: Johns Hopkins University Press, 1996.

Parks, Rosa, with Jim Haskins. *My Story*. New York: Puffin, 1992.

Pinn, Anne H., and Anthony B. Pinn. *Fortress Introduction of Black Church History*. Minneapolis: Fortress, 2002.

Plutarch. *The Lives of the Noble Grecians and Romans: Theseus*. Translated by John Dryden. Great Books of the Western World, vol. 14. Chicago: Encyclopedia Britannica, 1952.

Powell, Dennis M. "Wake Up, America: Laughter Is Healing." *Hill*, March 4, 2021. https://tinyurl.com/572ncumx.

Price, Michael. "These Asian Hunter-Gatherers May Have Been the First to Domesticate Horses." *Science*, May 9, 2018. https://tinyurl.com/ythf964f.

Robertson, James I . "The Civil War: Debate over Confederate Monuments." C-Span, July 28, 2018. https://tinyurl.com/yckssbpa.

———. *General A. P. Hill: The Story of a Confederate Warrior.* New York: Vintage, 1987.

Roosevelt, Theodore. "The Duties of American Citizenship." In *The Works of Theodore Roosevelt, National Edition*, vol. 13. New York: Scribner's, 1926.

———. "International Duty and Hyphenated Americanism." In *The Works of Theodore Roosevelt, National Edition*, vol. 18. New York: Scribner's, 1926.

———. "True Americanism." In *The Works of Theodore Roosevelt, National Edition*, vol. 13. New York: Scribner's, 1926.

Rousseau, Jean-Jacques. *The Social Contract and Other Later Political Writings.* Edited by Victor Gourevitch. Cambridge: Cambridge University Press, 1997.

Royster, Vermont. "*In Hoc Anno Domini.*" *Wall Street Journal*, December 22, 2023. https://tinyurl.com/ycywaw3b.

Russell, Bertrand. *The History of Western Philosophy.* 1945. Reprint. New York: Touchstone, 1973.

Russell, Colin A. "The Conflict of Science and Religion." In *Science and Religion: A Historical Introduction*, edited by Gary B. Ferngren. Baltimore: Johns Hopkins University Press, 2002.

"Russell Kirk: Voice for Conservatism." *Los Angeles Times*, April 30, 1994. https://tinyurl.com/bdebs9z3.

Ryn, Claes. *The Failure of American Conservatism and the Road Not Taken.* New York: Republic, 2023.

Sacks, Jonathan. *Morality: Restoring the Common Good in Divided Times.* New York: Basic Books, 2020.

Schleifer, James T. "Tocqueville, Religion, and Democracy in America: Some Essential Questions." *American Political Thought* 3, no. 2 (Fall 2014): 254–72.

Schweiger, Beth Barton. "Seeing Things: Knowledge and Love in History." In *Confessing History: Explorations in Christian Faith and the Historian's Vocation*, edited by John Fea, Jay Green, and Eric Miller. Notre Dame: University of Notre Dame Press, 2010.

Seidel, Andrew L. *The Founding Myth: Why Christian Nationalism Is Un-American.* New York: Sterling, 2019.

Sellers, Charles. *The Market Revolution: Jacksonian America, 1815–1846.* New York: Oxford University Press, 1991.

Seow, C. L. *Ecclesiastes: A New Translation with Introduction and Commentary.* Anchor Bible, vol. 18c. New York: Doubleday, 1997.

"Sergeant Henry Johnson, Medal of Honor, World War I." U.S. Army, https://tinyurl.com/3ydx5ahp.

Serwer, Adam. "The Fight over the 1619 Project Is Not about the Facts." *Atlantic*, December 23, 2019. https://tinyurl.com/3y2fkbb8.

Shain, Barry Alan. *The Myth of American Individualism: The Protestant Origins of American Political Thought*. Princeton: Princeton University Press, 1994.

Shakespeare, William. *Hamlet, Prince of Denmark*. Edited by William George Clarke and William Aldis Wright. Great Books of the Western World, vol. 27. Chicago: Encyclopedia Britannica, 1952.

———. *The Life of King Henry V*. Edited by William Aldis Wright. New York: Doubleday, 1936.

Sherwood, Samuel. "The Church's Flight into the Wilderness." In *Political Sermons of the American Founding Era, 1730–1805*, edited by Ellis Sandoz. Indianapolis: Liberty Fund, 1991.

Smith, Anthony D. *Chosen Peoples: Sacred Sources of National Identities*. New York: Oxford University Press, 2003.

Smith, Steven B. *Reclaiming Patriotism in an Age of Extremes*. New Haven: Yale University Press, 2021.

Snead, O. Carter. *What It Means to Be Human: The Case for the Body in Public Bioethics*. Cambridge, MA: Harvard University Press, 2020.

Stark, Rodney. *America's Blessings: How Religion Benefits Everyone, Including Atheists*. West Conshohocken, PA: Templeton, 2012.

———. *The Victory of Reason: How Christianity Led to Freedom, Capitalism, and Western Success*. New York: Random House, 2005.

Stephanson, Anders. *Manifest Destiny: American Expansion and the Empire of Right*. New York: Hill & Wang, 1995.

Street, Nicholas. "The American States Acting over the Part of the Children of Israel in the Wilderness and Thereby Impeding Their Entrance into Canaan's Rest." In *God's New Israel: Religious Interpretations of American Destiny*. 1971. Reprint, Chapel Hill: University of North Carolina Press, 1998.

Swedberg, Richard. *Tocqueville's Political Economy*. Princeton: Princeton University Press, 2009.

Tacitus, P. Cornelius. *The Annals*. Translated by Alfred John Church and William Jackson Brodribb. Great Books of the Western World, vol. 15. Chicago: Encyclopedia Britannica, 1952.

Tessitore, Aristide. "Alexis de Tocqueville on the Natural State of Religion in the Age of Democracy." *Journal of Politics* 64, no. 4 (November 2002): 1137–52.

Thompson, C. Bradley. *America's Revolutionary Mind: A Moral History of the*

American Revolution and the Declaration That Defined It. New York: Encounter, 2019.

Thoreau, Henry David. *Walden.* With an introduction by Bill McKibben. Boston: Beacon, 2004.

Thucydides, *The History of the Peloponnesian War.* Translated by Richard Crawley. Great Books of the Western World, vol. 6. Chicago: Encyclopedia Britannica, 1952.

Tocqueville, Alexis de. *The Ancien Regime and the French Revolution.* Edited by John Elster. Translated by Arthur Goldhammer. New York: Cambridge University Press, 2011.

———. *Democracy in America.* Edited by Eduardo Nolla. Translated by James T. Schleifer. 2 vols. Indianapolis: Liberty Fund, 2010.

———. *Letters from America.* New Haven: Yale University Press, 2010.

Tuveson, Ernest Lee. *Redeemer Nation: The Idea of America's Millennial Role.* Chicago: University of Chicago Press, 1968.

Vanhoozer, Kevin J. *Pictures at a Theological Exhibition: Scenes of the Church's Worship, Witness, and Wisdom.* Downers Grove, IL: IVP Academic, 2016.

Viereck, Peter. *Conservatism: From John Adams to Churchill.* Princeton: Nostrand, 1956.

———. *Conservatism Revisited: The Revolt against Ideology.* Reprint, New Brunswick, NJ: Transaction, 2005.

———. "Conservatism under the Elms." *New York Times*, November 4, 1951. https://tinyurl.com/fahh5h63.

———. *Metapolitics: From Wagner and the German Romantics to Hitler.* Expanded ed. New Brunswick, NJ: Transaction, 2004; original 1941.

———. *The Unadjusted Man: A New Hero for Americans; Reflections on the Distinction between Conforming and Conserving.* Boston: Beacon, 1956.

———. *Unadjusted Man in the Age of Overadjustment: Where History and Literature Intersect.* New York: Transaction, 2004.

Villa, Dana. "Tocqueville and Civil Society." In *The Cambridge Companion to Tocqueville*, edited by Cheryl B. Welch. Cambridge: Cambridge University Press, 2006.

Walker, Lee H. *Rediscovering Black Conservatism.* Chicago: Heartland Institute, 2009.

Weaver, Richard M. *Ideas Have Consequences.* 1948. Reprint, Chicago: University of Chicago Press, 1984.

———. "Lord Acton: The Historian as Thinker." In *In Defense of Tradition:*

Collected Shorter Writings of Richard M. Weaver, 1929–1963, edited by Ted J. Smith III. Indianapolis: Liberty Fund, 2000.

———. "The Role of Education in Shaping Our Society." In *In Defense of Tradition: Collected Shorter Writings of Richard M. Weaver, 1929–1963*, edited by Ted J. Smith III. Indianapolis: Liberty Fund, 2000.

Webster, Daniel. *Adams and Jefferson: Discourse in Commemoration of the Lives and Services of John Adams and Thomas Jefferson, Delivered in Faneuil Hall, Boston, on the 2d of August, 1826*. English Classic Series, vol. 51, edited by Albert F. Blaisdell. New York: Clark & Maynard, 1885.

White, Andrew Dickson. *The Warfare of Science*. London: King & Co., 1876.

Whitehead, Andrew L. *American Idolatry: How Christian Nationalism Betrays the Gospel and Threatens the Church*. Grand Rapids: Brazos, 2023.

Whitehead, Andrew L., and Samuel L. Perry. *Taking America Back for God: Christian Nationalism in the United States*. New York: Oxford University Press, 2020.

Williams, Tarah, Andrew Bloeser, and Brian Howard. "Large Numbers of Americans Want a Strong, Rough, Anti-democratic Leader." *Nextgov*, February 7, 2023. https://tinyurl.com/2atemcfp.

Wilsey, John D. *American Exceptionalism and Civil Religion*. Downers Grove, IL: IVP Academic, 2015.

———. "At Its Best, American Patriotism Is Blessed with Two-Dimensional Vision." *Christianity Today*, July 1, 2021. https://tinyurl.com/2n2sw2jk.

———. "The Christian Prince against the Dad Bod: An Assessment of the Case for Christian Nationalism." *London Lyceum*, April 28, 2023. https://tinyurl.com/2s4f4m23.

———. *God's Cold Warrior: The Life and Faith of John Foster Dulles*. Library of Religious Biography. Grand Rapids: Eerdmans, 2021.

———. "The Many Faces of Christian Nationalism." *Law and Liberty*, September 26, 2021. https://tinyurl.com/ycya4mwc.

———. *One Nation under God: An Evangelical Critique of Christian America*. Eugene, OR: Pickwick, 2011.

———. "Public Spirit as Mediating Influence between Tocqueville's 'Spirit of Religion' and 'Spirit of Freedom.'" In *The Palgrave Handbook of Religion and State: Theoretical Perspectives*, vol. 1, edited by Shannon Holzer. Cham, Switzerland: Palgrave Macmillan, 2023.

Winthrop, John. "A Modell of Christian Charity." In *God's New Israel: Religious Interpretations of American Destiny*, edited by Conrad Cherry. 1971. Reprint, Chapel Hill: University of North Carolina Press, 1998.

Wolfe, Stephen. *The Case for Christian Nationalism*. Moscow, ID: Canon, 2022.

Wood, Gordon S. *Revolutionary Characters: What Made the Founders Different.* New York: Penguin Books, 2006.

_____. *The Idea of America: Reflections on the Birth of the United States.* New York: Penguin Books, 2011.

Young, Neil J. *We Gather Together: The Religious Right and the Problem of Interfaith Politics.* New York: Oxford University Press, 2016.

Zitner, Aaron. "America Pulls Back from Values That Once Defined It, WSJ-NORC Poll Finds." *Wall Street Journal*, March 27, 2023. https://tinyurl.com/465e4cs7.

Zuckert, Catherine. "Not by Preaching: Tocqueville on the Role of Religion in American Democracy." *Review of Politics* 43, no. 2 (April 1981): 259–80.

Index

Index

Index